PC Magazine®
Home Networking Solutions

PC Magazine®
Home Networking
Solutions

Les Freed

Wiley Publishing, Inc.

PC Magazine® Home Networking Solutions

Published by
Wiley Publishing, Inc.
10475 Crosspoint Boulevard
Indianapolis, IN 46256
www.wiley.com

ISBN-13: 978-0-471-74754-3
ISBN-10: 0-471-74754-8

Manufactured in the United States of America

10 9 8 7 6 5 4 3 2 1

1MA/TR/QY/QV/IN

For general information on our other products and services or to obtain technical support, please contact our Customer Care Department within the U.S. at (800) 762-2974, outside the U.S. at (317) 572-3993 or fax (317) 572-4002.

Wiley also publishes its books in a variety of electronic formats. Some content that appears in print may not be available in electronic books.

Library of Congress Cataloging-in-Publication Data

Freed, Les.
  PC magazine home networking solutions / Les Freed.
      p. cm.
  Includes index.
  ISBN-13: 978-0-471-74754-3 (paper/website)
  ISBN-10: 0-471-74754-8 (paper/website)
  1. Home computer networks. I. Title: Home networking solutions. II. PC magazine (New York, N.Y.) III. Title.
  TK5105.75.F744 2005
  004.6'8—dc22
                            2005021554

About the Author

Les Freed has been a contributing editor at *PC Magazine* since 1994 and a frequent contributor since 1990. Before joining *PC Magazine*, Les was founder and CEO of Crosstalk Communications, developers of the popular Crosstalk data communications program for PCs—back in the days before the Internet made communications software obsolete. Prior to founding Crosstalk, Les was a Senior Technician and Videotape Editor at CBS News from 1976 to 1981 and a Cameraman and News Editor at WTVJ-TV in Miami from 1972 to 1976. He graduated from the University of Miami in 1974 with B.A. in Electronic Journalism. Les is the author or co-author of 14 books on networking, computing, and digital photography.

Les and long-time collaborator Frank Derfler shared the 1993 Computer Press Association award for Best How-To Book for their book *How Networks Work*, still in print in its 6th edition.

Credits

EXECUTIVE EDITOR
Chris Webb

DEVELOPMENT EDITOR
Tom Dinse

TECHNICAL EDITOR
Barry Press

PRODUCTION EDITOR
Pamela Hanley

COPY EDITOR
Susan Hobbs

EDITORIAL MANAGER
Mary Beth Wakefield

PRODUCTION MANAGER
Tim Tate

VICE PRESIDENT & EXECUTIVE GROUP PUBLISHER
Richard Swadley

VICE PRESIDENT AND PUBLISHER
Joseph B. Wikert

PROJECT COORDINATOR
Erin Smith

GRAPHICS AND PRODUCTION SPECIALISTS
Sean Decker
Lauren Goddard
Jennifer Heleine
Melanee Prendergast

QUALITY CONTROL TECHNICIANS
Leeann Harney
Jessica Kramer
Joe Niesen
Dwight Ramsey

PROOFREADING AND INDEXING
TECHBOOKS Production Services

Contents at a Glance

Contents

Preface

Home networks are a hot topic. When I installed my first home LAN in the late 1980s, I was the only person on my block—and probably in the entire city—to have a home network. Today, virtually every computer and electronics store has an aisle or two devoted to home networking products.

There are three factors driving the home networking bandwagon. The first is the ever-increasing number of multiple-PC homes, thanks to a drastic drop in PC prices over the past few years. As more people bring home that second or third PC, they often wish that it were possible to share files, printers, and an Internet connection among all the computers in the home. The second factor is the rapid rise in the use of broadband home Internet connections. Broadband cable and DSL Internet connections can easily handle two or more simultaneous users, but you need a network to share the connection.

The third and most important driver for home networking is the arrival of inexpensive, reliable wireless networking equipment. Many potential network users have been put off by the difficulty and expense involved with installing the cables necessary to create a home network. Wireless networks don't need cables at all, and this greatly reduces the effort and expense required to set up a home network.

A home network provides a simple, inexpensive way to share an Internet connection, files, and even printers among all of the computers in your home. Manufacturers have responded to the mushrooming demand for home network products by delivering products that are inexpensive and easy to install and use.

The increasing popularity of home networks has also caught the attention of the home entertainment industry. The result is a new breed of home entertainment devices that operate over a home network.

Who Should Read This Book?

If you've been thinking about installing a home network, this is the only book you'll need, regardless of your level of computer expertise. In this book, I provide the background you need to understand, purchase, install, and use your own home network.

What's in the Book?

This book is divided into four parts:

In Part I, I tell you why you need a network and show you how you can use a network to share an Internet connection, files, and printers. I also explain the basics of networking technology.

In Part II, we go on a shopping trip. I walk you through the maze of competing and complementary technologies you can use to build a home network, and I show you when to use wired and wireless networking products to design the perfect network for your home.

Part III shows you how to connect and configure the components of your home network. I show you how to install wired and wireless networks, and I explain what you'll need to do to prepare your computers for use on a network.

Part IV shows you how to use your network to share Internet access, files, and printers. I also introduce you to some interesting new products that extend your network to include video games, home security, and home entertainment devices.

At the end of the book, you'll find lots of useful reference information, including a hands-on Networking Cookbook, a troubleshooting guide, a list of online resources, and a complete glossary. I hope you enjoy reading this book as much as I enjoyed writing it. I think you'll find it a very useful tool for building, using, and expanding your own home network.

Acknowledgments

Every book is a group effort, although one person gets all of the credit. My heartfelt thanks go to:

Ron and Maria Cordell
Frank Derfler
Becky Freed
Michael Miller
Bradley Morse
Karen Sohl
Chris Webb
D-Link Systems, Inc.
Linksys Corporation

Part I

Why You Need a Network

Chapter 1

What Is a LAN?

Not long ago, home local area networks (LANs) were proof of their owner's geekhood. They were expensive, cantankerous, difficult to set up, and useful for only a very few advanced home users (mostly for programmers and writers). Thanks to falling prices and vastly improved software, home LANs aren't just for geeks anymore. In this chapter, you'll find the following:

- A typical home LAN

- Basic LAN building blocks

- The difference between LANs and WANs

As you'll see, building a home LAN isn't rocket science. Thanks in large part to the explosive growth of broadband Internet connections and the proliferation of multi-PC homes, there are hundreds of networking products made specifically for home and small-business users. These products are simple to install and operate, so you don't need a computer science degree to set them up. In fact, many home networking devices simply "plug and play" right out of the box, with little or no setup or configuration required.

Note

At PC Magazine, we've been talking about "Media Convergence" for many years, and it's finally here. Network-based home entertainment devices such as TiVo and Microsoft's Media Center PC blur the line between computing devices and home entertainment devices, making a home LAN more useful than ever. I'll show you how home media devices work in Chapters 2 and 12.

It's Simpler Than You Might Think

What is a network? It's simply two or more devices that communicate with one another over some type of electronic connection. The connection itself can be copper wire, fiber optic cable, or radio waves. There are all sorts of networks in use today, including the broadcast and cable television networks, the public telephone network, several cellular telephone networks, and the Internet. A *local area network* (LAN) is a network of computers, located physically close to one another. (The Internet, by the way, is a WAN, or *wide area network*, that connects millions of LANs.)

A LAN consists of two or more computers, each equipped with a communications device called a *network interface* or *network adapter*. The network interfaces are connected to one another by some type of communications medium, which provides a pathway for electrical signals that connect all of the computers on a LAN. The most widely used, cost-effective, and highest-performance network medium in use today is twisted-pair Ethernet cable, often called CAT5 or CAT6 cable. (CAT is short for category—several grades of cable can be used for Ethernet LANs.)

A relatively new technology called *wireless Ethernet* uses radio signals instead of copper cable as the communications medium. Early wireless devices were slow, expensive, and unreliable. Worse still, there were no industry standards, so products from one manufacturer didn't always work with products from another. In the late 1990s, most of the wireless equipment manufacturers formed a trade association called the WiFi Alliance to set technical standards and to certify interoperability. The current generation of WiFi devices offers excellent speed and reliability at very low prices, so your LAN no longer requires hardwiring between components. As you'll see in Chapter 6, you can use a mix of wired and wireless Ethernet connections on the same LAN.

Wired Ethernet interfaces are standard equipment on most modern desktops and laptops, and some high-end laptops include wired and wireless Ethernet interfaces as standard equipment. If your computer didn't come with a network adapter, there are several inexpensive ways to add one to your existing computer. There are different types of network adapters for different types of communications media; I cover them in detail in Chapter 4. Figure 1-1 shows a simple two-computer Ethernet LAN.

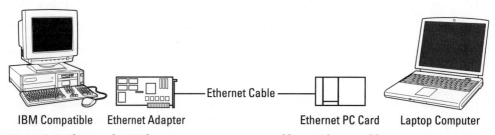

IBM Compatible   Ethernet Adapter   —— Ethernet Cable ——   Ethernet PC Card   Laptop Computer

Figure 1-1: This simple LAN has two computers connected by an Ethernet cable.

The example in Figure 1-1 shows a desktop computer on the left and a laptop computer on the right. The desktop is equipped with an internal Ethernet adapter card, and the laptop with a PC Card Ethernet adapter. The two Ethernet adapters are connected by a single cable. In many cases, you can create such a network simply by connecting an Ethernet cable between the two computers (assuming that the computers came from the factory with Ethernet adapters already installed).

While the LAN in Figure 1-1 is perfectly functional, it is also very limited because it provides connections for only two computers. To add a third computer or other device to the LAN, you would need to add an Ethernet switch to the network. For now, you can think of a switch as a sort of signal splitter for Ethernet connections. I'll explain switches in detail in Chapter 4.

The diagram in Figure 1-1 is deceptively simple because it doesn't show the complex interaction between the PC computer's operating system and the network adapter. Early versions of Windows (before Windows for Workgroups 3.1) didn't include the software necessary for computers to communicate over a LAN. Fortunately, Mac OS/X, Windows 98, Me, 2000, and XP all include built-in networking features as a standard part of the operating system. These features allow computers to share files, printers, and Internet connections over a LAN. I'll discuss these features in detail in Part IV.

Note

The step-by-step examples in this book assume that you are using Windows XP or Mac OS/X, but the basic networking concepts are universal and apply to all versions of Windows and the Mac OS. Windows XP and Mac OS/X contain many features designed to make networking simpler, including easier networking installation and setup, and built-in support for wireless networking.

So far, I've only discussed connecting computers to a LAN. If you have a broadband Internet connection, you'll almost certainly want to share that connection among all the computers on your home network.

Note

You can connect a cable or DSL (digital subscriber line) modem directly to a LAN, but for security reasons I don't recommend it.

Home networks aren't just for computers anymore. If you have a TiVo, Xbox, or Sony PlayStation, you may want to connect those devices to your LAN too. As you'll see in Chapters 2 and 13, the worlds of computing and home entertainment are converging, with the Internet—and the home network—as their meeting point.

A Guided Tour of Les's LAN

As you might expect, my own home is pretty well wired, and I thought you might find it interesting to see what my home LAN looks like. Figure 1-2 shows what's on my network.

So what is all this stuff, and what does it do? The equipment at the center of the diagram (the cable modem, firewall, Ethernet switch, and wireless access point) makes up the core of the network. These four devices provide and manage the connection among the devices on the LAN, and between the LAN and the Internet. The devices at the edge of the network (the PCs, Macs, laptops, TiVo, Media Center Extender, Windows 2000 Server, and printers) fall into two further classes: They either provide services for other devices on the LAN, or they use services that are provided by those devices. As you probably know, devices that provide services are called *servers*, and devices that use services are called *clients*.

For example, the Windows 2000 server (with its attached printer) provides file sharing and printing services for the other computers on the LAN. If I am working on my desktop PC and need to print a photograph, I can send the print job to the photo printer attached to the server. In this example, the Windows 2000 system is a server, and my desktop PC is a client. (Some devices can be both a client and a server, as I'll explain in Chapter 3.)

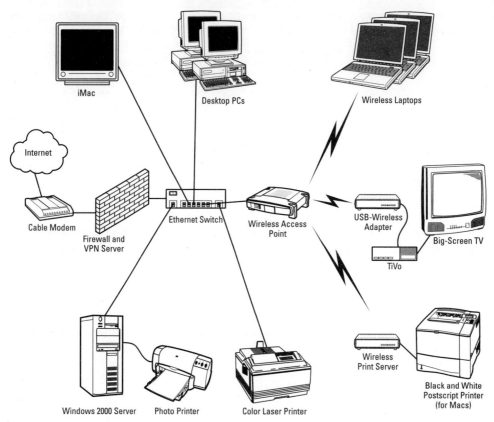

Figure 1-2: My home LAN has grown from a few desktop PCs to something a little more complex.

JOURNEY TO THE CENTER OF THE LAN

The device in the center of the diagram is an *Ethernet switch*, and it is the heart of the network. Ethernet switches have anywhere from a few to a few dozen connectors on them. All of the wired devices on the LAN connect to one of the sockets (called *ports*) on the Ethernet switch. The switch analyzes the data coming in on each port and reroutes the data to the appropriate device connected to another port. This enables any two devices on the LAN to exchange data with each other. Six devices are connected to the switch in Figure 1-2.

The wireless access point, or AP, to the right of the Ethernet switch does for wireless devices what the Ethernet switch does for wired devices. The AP is connected to the Ethernet switch so wireless devices can communicate with any of the wired devices on the LAN, and vice versa.

The cable modem and firewall to the left of the Ethernet switch work together to provide secure Internet access for all of the devices on the LAN. The cable modem provides a fast, always-on connection to the Internet. As you've probably heard, high-speed connections like cable and DSL modems tend to attract hackers and snoopers, so a firewall is an essential item on any Internet-connected LAN.

Note

Firewall products designed for the home market are actually two devices—a router and a firewall—in one package. A router directs traffic on a network; a firewall protects the network from outside attacks.

The firewall acts as an electronic gatekeeper between the LAN and the Internet. Outgoing connections (such as Web browser and e-mail client connections) going from the LAN to the Internet pass directly through the firewall unimpeded, just as if the firewall wasn't even there. Incoming connections are blocked to keep intruders out of your home network, unless you specifically configure your firewall to allow incoming connections.

Cross-Reference

See Chapter 13 for details about securing your network.

The router portion of the firewall serves another important role: As you'll see in Chapter 3, every device connected to the Internet must have a unique IP address. My cable modem provider (like most broadband providers) only assigns a single IP address to my cable modem, but I have over a dozen devices connected to the LAN. Using a technique called Network Address Translation (NAT), the firewall leverages that single IP address into any number of private IP addresses. The firewall keeps track of all traffic coming from and going to the Internet and routes the traffic to the appropriate device on the LAN.

Note

If this seems like a lot of equipment, relax. My network uses a separate Ethernet switch, wireless AP, and firewall, but you don't have to. Most network equipment manufacturers offer products that combine these three functions into a single unit costing less than $200. Figure 1-3 shows a typical product from D-Link. I prefer the separate units for my own home LAN because I do a lot of product testing and I need to be able to test a new firewall or Ethernet switch without reconfiguring the entire LAN.

OUT ON THE EDGE

The devices on the outside edges of the LAN diagram (the PCs, Macs, laptops, TiVo, and other devices) are either clients or servers. Most of these devices can communicate with one another, but some can't. Even though two devices may be connected to the same LAN, there's no guarantee that they'll have much to say to one another. What would a big-screen TV and a printer have to discuss?

Different types of devices communicate using different communications protocols. A *protocol* is essentially a digital language that defines the way that devices communicate over a network. There are hundreds of communications protocols in use today, including TCP/IP, NetBEUI, NetWare, and AppleTalk. It is possible—and actually quite common—for a single LAN to use several communications protocols at once.

Figure 1-3: D-Link calls its model DI-624 a Wireless Broadband Router. It combines a four-port Ethernet switch, a wireless access point, a router, and a firewall into one compact, inexpensive unit.

For example, Windows PCs share files and printers using the NetBIOS protocol. The Internet (and everything connected to the Internet) uses the IP protocol. Web servers and browsers use the Hypertext Transfer Protocol (http), which is one of hundreds of protocols that define how devices communicate over an IP network.

You may be wondering why I have a Windows 2000 server on my home LAN. I have a mix of PCs and Macs on my home LAN. Before the release of Mac OS/X, Macs couldn't easily share files with Windows-based PCs. Windows 2000 (and its successor, Windows 2003) include support for Appletalk-based file and printer sharing, making it possible to easily move files back and forth between the Mac and Windows universes. Fortunately, Mac OS/X now includes Windows file and printer sharing capabilities as a standard feature. I don't really need the Windows 2000 Server machine any more, but I have thousands of Mac and PC files stored on that system, so it acts as a central repository for my older, inactive files.

Summary

I hope this first chapter has shown you that you don't need a computer science degree to set up a home network. I'll admit that you'll have to learn some new acronyms, but the most important things to take away from this chapter is a broad idea of what a home LAN does and what kinds of components it links together.

The key points in this chapter are as follows:

- A network is any combination of computers and other devices connected by an electronic communications medium.

- There are two main types of home networks: wired and wireless.

- You can mix and match wired and wireless components as your needs dictate.

- Equipment manufacturers have a broad array of products to help get your home networked with a minimum of effort, and at a very low cost.

- A firewall is essential for sharing Internet access on any LAN.

At this point, you now know the basic elements of a LAN. In Chapter 2, I'll show you how these elements work together, and I'll also show you what you can do with a LAN.

Chapter 2

What Can You Do with a Network?

The majority of new home networks are purchased and installed by people who want to share an Internet connection. After you've installed a home network, you can use it for a more than Internet access. In this chapter, I'll show you some of the things you can do with your new network, including:

- Share your Internet connection
- Share files and printers
- Enjoy multimedia convergence
- Play network games

The list of things you can do with a network continues to grow as equipment makers dream up new ways to harness the power of a home network. For example, several companies, including General Motors, have demonstrated prototype car audio systems that use a wireless network to download new MP3 audio files into a car stereo system. And a new breed of telephones called IP Telephones hit the market in 2004. These telephones use a home network and broadband Internet connection to place and receive telephone calls without a conventional telephone line. This chapter introduces you to some of the more common uses of a home network.

Sharing Your Internet Connection

Although you can connect your home network to the Internet using a dial-up modem, the benefits of a broadband or DSL connection are enormous. After you've used a broadband cable modem or DSL connection, you'll never want to go back to dial-up. Broadband connections are many times faster than dial-up, and they're more reliable. Because they are always connected to the Internet, there's no waiting for your modem to connect. Best of all, broadband connections don't tie up your phone line, so you can still use the phone while you're online.

But there's a dark side to the story too. I call it broadband envy.

The problem is that most home broadband customers have their cable or DSL modem connected to a single PC. As a result, many home users enjoy broadband Nirvana on one PC, while the other users in the home have to wait to use the sole connected PC.

A home network solves broadband envy by allowing all of the PCs on the network to share a single Internet connection. Even if you don't have a broadband connection, you can use a home network to share a dial-up modem connection.

Caution

Before you begin sharing your Internet connection on your home network, check with your broadband provider to ensure that you won't violate your provider's acceptable use policy. Some providers specify that you may only connect a single computer to the service, and many providers charge an additional monthly fee for shared connection. Fortunately, the monthly fee is usually reasonable.

There are several ways to share an Internet connection with more than one computer. Figure 2-1 illustrates three options for a shared Internet connection(Ethernet switch, proxy server, and router). The following sections explain each option in detail.

Multiple IP Addresses (Ethernet Switch)

The left part of Figure 2-1 shows a small LAN directly connected to a modem. As you'll see in Chapter 3, every device connected to the Internet must have a unique *IP address*.

Some broadband Internet service providers (ISPs) can assign multiple IP addresses to a single cable or DSL modem, so users can connect several computers to the modem using a simple Ethernet switch. This approach has one big advantage but several large disadvantages.

The big plus is that each computer on the network can have its own, *fully routable* IP address. This means that each computer can be reached from any other device on the Internet. This is very useful in a business environment, where you might want to have a Web server, e-mail server, or other publicly available server in your office. But most home ISPs prohibit running such servers, so there's no real advantage to having a fully routable address for each computer on your LAN.

The disadvantages of the multiple-IP-address approach outweigh the benefits for home users. First, relatively few ISPs offer multiple addresses for home users, and those that do charge a hefty monthly premium for the extra addresses. Second, because each computer is directly connected to the Internet, the network is open to attacks from hackers. You can circumvent this problem by installing firewall software on each PC or by installing a firewall between the Internet and the LAN. But as I'll explain shortly, there's a better, simpler, cheaper way to accomplish the same thing.

Using Windows XP's Internet Connection Sharing (Proxy Server)

The middle illustration in Figure 2-1 shows a method of Internet sharing called a *proxy server*. The availability of inexpensive router/firewall devices has made the proxy server nearly extinct, but it is still a viable Internet-sharing solution for very small networks. Microsoft includes a proxy server called Internet Connection Sharing (ICS) with Windows XP.

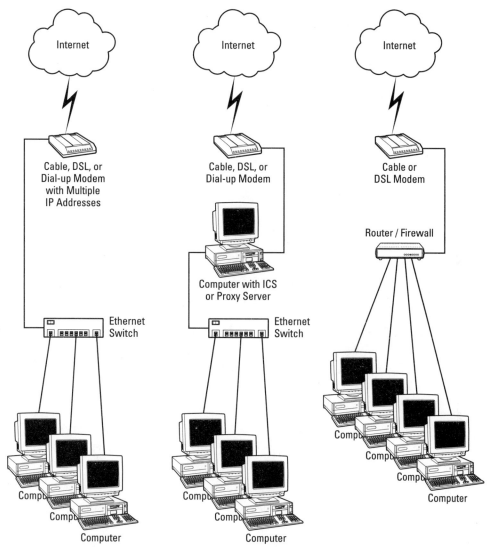

Figure 2-1: Some ISPs provide multiple IP addresses, so you can share the Internet connection using a simple Ethernet switch (left). A proxy server (middle) shares a connection attached to one PC on your LAN, and a router (right) is your best choice for a shared broadband connection.

ICS is a small piece of software that runs on a PC. The PC running the ICS server is called the *ICS Host*. The ICS Host PC must have two network interface cards installed in it, or one network interface and a dial-up modem connection. In most cases, you'll need to open up your PC and install a second Ethernet adapter (or use a slower external USB Ethernet adapter) before you can use ICS to share a broadband connection.

Microsoft's ICS takes only a few minutes to install, and it is very easy to configure. Figure 2-2 shows the main ICS configuration screen.

Figure 2-2: Microsoft's Internet Connection Sharing (ICS) feature is included with Windows XP and takes only a few minutes to install.

The ICS Host acts as a gateway between the Internet and the local network. The ICS Host uses a single IP address to communicate with the Internet. The computers on the LAN side of the ICS Host use private, nonroutable addresses to communicate with one another and with the ICS Host. (I'll explain more about nonroutable addresses in Chapter 3.)

All traffic coming from and going to the Internet passes through the ICS Host. You can continue to use the ICS Host system for normal computing tasks, with a few caveats. While the ICS software doesn't slow down the host PC, the reverse isn't always true. A resource-intensive program (like a 3-D game or a disk-defragmenter program) running on the ICS Host will slow down the Internet connection for all the users on the network.

As you've probably guessed, the ICS Host must be powered up and running in order for the other PCs to connect to the Internet. If the ICS Host PC crashes, all the other users will lose Internet access until the host PC is restarted.

Despite these limitations, ICS is a handy (and free!) tool if you want to share an Internet connection with a small number of PCs. While most router/firewall devices work only with cable or DSL connections, ICS works with just about any type of Internet connection, including dial-up connections, so you can use it with wireless and FireWire connections as well as traditional wired Ethernet. Because it is based on Windows, ICS is somewhat less secure than a standalone hardware firewall.

The low cost of hardware firewalls (combined with their lower power consumption) makes ICS less of a bargain than you might think. ICS is explained in greater detail in Chapter 9.

Note

Although the diagram in Figure 2-1 shows several PCs connected to an Ethernet switch, you don't need even the switch to connect two (and only two) PCs for Internet sharing, but you'll need a special cable called a *crossover cable* to connect the two computers. Most computer and electronics stores carry crossover cables. If you buy one, make sure it is a different color from your other network cables so you'll be able to tell the crossover cable from all of your other cables!

Using a Router/Firewall (Router)

The diagram on the right side of Figure 2-1 shows several computers sharing an Internet connection using a combination router/firewall/Ethernet switch. Devices such as this one are commonly used on home networks since they combine three functions—router, firewall, and switch—into a single, compact device. These devices are easier to install and take up less space than a separate router, firewall, and switch, but they are functionally identical.

The router is connected to the broadband modem, and the computers are connected to the Ethernet switch built into the router. As with the proxy server, the router uses a single IP address to communicate with the Internet, and it uses a range of private IP addresses to communicate with the devices on the LAN. These devices can include Windows and Linux-based PCs, Macs, TiVo Digital Video Recorders, and any other device that communicates using the IP protocol.

Each computer can access the Internet independently of the others, and all of the computers can connect to the Internet at the same time. Because the computers are all connected to the same Ethernet switch, they can also share files and printers with one another, as you'll see in the next section of this chapter.

Tip

Most routers are designed specifically for cable or DSL broadband connections, but a few manufacturers offer models that work with dial-up connections too. These products typically have an RS-232C serial interface in addition to an Ethernet connection, and the serial interface can be used to connect an external modem for dial-up connections.

Some routers—such as Apple's AirPort Extreme—include a built-in dial-up modem so that you can connect the router directly to a phone line. If you do eventually upgrade to broadband, you can still use the modem as a backup connection if the broadband connection goes down.

A router/firewall device is the simplest way to share an Internet connection on a LAN. Most routers offer true plug-and-play operation, so setup usually takes just a few minutes. All home routers provide automatic IP address configuration for all of the computers on the LAN. As you'll see in Chapter 3, automatic IP addressing is a very nice feature to have on your LAN since it frees you from the task of manually assigning and configuring an address for every device on your network.

In addition to providing a way to share an Internet connection, a router/firewall also provides protection against hackers and intruders for all of the computers on the LAN. The firewall acts as an electronic gatekeeper for the LAN, allowing only authorized traffic to pass through the firewall. Some firewalls provide parental control, content control, and time-of-day filtering features that allow you to control or restrict access to certain Web sites or to restrict access to certain times of day.

Tip

Most broadband Internet connections are more than fast enough to share among several users with no noticeable slowdown in connection speed. If you live in a house full of Internet junkies, check with your service provider to see if it offers an upgraded connection package for multiple-PC homes. Many broadband providers offer faster connection speeds for a small monthly premium.

Router/firewalls have become very popular with broadband users thanks to their simple setup, all-in-one convenience, and low price. Manufacturers have responded to market needs with a wide variety of router products, including models with built-in wireless access points, Ethernet switches, and print servers.

Sharing Files and Printers

Home networks are great for sharing an Internet connection, but there are other benefits to having a LAN in your home. When you install the hardware and software necessary for Internet sharing, you've also installed almost everything you need to share files and printers among all the computers in your home.

File and printer sharing is popular in the corporate world, and it is equally useful on a home network. Unfortunately, many home network users aren't aware of the benefits of file and printer sharing, but the next two sections will clue you in.

File Sharing

Simply put, file sharing lets you use files stored on another computer connected to the LAN. Windows XP and Mac OS/X both provide built-in file-sharing features, so you don't need to purchase any additional software. Any computer on the network can share files with any other computer.

If you routinely work on more than one computer, file sharing can help you keep your files organized. For example, I frequently switch between my desktop and laptop PCs, but the majority of my work-in-progress files reside on my desktop machine. When I'm working on my laptop and need to open a file stored on the desktop PC, I use file sharing to open the stored file from my laptop PC.

Note

The machine on which the files reside must be powered up in order to share files on the network.

I also use file sharing on my home network to maintain a backup copy of my important files on a dedicated file server PC. Like many PC users, I dread the inevitable day when my laptop or desktop PC's hard drive dies. Unlike most home users, I'll be prepared (and possibly even a little smug) because I won't lose any of my important files.

Figure 2-3 shows an overview of file sharing on my own network.

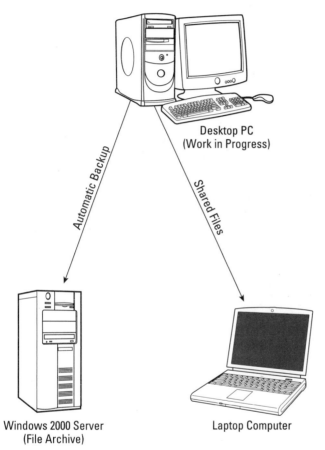

Desktop PC
(Work in Progress)

Automatic Backup

Shared Files

Windows 2000 Server
(File Archive)

Laptop Computer

Figure 2-3: I store frequently used files on my desktop PC (top). File sharing allows me to use those files from my laptop or from other PCs in the house. Older, archived files are automatically moved over to my file server.

If you're concerned that you'll have to learn a lot of new techniques to use your network, you can relax. Windows XP uses the familiar Windows Explorer interface for most networking tasks, and Mac OS/X integrates networking tasks into the Finder. These are the same drag-and-drop user interfaces that you already use for moving, renaming, and deleting files.

Tip

Windows XP Users: After you install your network, you'll probably want to enable the My Network Places icon on your desktop. Most computer makers ship their systems with this icon turned off. To add the Network Places icon to your desktop, follow these steps:

1. Open the Control Panel and double-click on Display.
2. Select the Desktop tab at the top of the Display Properties control panel.
3. Click on Customize Desktop.
4. Check the My Network Places icon and click OK.

While you're adding items to your desktop, you may want to enable the My Computer and My Documents desktop icons too.

On a Windows XP system, shared network files and folders appear in the Explorer interface as objects under My Network Places, as you can see from Figure 2-4.

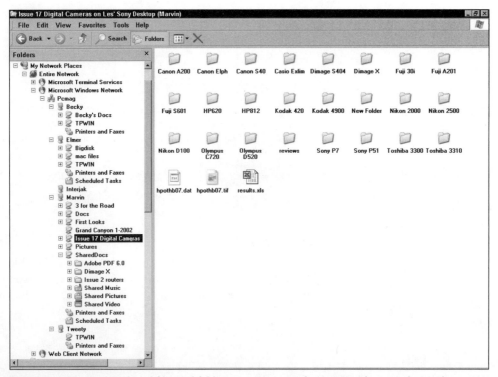

Figure 2-4: You can see shared files and folders on your network using Windows Explorer. The highlighted folder in this example is located on the computer named Marvin.

The left side of the Windows Explorer screen shows a tree view of the shared resources on the network. Each computer on the network must have a unique name, and each network must also have a name. As you can see in Figure 2-4, my network's name is Pcmag. Each computer on the network appears underneath the network's name, and the shared resources on each computer appear below the computer. In the example, I have selected a shared folder called Issue 17 Digital Cameras on the computer named Marvin. Many of the other computers on the network have shared folders, and a few also have shared printers.

Mac OS/X systems integrate network features directly into the Finder. Figure 2-5 shows how networked computers appear on a Mac.

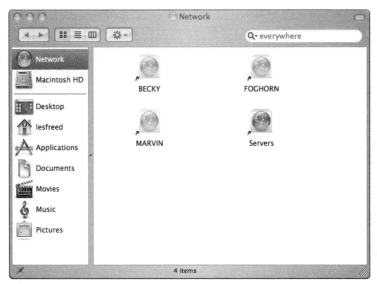

Figure 2-5: On Mac OS/X systems, available network computers appear as icons when you click "Network" in the finder menu.

In the example shown in Figure 2-5, the computers named Marvin, Becky, and Foghorn are all Windows XP-based systems.

All this sharing is a good thing, but you probably won't want everyone on the network to be able to see or have access to every shared file or folder. Windows XP includes security features that let you keep your files private, and it also includes features to help you keep track of shared files on portable computers. I'll explain these features in detail in Chapter 10.

Tip

If you plan to use file sharing, it is vitally important that you have a firewall on your network. Without a firewall, anyone on the Internet can connect to your PC and open, modify, or even delete files on your PC.

Printer Sharing

Internet sharing can prevent family strife, and file sharing can make your life a little less complicated. But printer sharing can save you money—and valuable desk space too. In most cases, having a multi-PC home means having a multiprinter home as well. And if you have more than one printer, the odds are pretty good that each of your printers takes a different set of ink cartridges.

You can use your home LAN to share each printer with the other computers on the network. And since everyone can use the same printer, you may be able to get rid of a printer or two and reclaim some desk space.

There are three distinct ways to share a printer on a Windows network, as you can see in Figure 2-6.

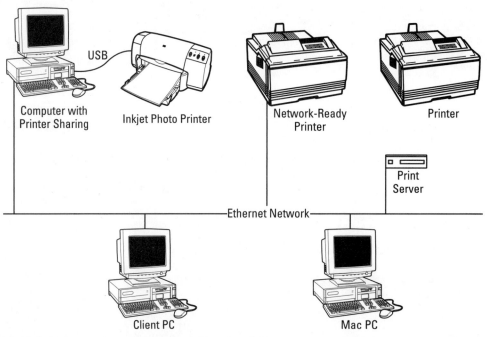

Figure 2-6: You can share a printer attached to a PC (left), or you can add an inexpensive print server device to most any printer (right). Many newer printers are "network-ready" (center), so they can attach directly to the LAN.

The leftmost printer in Figure 2-6 is connected to a Windows-based PC using a high-speed USB (universal serial bus) connection. For most home network users, this is the most effective and least expensive way to share a printer, since it does not require any additional hardware or software. You can share virtually any printer using this method. There are two drawbacks to this approach, though. First, the PC must be running in order for the printer to be available to the other users on the network. If the PC is off, the printer isn't available. Second, because of the limited length of printer cables (usually 10 to 16 feet maximum), the shared printer must be located relatively close to the PC. This limits your options and may require that you place the printer in an inconvenient location like a bedroom.

The middle printer in Figure 2-6 is attached directly to the network. Many midrange and high-end printers come with a built-in Ethernet interface and don't require an attached PC for file sharing. These printers are designed to be shared on a network and can accept print jobs from several users at once. Because they don't require an attached PC, you can place them wherever you like. Most network-ready printers work with Windows and Mac PCs, but Mac users should check carefully before buying a network printer, since some printers only work with Windows PCs.

Many newer network printers use a Web browser interface to control and monitor the printer. This is a very nice feature to have because you can check the status of the printer (including ink and paper levels) without leaving your desk. Figure 2-7 shows the status screen from a typical network printer.

The rightmost printer in Figure 2-6 is connected to the network using a device called a *print server*. Print servers are available in a variety of configurations to connect to wired or wireless networks and to printers with USB or parallel connections. Figure 2-8 shows a typical print server.

Print servers like this one can turn almost any printer into a network printer. There are a few exceptions, though. Some very inexpensive printers (often called *controllerless printers*) use the attached PC to generate the printed image and will not work with a print server.

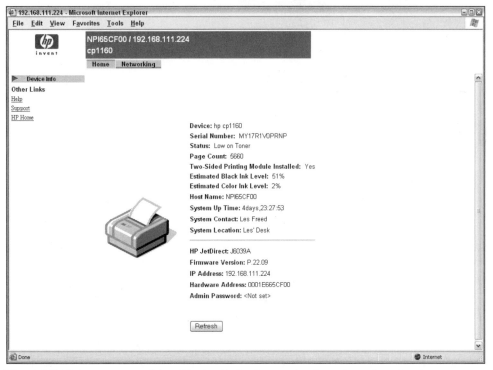

Figure 2-7: This status screen from a Hewlett-Packard network printer shows the printer's status at a glance.

Figure 2-8: This network print server is about the size of a deck of playing cards and operates with wired or wireless networks. The small connector on the left side of the picture is for a wireless antenna; the rear panel provides connections for wired Ethernet (left), a parallel printer (center), and the power cord.

Server-connected printers work much like their PC-connected counterparts, with two important differences. First, the print server isn't directly attached to each PC on the network, so the Plug and Play driver installation isn't possible. You will need to manually install the printer driver on each PC or Mac that will be using the shared printer. Second, many printers come with a status monitor program that shows the amount of paper or ink, or both, remaining in the printer. As a rule, status monitor programs can only operate over a USB or parallel cable connection, so they won't work through the print server.

Tip

If your printer has both USB and parallel connections, you'll want to buy a print server with a USB connection. Parallel printer connections are relatively slow and should be avoided when possible. This is especially true for photo printers because of the large amount of data transferred from the PC to the printer during the printing process.

Although print servers provide a high degree of convenience, they can also cause some logistical problems for users. When you're using a printer directly connected to your PC, you can tell at a glance what size and type of paper (if any) is installed in the printer. When you're using a remote network printer, you may not be able to see the printer from your desk. You may think you're printing to that sheet of expensive photo-quality paper you just put in the printer. But by the time you get back to your desk, your son may have decided to print his homework to the same printer—thereby wasting that 50-cent sheet of 8 × 10" glossy paper.

Tip

As a rule, I recommend using shared printers for plain-paper printing only. If you have a photo-quality printer, you'll be better off doing all your photo printing from the PC or Mac directly attached to the photo printer (or at least when you're alone in the house).

If you want to print a picture located on another computer elsewhere in the house, you can always use file sharing to open the image file on the remote computer.

Until recently, many printer makers completely ignored the home network market by offering network connections as an option only in their business-class printers. But a few printer makers—notably HP and Epson—now offer network-ready home printers and/or integrated print servers designed specifically for their home market printers. For example, some HP printers can accept a print server module that simply snaps into the rear of the printer.

Enjoying Multimedia Convergence

If you've picked up a copy of *PC Magazine* in the past five years, you've probably seen the term *multimedia convergence*. The basic idea behind convergence is that all of the computing and home entertainment devices in a typical home—including the PC, television, audio, and other electronic devices—will converge into a single, unified system.

Early convergence PCs from Sony and other video-savvy manufacturers simply grafted basic functions like a TV tuner and DVD player into a typical desktop PC. These products used the PC as the viewing platform for multimedia content. The problem is that after spending all day at their computers, most people don't want to come home and watch TV on a computer monitor.

A new wave of true convergence products is turning the tables. Rather than making the PC the center of the entertainment system, these products use the PC as an accessory to your existing home entertainment system . . . so you can relax on the sofa and watch the latest Hollywood blockbuster without having to worry about getting popcorn butter all over your keyboard.

The new convergence products use a home network—often in conjunction with a broadband Internet connection—to transport digital audio, video, and still image data. As we move toward faster, more reliable wireless connection, you can expect to see all sorts of new convergence technologies hitting the store shelves.

Using Digital Media on a Home Network

Over the past few years, we've witnessed an explosion in the use of digital cameras, MP3 players, and digital camcorders. If you own one of these devices, you probably have loads of music, still pictures, and digital video files on your computer.

Thanks to the popularity of Napster, Kazaa, and other file-swapping services, the MP3 digital audio file has become part of mainstream life for millions of users. There are dozens of programs available to record, edit, and play MP3 files. And if you like your music on the run, there are hundreds of portable MP3 players on the market, including tiny wearable models, larger, hard-drive-based products (like Apple's iPod), and even trunk-mounted systems for cars.

The problem with all of these players is that they don't have enough storage space to hold a large music collection. Virtually all MP3 players use a USB cable connection so that users can store their main stash of files on a PC and download selected tracks to a portable or car player. But unless you're lucky enough to have your PC located within an arm's length of your stereo system, there's been no easy way to listen to those MP3 files on your home entertainment system.

Tip

An *MP3 file* is simply an audio recording that has been converted to digital form and stored in a standard file format. MP3 became the most popular file format for digital audio because it is part of a larger, public standard developed by the Motion Picture Experts Group, or MPEG. And if the name MPEG rings a bell, it's because they are the same folks who developed a standard method for storing and compressing digital video. MPEG video files are used to store video files on PCs; MP3 is simply an audio-only version of MPEG.

The Motion Picture Experts Group is part of ISO—a network of standards organizations in 147 countries. Visit their interesting Web site at www.iso.org for more information.

Digital still and video camera users face a similar problem: Now that you have all of your family memories committed to digital form, how do you show them to family members—short of having everyone crowd around your computer monitor?

In the next few sections, I'll introduce you to a trio of new products designed to free your media files from the PC and move them out into the real world. Each of these products represents a new class of network-connected consumer electronics devices.

Home Media Hubs

A *home media hub* makes it possible—and easy—to listen to your MP3 files and view your digital still pictures on your home entertainment system. Figure 2-9 shows how a typical media hub works.

There are dozens of media hub products on the market. Most media hubs connect to your home entertainment system using standard analog audio and video cables, and to your home network using a wired or wireless Ethernet connection.

Media hubs have no storage of their own. They can only work with files stored on a PC on your network. As part of the installation process, you must install a small program on your PC. The program watches for requests from the media hub and serves up music and still image files for playback on the media hub. The Linksys media hub uses a remote control and on-screen menus (on the TV, not the PC) to help you navigate through your collection of music and pictures.

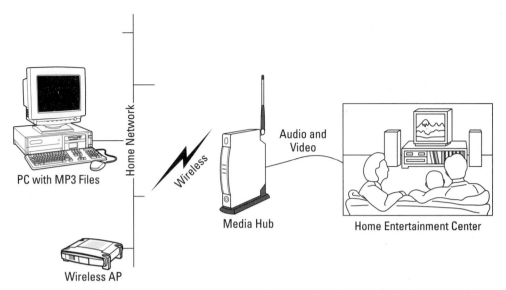

Figure 2-9: A media hub connects to your home wireless network. The media hub takes MP3 and digital image files stored on the PC and converts them into standard analog audio and video signals that you can connect to your home entertainment system.

The current generation of media adapters works with audio and still image files, but future models will include the ability to play back full-motion video from MPEG and other video file formats.

TiVo Series2

It's hard to explain the concept behind the TiVo system to someone who doesn't own one. Looking at the front of a TiVo recorder, shown in Figure 2-10, it's hard to tell what it is!

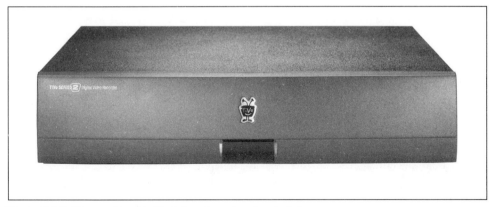

Figure 2-10: Okay, so it's a big black box, but what does it do?

©2002 TiVo Inc. All Rights Reserved.

The TiVo folks call their product a *digital video recorder*, and that's true enough—but that tells only part of the story. Basically, the TiVo DVR is like a hyperintelligent VCR that uses a large hard drive instead of videotape. Current models can hold up to 140 hours of content. Instead of programming the TiVo DVR using time and channel numbers (like you would on a VCR—if you actually could figure out how to program it), you simply pick a program from an on-screen program guide that shows a list of upcoming programs. You can also get a "season pass" that tells the TiVo system to record every episode of a particular program. The program display is updated daily (here's the home networking tie-in that you knew was coming) over the Internet. Figure 2-11 shows the rear panel of a TiVo recorder.

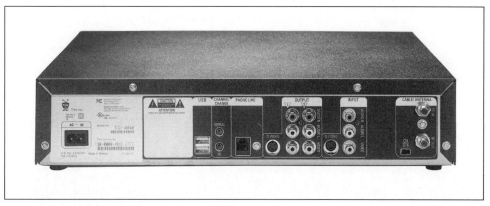

Figure 2-11: The rear panel has connections for your VCR, satellite receiver, cable box, TV set, stereo system, and two USB ports for add-ons like a broadband Internet connection.

The early model TiVo DVRs used a dial-up telephone line to make their daily (and very time-consuming) call in to the TiVo mother ship. But the newer TiVo Series2 systems can connect over your home network using a USB-connected Ethernet adapter.

As long as they were building a network connection into the machine, the folks at TiVo decided that it would be nice if you could use the TiVo DVR to play your MP3 files or to view your photo collection on your TV, so they added a new feature called Home Media Option to the basic TiVo service. If you're thinking that this sounds very much like the Linksys Media Adapter in the previous section, you're right.

Similar to the Linksys (and other media hub products), the TiVo DVR installs a program called the TiVo Server on your desktop PC. When you play back an MP3 or still image file on the TiVo DVR, the TiVo DVR fetches the file from your desktop PC.

TiVo Series2 machines also include two neat features that work only with TiVos connected to a home LAN. The first feature, called Multi-Room Viewing, allows you to record programs on one TiVo DVR and then watch them from another TiVo in a different room. Of course, you'll need two or more TiVos to use this feature, but it can help keep the peace in a TV-intensive household.

The second feature, called TiVoToGo, allows you to transfer recordings from your TiVo box onto a desktop or laptop PC. This feature allows you, for example, to record Leno or Letterman at night, transfer the recording to your laptop in the morning, and then watch the recording on the train during your morning commute.

The original TiVo products were offered only as standalone boxes like the one shown in Figure 2.10. TiVo has recently struck deals with several cable TV companies and home electronics vendors, and you can now purchase DVD recorders, satellite receivers, and cable TV set-top boxes with a built-in TiVo DVR.

Microsoft Media Center PC

Media Hubs are handy for sharing MP3 and digital still image files, and TiVo will change the way you watch TV—but the Media Center PC takes home media to the next level. A Media Center PC is a high-powered PC equipped with a large hard drive, large RAM memory, and a network connection. Most Media Center PCs also include a DVD player or recorder, audio and video inputs and outputs, a wireless remote control, and radio and TV tuners. Media Center PCs run a special version of Windows XP called XP Media Center Edition.

A fully-equipped Media Center PC can operate as a digital video recorder, DVD player, digital photo repository, and a digital music center. Most Media Center PCs come equipped with standard audio and video output connectors so you can connect them to a home entertainment system. Media Center uses a simple point-and-click interface that you can operate from your PC's keyboard or from the wireless remote. Figure 2-12 shows the main Media Center screen.

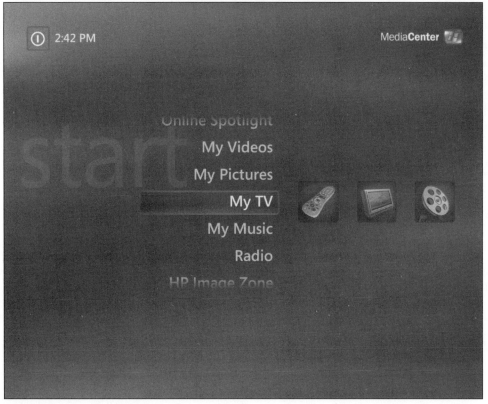

Figure 2-12: The main Media Center screen provides access to all of your home media, including TV, videos, digital images, and digital music.

Many Media Center PCs feature ultra-quiet cooling fans and hard drives so you can place them in your living room or home theater room. Some manufacturers even offer PCs packaged in cabinets designed to fit into a standard audio/video equipment rack. Media Center provides digital video recorder (DVR) features that rival TiVo's, but without the monthly fee.

If you don't want a PC in your living room, you can use a Media Center Extender (MCE) instead. An MCE is a small box (shown in Figure 2-13) that connects to your home entertainment system and to your home LAN.

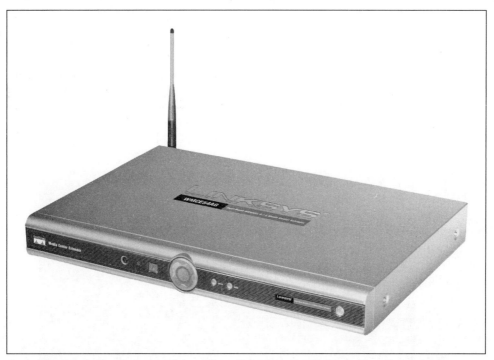

Figure 2-13: A Media Center Extender—such as the Linksys model shown here—brings Media Center PC features to any TV in your home. (Photo courtesy of Linksys.)

The rear of the MCE has standard audio, video, and digital audio connectors that connect to your TV and audio amplifier. The MCE acts as a bridge between your home entertainment system and a Media Center PC. You can use the MCE to watch live or recorded TV, play DVDs, listen to MP3 files, and view digital photos stored on your PC.

The user interface on the MCE is virtually identical to the Media Center screen shown in Figure 2-12. Most MCE devices can operate over wired or wireless LANs, so you don't need to run any new cables to connect the MCE box to your home LAN.

Playing Head-to-Head Games

Computer games have come a very long way from Adventure, the text-based role-playing game that wasted much of my time back in the 1980s. Today's games feature realistic animated graphics, stereo surround sound, and head-to-head multiplayer competition, either over the Internet or a LAN.

Not surprising, serious computer gaming requires top-end performance. Many computer makers now offer ultra-high-performance PCs designed specifically for serious computer game players.

The new generation of multiplayer games also requires a fast, responsive Internet connection. If you read any of the dozens of computer gaming discussion boards on the Internet, you'll hear a lot of tech terms like *latency* and *ping time*. These terms describe the amount of time it takes for data to travel over the Internet. Long latency is the kiss of death for gaming. If your opponent has lower latency times, you're toast.

Most home network firewalls are designed to block all incoming connections. This poses a problem for gamers, since many multiplayer games create a direct connection between the two players' computers. If you are into multiplayer games, you'll want to make sure that you purchase a router with a configurable firewall, so that you can customize the firewall's settings to allow incoming connections for specific game programs. Figure 2-14 shows a configurable firewall settings screen from a D-Link router.

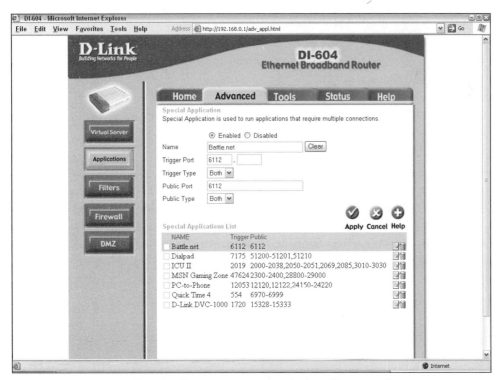

Figure 2-14: Many home firewalls allow you to customize the firewall's settings for computer gaming.

The network computer gaming market has become so hot that many network equipment makers maintain a list of popular games and their necessary firewall settings. If gaming is a big part of your computing life, you may need to do a little research before you purchase a firewall to make sure that you select a firewall that is compatible with your favorite games.

Summary

Now you know all the cool things you can do with a home network. I hope this chapter has given you some ideas on how to make the most of your home network system.

The key points in this chapter are as follows:

- Home networks aren't just for the Internet anymore.

- You can use file sharing to move, store, and archive files to and from any PC on your home network.

- By using printer sharing, you may be able to reduce the number of printers in your home.

- The worlds of home entertainment and home computing are growing closer because of media convergence.

- Multiplayer game programs place special demands on home network connections.

So now you know what a network can do for you. In Chapter 3, I'll explain the basics of how networks work, and I'll introduce you to some key networking concepts.

Chapter 3

A Networking Crash Course

The number of small-business and home networks has mushroomed over the past few years. Microsoft, Apple, and the leading network equipment manufacturers have responded to the demand by making networks simpler and easier to use than ever before. In fact, many office workers (and you may be one of them) use networked Macs and PCs every day without even realizing that they're using a network. This is called "seamless" networking, and it is the goal of every corporate network administrator.

Your home network can be just as seamless and as easy to use, but you'll have to be your own network administrator. Fortunately, you don't need a great deal of networking knowledge to set up your network, but you do need to know what a network is, what it does, and the basics of how it works. This chapter covers two major topics:

- The essentials of network communications, including Internet Protocol and IP addressing

- The basics of client-server and peer-to-peer networks

This is one of the more technical chapters in the entire book. After you've finished this chapter, you'll have a good working knowledge of basic networking concepts . . . maybe enough to impress the network guru at your office the next time he or she comes to fix your computer!

Network Connection Basics

If you could see the signals flowing inside an Ethernet cable, you would witness an incredibly complex and perfectly timed ballet of data flowing back and forth through the cable at an almost unimaginable speed. Wireless networks are even more complex because they must carry out the same complex data interchange using radio waves instead of cable.

Internet Protocol

The data traffic on any network is governed by a set of rules called a *network protocol*. A protocol defines the way data travels over the network and how to handle specific situations—like when two computers attempt to "talk" at the same time.

Different types of protocols define different aspects of a network's operation. Network designers often categorize protocols by their closeness to the communications hardware; the lowest-level **31** protocols deal directly with the communications hardware, while the highest-level protocols address the interaction between the computer and the users. At the lowest level, protocols like Ethernet define how to move a series of messages called *packets* over the network.

These low-level protocols are primarily concerned with transporting packets of data from one place to another, so they don't attempt to make sense of the data they are carrying. Higher-level protocols address specific tasks once the data arrives at its destination.

There have been dozens of protocols used for computer networking over the years. For many years, Novell's IPX protocol was widely used (usually in conjunction with Ethernet) on corporate LANs that used Novell NetWare file servers. IPX and many other protocols were either proprietary to or at least closely aligned with a specific manufacturer.

The *Internet Protocol* (almost always called *IP*) is the underlying protocol used to carry traffic over the Internet. IP doesn't belong to any specific manufacturer or software vendor, so it can be freely used by anyone. A group called the Internet Engineering Task Force (IETF) develops and maintains standards for IP and the associated protocols to ensure compatibility with existing and future applications.

Note

The IETF (www.ietf.org) is an international community of network designers, service providers, hardware manufacturers, and researchers. Their primary mission is to ensure and facilitate the continuing evolution of the Internet. The IETF is itself part of the Internet Society (www.isoc.org). Both Web sites contain a treasure trove of information about IP and the Internet in general.

IP is often used in conjunction with another protocol called the *Transfer Control Protocol*, or TCP. In fact, the two protocols are so often used together that network old-timers still refer to them as TCP/IP. TCP enables two devices on the Internet to create a connection between them. TCP contains error-checking and retransmission features to ensure that no data is lost as it travels over the Internet.

The beauty of the IP protocol is that it is *extensible* (that is, it can be extended to add new capabilities). One of the most significant extensions ever made to IP was the *Hypertext Transfer Protocol*, the protocol you know as the "http" at the beginning of a Web address. Other widely used IP-based protocols include the Post Office Protocol (POP3) used to pick up your e-mail, the File Transfer Protocol (FTP) used for file transfers, and the Simple Message Transfer Protocol (SMTP) used to send outbound e-mail. These and other protocols provide a traffic system for all the data crisscrossing the Internet.

IP Addressing

Every single device connected to the Internet—including Web and mail servers, computers of all sizes, and even many Web-enabled phones—must have a unique address; this unique addressing ensures that any two devices on the Internet will be able to communicate with each other. An *IP address* is a series of four numbers between 0 and 255, separated by periods. For example, 192.168.1.2 and 24.2.3.33 are typical IP addresses.

At the time the IP protocol was created, there were only a few hundred thousand computers on the entire planet, and only a tiny fraction of those were connected to the ARPANET (the predecessor to the Internet, constructed by the U.S. Department of Defense). Thanks to the incredible foresight of the Internet's designers, the four-number IP address scheme allows for over 4 billion unique addresses (score one point for engineering overkill!).

While 4 billion sounds like a huge number, it isn't. Because of inefficiencies in the way addresses are assigned, there aren't enough addresses to go around. Experts estimate that the supply of IP addresses will be exhausted in 2008 or 2009. There are two solutions to this address shortage problem. In the long term, the Internet will move to a new addressing scheme called IP Version 6 (IPv6 for short) that will provide a staggering 35 trillion unique addresses. But until the eventual switch to IPv6 takes place, two stopgap technologies called *Dynamic Host Configuration Protocol* (DHCP) and *Network Address Translation* (NAT) will get us through. I'll discuss these two technologies later in this chapter.

Note

No one knows exactly how long it will take to transition to IPv6, but most experts expect the complete transition to take 10 to 15 years. In the meantime, IPv6 is fully backward-compatible with the existing IPv4, ensuring complete Internet connectivity between different-generation devices. For complete details on IPv6, visit www.ipv6.org.

There are two basic types of IP addresses: public and private. Virtually all small networks (like the home LAN you're about to install) use a single *public* IP address to connect to the Internet and a pool of *private* IP addresses for the computers on the LAN. The private addresses on the LAN side of the connection are typically supplied by a NAT firewall/router. The major difference between public and private IP addresses is a simple but important one. Public addresses are unique and can be reached from any other computer on the Internet. Private addresses are not unique (although all of the private addresses on a single LAN must be unique) but are not reachable via the Internet. As we'll see in Chapter 9, many home routers allow you to pass connections from the public Internet through to a private address on your LAN.

Note

Many universities and private corporations own large blocks of IP addresses. In the early days of the Internet, it was common practice to assign a unique public address to each device on the LAN.

PUBLIC IP ADDRESSES

One of the original design goals for the Internet was that any device on the Internet be able to connect directly to any other device. This design goal requires that every computer on the Internet must have a unique IP address. It also requires that public addresses be carefully coordinated so that no two devices have the same address.

Machines are good at remembering numbers, but humans aren't, so each public IP address may have a *host name* associated with it. For example, when you connect your Web browser to the Web server (host) named www.pcmag.com, you are actually connecting to IP address 63.87.252.186. The conversion from a human-friendly host name to a machine-readable IP address is performed by a *Domain Name Server*, an online database of host names and IP addresses.

In the early days of the Internet, there were very few personal computers, and the idea of a portable computer was still science fiction. As the Internet grew in the early 1990s, an important transition took place. Suddenly, the majority of computers on the Internet were transient rather than permanent. Instead of being installed and operated by computer scientists, they were being installed and used by mere mortals with little or no knowledge of IP and its inner workings. The huge increase in demand for Internet access put a strain on the pool of available IP addresses.

Note

With over four billion addresses, you'd think there would be plenty to go around—but there aren't. The problem is not with the number of addresses but rather with the way they are assigned. Some North American universities and corporations actually have more assigned addresses than entire large countries such as China and Japan. The transition to IPv6 will fix the address shortage once and for all. For more information on how IP addresses are allocated, visit the Internet Center for Assigned Names and Numbers (ICANN) at www.icann.org.

Most ISPs have temporarily dodged the IP address crunch by distributing reusable IP addresses on demand. The Dynamic Host Configuration Protocol (DHCP) is an extension to TCP/IP that defines a way for individual devices to request and obtain a temporary IP address. When you use a cable, DSL, or dial-up modem to connect to the Internet, your computer or router requests a public address from your ISP. Each ISP owns a large block of IP addresses, and the ISP assigns your connection an address from that pool of available addresses.

The address assigned by DHCP is unique but temporary, thus allowing ISPs to assign users an IP address from a pool of available addresses. DHCP makes life easier for Internet users because it eliminates the need for each computer to be manually configured with a specific IP address. DHCP users can simply turn on their computers, connect to the Internet, and surf the Web without knowing a thing about IP addresses.

PRIVATE IP ADDRESSES

DHCP and reusable addresses have helped to deal with the IP address shortage, but they are only a partial solution. If you're setting up a small LAN, you'll need a unique IP address for each computer on your network—but there's a catch. Most ISPs only supply one IP address per connection. If you have a dial-up, cable, or DSL connection to the Internet, your ISP assigns a single IP address to your connection. If you have more than one computer on your LAN, you'll need some more addresses.

The solution is to use a single, public IP address to communicate with the Internet while using a range of private addresses for the computers on your LAN.

Fortunately, the Internet's designers set aside several blocks of IP addresses for use on private networks. When you set up your home LAN, you can use any of these private address ranges for your PCs. Table 3-1 lists the private IP address ranges.

Table 3-1   Private IP Address Ranges

Address	Number of Available Networks and Addresses
10.0.0.0–10.255.255.255	1 network with over 1 billion addresses
172.16.0.0–172.31.255.255	16 networks with 65,535 addresses on each network
192.168.0.0–192.168.255.255	256 networks with 254 addresses on each network

The 10.0.0.0 network address range allows you to create a single network with a billion addresses. Obviously, you don't need a billion addresses on your private LAN. Most home networking equipment comes from the factory preconfigured to use the 192.168.x.x address range, but you can use any of the three private address ranges for your home LAN.

Routers designed for small networks use a technique called *Network Address Translation* (NAT) to funnel traffic from several private IP addresses into a single public address. I'll explain NAT in detail in Chapter 9.

The majority of home networks use the 192.168.x.x private addresses, primarily because that is the default setting on most home routers. Figure 3-1 shows a typical home LAN using private IP addressing.

The router in Figure 3-1 acts as a DHCP client to obtain a public IP address from the ISP. When the router first powers up, it sends a DHCP request to the ISP. The ISP's router responds with a public IP address, and the router uses that address to communicate with the Internet. The public address remains assigned to that particular connection for a period of time determined by the ISP, usually until the connection or the router is reset.

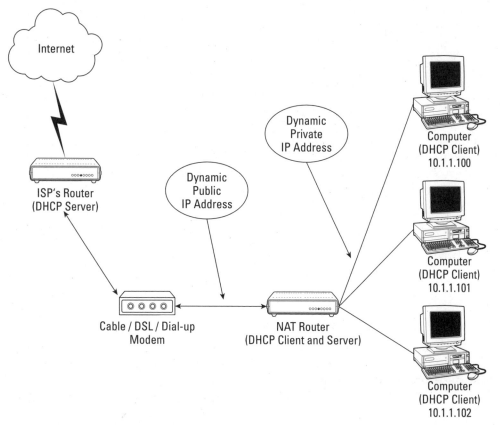

Figure 3-1: A NAT router provides a simple way to share Internet access using a single public IP address.

The router also acts as a DHCP server for the clients on the LAN. This arrangement allows for hands-off plug-and-play configuration of all the PCs on the LAN. When each PC is powered up, it sends a DHCP request to the router; the router responds with a private IP address for the PC to use. In most cases, the LAN DHCP server also provides the clients with all the information they will need to connect to the Internet. Figure 3-2 shows the information that a Windows XP PC needs to connect to the Internet.

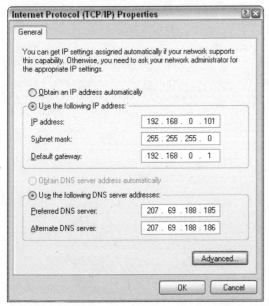

Figure 3-2: You can use the Windows XP TCP/IP Properties
screen to manually enter your network's IP configuration.

In the example in Figure 3-2, I have chosen to manually configure the IP settings. If your network has a DHCP server, you can just check the box marked "Obtain an IP address automatically" and let your network's DHCP server do all the work for you.

Mac OS/X computers have a similar network settings dialog box, found in the Network section of the system preferences. Figure 3-3 shows the Mac network settings control panel.

Note

If you look closely at the Mac network settings control panel, you'll see that OS/X already has support for IPv6. As you can see from the example, IPv6 addresses are very, very long!

In most cases, it is easier and simpler to use automatic DHCP addressing on a home LAN. If you choose to use manual addressing, you'll need to manually enter the IP address, subnet mask, router address, and DNS server names for each computer on your LAN. You'll also need to keep track of each computer's IP address, since no two computers can have the same address. In either case, you may find it helpful to know what these settings are and what they do. Table 3-2 explains the IP configuration settings.

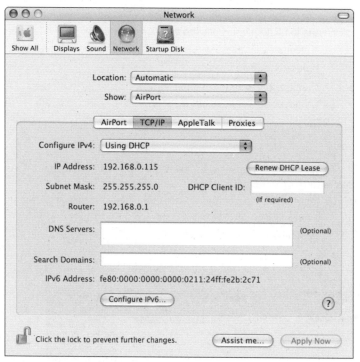

Figure 3-3: The Mac OS/X Network settings control panel allows you to select manual or automatic IP addressing for each network connection. This example shows the IP settings for an AirPort wireless network connection.

Table 3-2   IP Configuration Settings

Setting Name	Contents and Purpose
IP Address	Assigns an IP address to the connection.
Subnet Mask	Indicates how many other computers are on the same network. Computers on the same network can be reached directly without going through the router, so this setting is used to let each computer know how to reach other computers on the LAN

Continued

Table 3-2   IP Configuration Settings *(continued)*

Setting Name	*Contents and Purpose*
Default Gateway (Windows) or Router (Mac OS/X)	Tells the computer how to reach other IP addresses that are not on the local network. Traffic bound for addresses not on the local network is passed on to this address
Preferred DNS Server (Windows) or DNS Servers (Mac OS/X)	Tells the computer which DNS server(s) to use to resolve host names into IP addresses
Alternate DNS Server	Contains the address of a backup DNS server to use if the preferred server does not respond

Most home network routers use DHCP to obtain a public IP address from the ISP. The majority of ISPs also provide a list of DNS servers to the router along with the IP address.

When the router responds to DHCP requests from clients on the LAN, the router issues a private IP address from its own pool of IP addresses, and it also passes on the DNS information it received from the ISP. Figure 3-4 shows the status screen from a Linksys router.

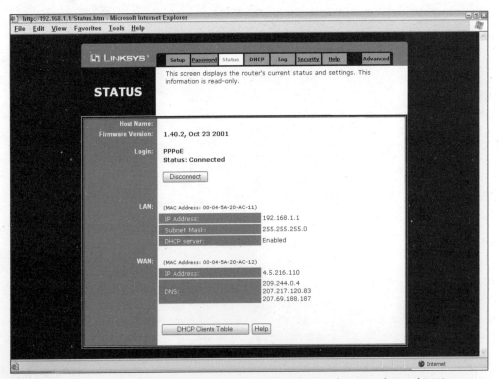

Figure 3-4: This status screen from a Linksys router shows the currently assigned IP and DNS server information.

The screen in Figure 3-4 shows the router's current LAN and WAN (wide area network, or Internet) status. The LAN settings show that the router itself is using an address of 192.168.1.1 and that the LAN DHCP server is enabled. The DHCP settings screen (not shown here) allows the network administrator to choose a range of IP addresses for the computers attached to the LAN.

The WAN settings section of Figure 3-4 shows the current IP address and DNS server as provided by the ISP—in this case, using a DSL modem. The ISP has issued an address of 4.5.216.110, and the ISP has also provided the addresses of three DNS servers.

HOW IP ROUTING WORKS

So far, I've mentioned routers about a dozen or so times without explaining why they are called routers in the first place. As the name implies, a *router* is a device that routes traffic between two or more networks. On home networks, the router connects your LAN to the Internet. The router's primary job is to watch all traffic coming and going on the local network, and to direct the traffic to the appropriate destination.

TCP/IP traffic travels over the Internet in chunks called *packets*. In addition to the actual data being transferred, each TCP/IP packet contains information to help the packet move through the Internet.

Imagine that you were going to mail a page of information from one place to another. You'd put the page in an envelope, and you'd write your return address at the top and the recipient's address in the middle of the envelope. TCP/IP packets work in much the same way. The packet is the envelope, and the page of information is the data. Each IP packet is preceded by a block of information called a *header*. The IP header contains information about the data being sent, the most important of which are the *source address* and the *destination address*. As you may have guessed, the source address is the IP address of the computer that sent the packet, and the destination address is the IP address of the ultimate recipient of the packet.

Traffic on a small LAN contains a mix of on- and off-LAN traffic. Communications between computers directly attached to the LAN, like the three computers on the right side of the diagram in Figure 3-1, travel directly from the source to the destination address. For example, if you print to a network printer attached to the LAN, the data travels directly from your PC to the printer, and the router does not manage the traffic flow between them.

In contrast, let's say that you've opened your Web browser and typed in the address of a Web server. The Web server's address isn't on the local network, so the PC sends the traffic to the *Default Gateway* address as specified in the computer's TCP/IP settings. The default gateway router determines how to send the data to the destination address. Home LAN routers simply pass the data on to the ISP's router. Larger routers—like the ones at your ISP's data center—are very complex devices that use sophisticated techniques to determine how best to get your data to its destination.

IP SECURITY ISSUES

The Internet has always been an open platform, both from a technical and a content perspective. In the early days of the Internet, it was common practice for every Internet user to have a shared files folder open to all users on the Internet. Anyone who wanted to could look through the public folder and upload or download files. The early Internet was a very small community of researchers and computer scientists at major universities, so there was really no need for elaborate security measures. As a result, many of the core Internet protocols—including IP and the SMTP mail transfer protocol—have very few inherent security features.

Today, hardly a week passes without a headline-making Internet attack, virus outbreak, or major security breach. A lack of security features in SMTP has made it trivially easy for spammers and scammers to hijack legitimate e-mail accounts in order to propagate millions of spam e-mails every day. Network hacking has become a competitive sport, with some hacker groups even staging hacking contests to see who can break into the most systems in a 24-hour period. If you think that hackers only target large, high-profile computers like the Department of Defense or the White House, think again: The always-on nature of home broadband Internet connections like DSL and cable modems makes them a favorite target of hackers.

Note

Technically, a hacker is anyone who scours the Internet looking for security flaws. Many hackers actually perform a public service by detecting and reporting security flaws. A cracker is someone who looks for security flaws as a way to exploit, intercept, or steal data.

Fortunately, the NAT connection sharing technique used by most home broadband routers provides good protection against intruders. Computers connected to a NAT router aren't directly reachable over the Internet, and many NAT routers include "stealth" features that make them appear invisible to hacker probes. When an intruder attempts to connect to one of the computers on your LAN, the NAT firewall refuses the connection.

Tip

It is important to remember that a NAT firewall offers no protection at all against computer viruses. Many newer viruses are network-aware, meaning that they actively seek out and infect other computers on the local network. If one user gets the virus, it is often only a matter of minutes before all of the other computers on the LAN are infected. You should plan to install a good, reliable antivirus program on each computer on your LAN—and make sure you keep the antivirus software updated on a regular basis. Most antivirus programs have an automatic update feature to ensure that you always have the latest and most complete virus protection.

Understanding Client-Server and Peer Networks

Back in the early days of PC networks, hard drives and printers were very expensive. The earliest computer networks were designed to provide a way for many users to share those expensive disks and printers.

Those early computer networks were based on a *client-server* model, meaning that one or more servers on the network provided services for the client PCs on the LAN. Client-server LANs are still widely used in business networks, but they are overkill for most home users. All later versions of the Mac OS and all versions of Windows since Windows 3.1 include a feature called *peer networking*, which allows users to create a free-form network of clients and servers as necessary. Table 3-3 shows the major differences between server-based and peer networks.

Table 3-3   Server and Peer Networks Compared

Server Network	Peer Network
All shared files are located on one or more server computers.	Shared files may be located on any computer on the network.
Users must provide a user name and password before being granted access to the network.	User authentication is optional at the discretion of the system administrator.
Network server software can be expanded to offer additional services like e-mail, shared database, and centralized backup services.	Windows peer networking provides file and printer sharing only.
A server network requires a dedicated server PC; clients cannot provide shared files or printers for others to use.	Any PC may be a server or a client.
Server software is optimized for high performance.	The server feature is part of the operating system and may impact performance of the PC.

The largest practical difference between server and peer networks is one of control. Server-based LANs are typically controlled by one or more system administrators. The administrator exercises tight control over access to the LAN and also determines which users have access to which shared resources. The high level of control is essential in order to protect confidential data stored on the servers. For example, everyone in the human resources department may need access to the employee records database, but the highly sensitive nature of the data demands that it be well protected from snoopers.

In comparison, peer networks are more democratic, even anarchistic. Anyone can share any file on the network without first obtaining permission from a system administrator—if there even is an administrator. Most peer networks—including the file and print sharing features built into Windows—contain user authentication features, but few users bother to use them. In Chapter 10, I'll show you how to use these features to protect your own sensitive files from other users on your home network.

Client-Server Networks

As its name implies, a client-server LAN contains both *clients* and *servers*. A server provides a service for other computers to use; a client is a computer that makes use of those services. There are many types of servers in use today, including file servers, print servers, and database servers. Figure 3-5 shows a simple client-server network.

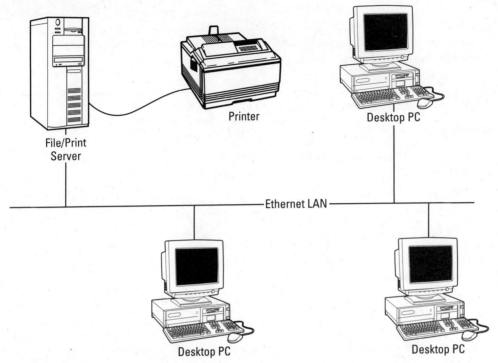

Figure 3-5: This client-server LAN has one server and three PCs. The server provides file and print sharing services for the client PCs on the LAN.

Client-server LANs aren't widely used on home networks but are still very popular in the business world. Most server operating systems include very strong user authentication features, automatic data backup, and redundant data storage capabilities. These features aren't necessary for most home networks but are essential for storing and protecting important business data.

The clients on a server-based LAN can connect to shared resources (drives, printers, and databases) located on the server, but they don't typically provide any shared resources to other clients on the LAN.

Although the client-server concept was first applied to network file sharing, it has since been adopted for other applications. Table 3-4 shows some common (and familiar) client-server systems.

Table 3-4   Common Client-Server Systems

Application	*Server*	*Client*
World Wide Web	Web server	Web browser
E-mail	SMTP server (outgoing mail), POP3 server (incoming mail)	E-mail client program (Outlook Express, and so on)
USENET discussion groups	NNTP server	Newsgroup client (Outlook Express, Forte Agent, and so on)

Application	Server	Client
Multiplayer games	Game system host	Game software with multiplayer features
Internet Relay Chat	IRC server	IRC client
Dynamic Host Configuration (DHCP)	DHCP server (usually embedded in routers or other network devices)	Any TCP/IP device

Peer-to-Peer Networks

Peer-to-peer networks are very popular with home and small-business network users because they are very flexible. On a peer network, any computer can be a server, a client, or even both at the same time. Windows XP and Mac OS X both have built-in networking that lets each machine share files and printers with the other computers on your network.

Note

You've probably heard the term *peer file sharing* used to describe Internet-based file swapping services like Kazaa and BitTorrent. While the names are very similar, peer-to-peer LANs and peer file sharing networks are two completely different things.

Peer networking was introduced in Windows with the release of Windows 3.1, and each successive release of Windows has offered substantially improved networking features. With earlier versions of Windows, you often got the impression that the networking features were added into Windows after the fact—because they were. The networking features in Windows 2000 and Windows XP are tightly integrated into the operating system and provide users with a nearly seamless network environment.

PEER FILE SHARING IN WINDOWS

Figure 3-6 shows a typical small peer-to-peer LAN with four PCs and one printer.

In Figure 3-6, the computer named Bugs is sharing two directories named Pictures and MP3s. The computer named Daffy is sharing a single directory named Articles. Computer Marvin, on the lower left of the diagram, is using the Pictures folder from Bugs and the Articles folder from Daffy. All of the shared folders on the network appear when you click on the My Network Places icon. To use a shared folder, you open My Network Places and navigate through the list of shared folders until you see the one you want.

If you frequently need access to a shared folder, you may want to use a mapped drive, which creates a virtual disk drive on a client computer that connects to a shared folder on another. Marvin's user has chosen to create mapped drives on Marvin that point to shared folders on Bugs and Daffy. In the example, Drive Z: on Marvin is mapped to the Pictures folder on Bugs, and Drive Y: is mapped to the Articles folder on Daffy.

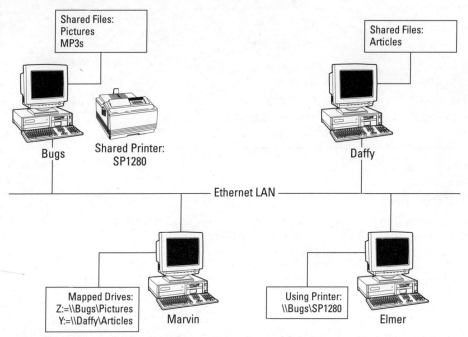

Figure 3-6: On a peer network, each PC can be a client, a server, or both at the same time.

There are two reasons to create a drive mapping. Some older Windows programs are not *network-aware*. These programs know how to deal with physical drive letters like C:, but they don't understand network drive names such as \\Bugs\Pictures. Drive mapping solves this problem by creating a virtual disk drive that connects to a shared network drive. As far as application programs know, Drive Z: is a local drive on Marvin. The second reason is simply one of convenience. It is a lot simpler to remember "Drive Y:" than "\\Daffy\Articles".

Naming Your Computers

Each computer on a Windows network must have a unique name (in addition to a unique IP address), so you might as well have a little fun with it. In case you hadn't noticed, most of the computers on my own LAN are named after Warner Brothers cartoon characters.

Other popular naming themes include the following:

- *Star Wars, Hitchhiker's Guide,* and *Star Trek* characters

- Greek and Roman gods and goddesses

- Presidents, kings, queens, outlaws, and so on

I'll show you how to change your computer's name in Chapter 8.

You create mapped drives by right-clicking on the My Computer or My Network Places icons on the Windows desktop. Figure 3-7 shows the Map Network Drive dialog box.

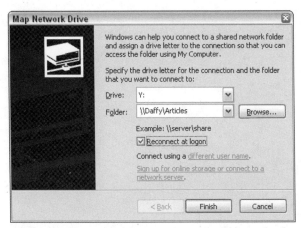

Figure 3-7: You use the Map Network Drive dialog box to create drive mappings.

When you create a mapped drive, you can tell Windows to automatically reconnect that mapping each time you start your computer. This saves you from having to manually map your favorite drives upon startup.

PEER PRINTER SHARING

In Figure 3-6, you may have noticed that the computer named Bugs is sharing a printer named SP1280, and the computer named Elmer is using the shared printer. Any computer on the LAN may print to any shared printer as long as the proper printer driver is installed on the computer using the shared printer. I discuss printer sharing in detail in Chapter 11.

FILE SHARING WITH MAC OS X

OS X includes built-in file sharing services very similar to those in Windows. In the early days of PC networking, it was very difficult to share files between Macs and PCs. Beginning with version 10.2, OS X now includes Windows-compatible file sharing. This feature provides for simple, easy sharing of files between Macs and Windows PCs on a LAN.

Note

There's more to file sharing than simply being able to move files from one machine to another. It is vitally important that both computers share a common file format. Thanks to standardization efforts on both sides of the Mac / PC divide, most PC applications can open files created on a Mac and vice-versa.

To enable file sharing on an OS X system, you click the sharing icon in the Internet & Networking section of System Preferences. You'll see a display like the one in Figure 3-8.

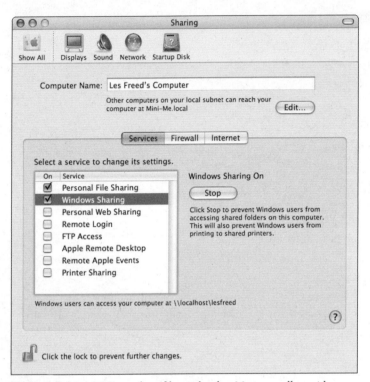

Figure 3-8: Mac OS X can share files with other Macs as well as with Windows PCs.

As you can see from Figure 3-8, OS X has separate settings to enable Personal File Sharing (for Mac-to-Mac file sharing) and Windows Sharing (for Mac-to-Windows sharing.) This setting only controls the Mac's ability to share files with Windows PCs. It does not need to be enabled to allow a Mac to use shared files stored on a Windows PC.

Summary

Thanks for sticking with me through this somewhat technical chapter. I hope you've learned a few key concepts about networking. As you've seen, configuring and managing your own home network doesn't really require an IT degree. As you progress through the process of building and using your network, you'll be glad you have these concepts under your belt.

The key points in this chapter are as follows:

- The IP protocol is the heart of the Internet and the basis for most LANs too.

- You only need a single public IP address to connect your entire LAN to the Internet.

- Most routers incorporate a DHCP server to automatically configure all the computers on your LAN.

- Network security is a concern for small LANs just as it is for large ones.

- Windows includes very flexible peer-to-peer networking features that are easy to use and understand.

In Chapter 4, I'll take the concepts you learned in this chapter and show you how to use them to design the perfect home network for your needs.

Part II

Designing Your LAN

Chapter 4

Designing Your Network

An almost overwhelming number of networking products are on the market today. During my research for this book, I spent some time browsing the network aisle of my favorite computer and electronics stores, watching customers trying to decide exactly what products to buy to build their home networks. A few customers knew exactly what they wanted and were out of the store in minutes. Others picked up nearly every box on the shelf, trying to make heads or tails out of the diagrams on the backs of boxes. More than a few left the store empty-handed.

Many of the salespeople I encountered weren't much help, either. While some were knowledgeable and helpful, others were nearly as clueless as their perplexed customers. My goal for this section of the book is to give you the information you need to make an intelligent, informed buying decision—so you can be one of those people who know exactly what they need. In this chapter, I cover the following:

- Deciding which networking technology is best for your home
- Designing an Ethernet (wired) network
- Designing a wireless network
- Alternative networking technologies

Wired, Wireless, or Both?

In a perfect world, we wouldn't need wired networks anymore, and I wouldn't need this section of this book. But although wireless networks have tremendous appeal—including simple installation, good speed, and excellent portability—they aren't the perfect solution for every home network.

Wired Ethernet networks are more difficult to install but offer higher speed and better reliability than wireless networks—at a much lower cost. Running cables can be difficult and expensive, however, which makes Ethernet a nonstarter for many home users.

Before you choose a network technology for your home, you need to know all the advantages—and the pitfalls—of each.

Note

Throughout this book, I'll use the term *Ethernet* to refer to wired networks and the terms *wireless* and *WiFi* when discussing wireless networks. When you're shopping for networking equipment, you may encounter the term *wireless Ethernet,* which may seem to be an oxymoron, but it isn't. WiFi wireless networks use a variant of the Ethernet networking protocol over a wireless communications link.

In many cases, the best networking solution may involve a mix of networking technologies. Fortunately, you can mix and match networking technologies to create a network that works best for your individual needs.

Is Wireless Best for You?

Wireless networks allow you complete freedom to place your computers wherever you want, without having to worry about how you're going to get a cable from your PC to your network. The newest generation of wireless LANs are faster, more secure, and more reliable than products from just a year or two ago—and they cost less too. They are very popular with laptop computer users because you can surf the Net from your sofa, your back porch, or just about anywhere you like.

Under ideal conditions, the fastest wireless LANs operate at about half the speed of Ethernet LANs. But in real-world conditions, wireless LANs often operate at far less than their theoretical maximum speed.

Many businesses have installed wireless LANs to allow workers to stay connected to the network while attending meetings, giving presentations, or collaborating with colleagues throughout the building. The emergence of wireless LANs has also attracted the attention of retailers and telecommunications providers. Many Starbucks, McDonald's, and independent coffee shops offer fee-based wireless access to customers. You can also get wireless Internet access in many airport departure lounges and hotels. Some large airports even offer free wireless Internet access throughout the terminal building. Thanks to a very well-defined industry standard, you can use your wireless-equipped laptop at home, at the office, and even on overseas business trips.

Warning: Keep Away from the Pool

Wireless LAN and laptop computer ads often show a happy laptop user sitting by the pool, sipping one of those tall, frosty drinks with an umbrella in it while supposedly doing productive work from home. I live in Florida, I have a wireless LAN in my house, and the wireless coverage even reaches out to the pool area.

There are three realities you'll need to face if you install a wireless LAN:

1. You can't see a laptop screen outside in the bright sun. I've tried it.

2. You can't get much work done if you're sipping umbrella-festooned drinks by the pool. I've tried that too.

3. Large bodies of chlorinated water and delicate laptop computers are a bad mix.

Wireless LANs are still in the evolutionary phase of their development cycle. In just a few years, wireless networks have increased in speed from 2 to 11 and now to 108 megabits per second (mbps). Engineers are always hard at work on the next generation of even faster wireless equipment. Fortunately, each successive generation of wireless equipment has been backward-compatible with previous generations. This allows users to keep much of their older, slower equipment while upgrading to a newer, faster wireless LAN.

Despite their enormous appeal, wireless LANs aren't the best solution for everyone. Because they rely on microwave radio signals, the working range of wireless LANs is very limited. Common electronic devices such as 2.4 GHz telephones and microwave ovens can disrupt the weak radio signal, causing a slowdown or even total blackout of the wireless LAN. Concrete block, stucco, and steel-reinforced construction are major obstacles for wireless LAN signals, as are the metal, interior wall studs used in place of wood 2×4s in many newer homes.

Tip

Sometimes, a few dollars worth of Ethernet cable can do the job that a wireless network can't. My neighbor Gene wanted to install a wireless LAN in his home so that he could connect his daughter Elizabeth's computer to their existing broadband connection in Gene's home office. The home office and Elizabeth's room are no more than 75' apart—far less than the 300' to 900' range claimed for most wireless networks. But when we installed a wireless network in the home office, the wireless signal did not reach Elizabeth's room. The culprit was the steel-reinforced concrete construction of the house, which completely blocked the signal. We solved the problem by running an Ethernet cable under the house from the office to the bedroom.

Should You Stick With a Wired Network?

Wired Ethernet is cheaper, faster, and more reliable than wireless and will continue to be so for some time to come. Ethernet components—the network adapters, switches, and cables you'll need to build a network—are far less expensive than their wireless counterparts. But in many cases, the added expense and inconvenience of getting a cable to each computer or other component makes Ethernet impractical.

This is especially true if you live in a high-rise condominium or co-op apartment. Your city building code, apartment lease, or condominium charter may prohibit you from drilling holes through walls to run your Ethernet cables. Some city building codes may even require that your cables be installed in metal conduits, adding hundreds of dollars to the cost of your LAN.

Installation costs aside, a wired Ethernet network costs about half as much as a comparable wireless network. For less money, you get much better performance and higher reliability. Wired networks are also inherently more secure than their wireless counterparts because a would-be intruder must have physical access to your network cable in order to connect to your network.

"No new wires" Alternatives

There are two lesser-known network technologies that you can use instead of (or in addition to) wired Ethernet and wireless LANs: HomePlug and phone line networks. These products use the existing telephone or AC power wiring in your house to create a wired network without having to run any new wires.

While these products aren't as fast as 10/100 Ethernet, they can be a lifesaver in situations where wireless won't work and where you can't install Ethernet cable.

HOMEPLUG

HomePlug is a relatively new networking technology that transmits data over the existing AC power wiring in your home or office. With a maximum data throughput of only 6 mbps, HomePlug isn't as fast as Ethernet, but it is faster than many wireless networks. HomePlug networking products cost about the same as their wireless counterparts. HomePlug offers better mobility than a wired Ethernet network since you can (at least in theory) plug any HomePlug device into any electrical outlet. But HomePlug doesn't offer the complete freedom of mobility provided by wireless networks.

HomePlug networks are fast and reliable—if they work in your home. While the HomePlug signal doesn't interfere with appliances and other devices plugged into your home's electrical system, the reverse isn't always true. Some appliances and power tools can interfere with the HomePlug system, slowing or completely disrupting the flow of data. In addition, many modern homes use two separate 110 V feeds from the power company. Some circuits in the house are connected to one of the 110V feeds, and the remainder connect to the other feed. The use of two feeds poses a problem for HomePlug networks.

You can use HomePlug in conjunction with conventional wired and wireless Ethernet networks. For example, you may want to put a computer or printer at the far end of your home where it is out of reach of your wireless network. You can use a HomePlug connection to reach that one problem component, and use your wireless network for the rest of the house. I cover HomePlug in more detail later in this chapter.

PHONE LINE NETWORKS

Phone line networks are similar to HomePlug, but phone line networks use your existing telephone jacks instead of the AC power wiring. I'm not a big fan of phone line networks for several reasons, but the most important reason is also the most obvious: You must have a phone jack near the computer to use phone line networking. If someone were able to get a phone wire into the wall, you could probably get an Ethernet cable to the same location.

I'd like these products a lot better if they were faster and more reliable. I've used them in small homes with decent results, but they often fail to work at full speed (or at all) on certain types of telephone wiring. They are also problematic if you have DSL service on your phone line because the phone line network and DSL signals interfere with each other.

Evaluating Your Options

Now that you have a basic understanding of the four major home networking technologies—Ethernet, wireless, HomePlug, and phone line—you'll need to map out a networking plan for your home. Table 4-1 presents the pros and cons of each networking technology at a glance.

Table 4-1   Networking Technologies Pros and Cons

Network Type	Cost	Speed	Pros	Cons
Ethernet	Low	Best	Excellent security Often built in on new computers	Requires cable to each computer Cable installation can be difficult and/or costly No mobility
Wireless	High	Slow (802.11b) to medium (802.11a and g) to pretty good (802.11b WiMax)	Very flexible; no cables required Complete mobility	Highest cost Technology Still developing Requires security vigilance
HomePlug	Medium	Slow	Exceptionally easy installation	Limited speed May not work in some homes or on some power outlets More expensive than Ethernet
Phone line	Medium	Slow	Simple installation	Requires telephone outlet near computer Limited speed May interfere with DSL service

In the following sections, I'll explain how each networking technology works in more detail.

Ethernet Networks

Ethernet is one of the oldest LAN technologies on the planet, and it is still the most widely used. It is fast, reliable, and inexpensive. Many desktop and notebook computers come with an Ethernet connection as standard equipment, as do virtually all wireless access points, cable modems, and DSL modems. Even if you've decided to build an all-wireless network, you'll still have at least one Ethernet connection on your network, connecting your cable or DSL modem to your wireless access point.

Early Ethernet LANs operated at a speed of 10 mbps over several different types of bulky, expensive cable. In the early 1990s, the Ethernet standards committee issued a new standard for a more reliable, less expensive Ethernet cabling system called 10Base-T. Today's Ethernet networks are variations on and improvements of the original 10Base-T technology.

The big attraction of 10Base-T was that it used inexpensive unshielded twisted pair (UTP) cable with an 8-pin modular plastic connector at each end of the cable. The modular connectors are inexpensive and easy to install using a special connector crimping tool.

10Base-T networks were the standard for many years but were made obsolete by 100Base-T networks in the late 1990s. As you've likely guessed, 100Base-T networks operate at 100 mbps, 10 times the speed of 10Base-T. 100Base-T (also called Fast Ethernet) networks use a higher grade of UTP cable called Category 5 or CAT5 cable—so named because it is the fifth generation of UTP Ethernet cable. CAT5 cable looks like standard telephone cable but is slightly thicker.

To maintain backward compatibility with the huge installed base of 10Base-T equipment, most 100Base-T Ethernet equipment can operate at 10 or 100 mbps. You'll likely encounter the term "10/100 Ethernet" when you're shopping for network products. 10/100 devices automatically switch between 10 and 100 mbps operation as necessary. In practical terms, nearly every Ethernet product sold today can operate at 100 mbps. Keep in mind that even the slower 10 mbps Ethernet products are many times faster than a cable or DSL modem connection, so they are still more than fast enough for Internet-sharing applications. If you plan to do a lot of file and/or printer sharing, you may find that 10 mbps is just too slow.

The next-generation Ethernet technology is called Gigabit Ethernet which operates at 10 times the speed of 100Base-T networks. Gigabit products typically cost more than 100 mbps Fast Ethernet, and most Gigabit products are designed for business networks. Unless you really need the additional speed of Gigabit, 100 mbps provides more than enough speed for 99 percent of all home network applications. The remaining 1% of you—the ones who need to move huge, multi-gigabit files (such as large video files) across your LAN—will find the extra cost to be money well spent.

Each device on an Ethernet network is connected to a central point on the network, called a *switch*.

Figure 4-1 shows a typical Ethernet network with a PC, a laptop, a router, and a network printer all connected to an Ethernet switch.

Which CAT?

When shopping for cable, you'll encounter several cable type designators with names like CAT5, CAT5e, and CAT6. CAT5 cable is the minimum required for Fast Ethernet. CAT5e cable is a higher-grade version of CAT5, and CAT6 cable is commonly used for Gigabit Ethernet, an up-and-coming version of Ethernet that operates at 10 times the speed of Fast Ethernet.

There is only a very small pricing differential between CAT5 and CAT5e, so many retailers no longer carry the older CAT5 cable. CAT6 cable costs more than CAT5e but is worth the extra money if you want to future-proof your cable installation.

While I'm on the subject of cable, be sure to get the right type of cable for your installation. If you will be running cable though an attic or crawl space, your local building code may mandate the use of *plenum* cable. This cable is fire-resistant and burns without releasing noxious chemicals, but it is much more expensive than standard cable.

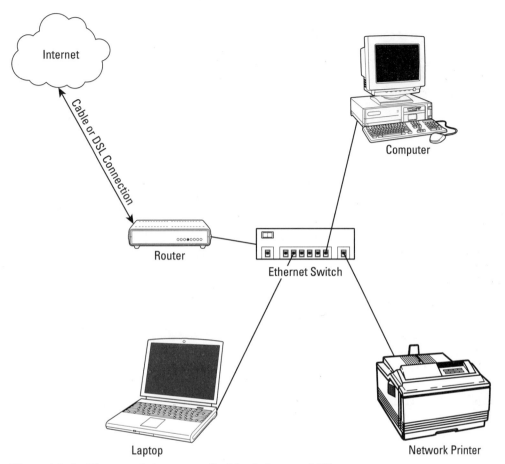

Figure 4-1: An Ethernet switch connects all of the devices on a LAN.

As you can see, the Ethernet switch is the center of the network; all traffic traveling between any two devices on the LAN must pass through the switch. Each network device has its own cable to the switch, so users can connect and disconnect to and from the network without disrupting the network traffic.

Switches come in a variety of sizes, with anywhere from 5 to 24 Ethernet connectors called *ports*. Most home network equipment makers offer two or three models designed for home LANs. Figure 4-2 shows a typical five-port Ethernet switch, with front and back views.

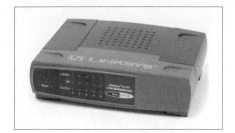 

Figure 4-2: This compact Ethernet switch from Linksys is about the size of a paperback book. The sixth connector (on the right) can be used to expand the network using a second switch.

One of the first decisions you'll need to make in designing your home network is deciding where to put the switch. Most people simply put the switch where it is the most convenient, usually near their main computer. This is fine, but you should bear in mind that each device on the network will have a cable to connect to the switch, so you may find yourself with a rat's nest of wires underneath your computer desk. If you are designing a network from scratch with components spread out around the house, you may be better off locating the switch in a central location in your home, perhaps in the attic, basement, or garage.

If you will have more than one computer or network device in a room (a home office, for example), you can install a second switch to service that one room and still have only a single cable connecting to the main switch located in the attic or basement. Figure 4-3 shows a typical two-switch network in a two-story home with a basement.

What's a Switch?

You may hear the terms Ethernet hub and Ethernet switch used interchangeably. They look alike on the outside, but they're very different on the inside.

Hubs are dumb devices that simply repeat everything they hear. When one computer sends a signal to the hub, the hub sends the identical signal back out to all of the other ports on the hub. This wastes network bandwidth because the majority of traffic on the LAN only needs to get from point A to point B (from a file server to a client, for example) without going to points C, D, E, and so on. Because all of the traffic is sent to all of the ports, it is possible (and in fact trivially simple) for an unauthorized user to capture and monitor all of the network traffic. This is a serious security problem for corporate users but not a major issue for home networks.

Switches are much more intelligent devices that analyze each packet coming in. The switch determines where the traffic needs to go and transmits it only on the port connected to the destination computer. This is a much more efficient use of the network's bandwidth, and it also prevents unauthorized users from intercepting traffic on the network.

Until recently, switches were much more expensive than hubs, but recent advances in switch technology have made hubs all but obsolete.

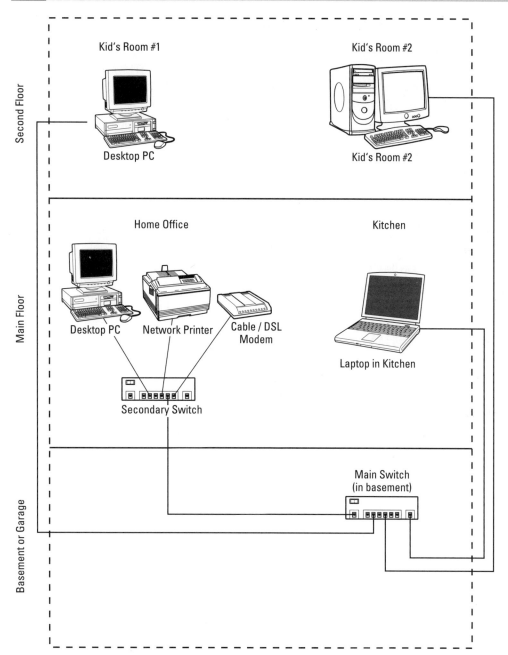

Figure 4-3: This two-switch network avoids cable clutter in the home office.

With only a single switch, the network in Figure 4-3 would have three cables coming from the two bedrooms and the kitchen into the home office. By using a second switch, only a single cable (to the basement switch) is required.

Need More Speed?

If you have several high-traffic devices (such as TiVo DVRs or Media Center Extenders) on your home LAN, you may want to consider Gigabit Ethernet as an alternative to 100 Mbps Ethernet. As the name implies, Gigabit Ethernet operates at 10 times the speed of 100 Mbps Ethernet. Gigabit operates over CAT6 twisted-pair cable, a higher-performance (and more costly) version of CAT5.

Gigabit products are more expensive than standard Ethernet, but gigabit prices are falling rapidly. Gigabit is most often used as the connection between two 100 mbps switches. In the example shown in Figure 4-3, it might make sense to use a gigabit connection between the main switch in the basement and the secondary switch in the home office area.

Ethernet switches are relatively inexpensive, so it often pays to buy a larger switch than you need. Having a few extra ports will cost you a few extra dollars but may save you from having to replace the switch with a larger one as your network grows.

Despite the tremendous advances in the price and performance of wireless networks, Ethernet is still my first choice for home networks.

Wireless Networks

Just a few years ago, wireless LANs were incredibly expensive, slow, and unreliable. Despite the drawbacks—and the well-publicized security issues associated with wireless LANs in the corporate workplace—wireless LAN products have become very popular with corporate and home users alike.

Today, you can buy everything you need to set up a wireless network in your home for just a few dollars more than a comparable Ethernet network. When you consider the potential cost and inconvenience of installing Ethernet cable, a wireless LAN may actually be cheaper.

Sorting Through the Standards

The Institute of Electrical and Electronic Engineers (IEEE) develops and maintains the standards for wireless networks. A separate industry trade group called the WiFi Alliance performs compatibility testing and issues certification—the WiFi Seal—for compatible products.

The WiFi certification assures buyers that WiFi products from one manufacturer will interoperate with equipment made by another. But many would-be buyers are confused by the maze of wireless products on the market. Much of this confusion is caused by the very similar IEEE standard names used to identify the different classes of wireless products.

Table 4-2 will help you sort out the different types of wireless products on the market.

Table 4-2   Wireless Network Standards

IEEE Name	Maximum Speed	Range	Radio Frequency	Performance	Price
802.11b	11 mbps	Good	2.4 GHz	Good	Low
802.11g	54 mbps	Good	2.4 GHz	Excellent	Medium
802.11a	54 mbps	Fair	5 GHz	Excellent	High
MIMO (proposed 802.11n)	108 mbps	Very Good	2.4 GHz	Excellent	Moderate

Structured Wiring

If you're building a new home, remodeling your existing home, or just looking for a project to keep you busy for a couple of weeks, you should consider installing structured wiring in your home.

Each structured wiring equipment maker has its own definition of exactly what structured wiring is. The basic concept is that every room in a house should have at least one and preferably two CAT5 UTP cables installed, along with one or two RG-6 coaxial cables for TV. All of the cables run back to a central point in the home (sound familiar?) to a device called a *patch panel*. The patch panel contains a jack for each cable, along with connections for telephone, cable or satellite TV, a DSL modem, and possibly other devices like an alarm or home control system. After the structured wiring is installed, you can connect telephones, computers, and televisions anyplace in the home without having to run new cables.

Many people (and companies) associate structured wiring with home automation systems that combine automated control of lights and appliances with a whole-house security system. Most automation systems require structured wiring, but you don't need such a system to take advantage of structured wiring.

Business networks have used structured wiring for many years. It is a great idea for homes too, although I'm not sure that you need two TV cables to every room in the house. But even though I'm a big fan of the concept, I don't have it in my 30-year-old home, and I don't plan to install it anytime soon.

The biggest problem with structured wiring is that it is very difficult to install in an existing home. Unless your home has a large attic above or a basement or crawl space below (my own home has neither), it can be very difficult to get cables to each room, and you'll need to find a place to put the patch panel.

New homes are a different story. You'll have to put telephone and cable TV wiring in your new home anyway, so you might as well do it right. An Internet search on "structured wiring" will provide you with all you could possibly want to know on the subject. Leviton Manufacturing has an excellent "how-to" guide on their Web site at www.levitonvoicedata.com.

802.11b was the first wireless standard to achieve critical mass in the market. As you can see from Table 4-2, 802.11b networks operate at 11 mbps, slightly faster than 10 mbps Ethernet. Thanks to the rapid price decrease of the faster 802.11g products, 802.11b is now essentially obsolete, although many public wireless hotspots still operate at 802.11b speeds.

A newer standard called 802.11g operates at up to 54 mbps, nearly five times the maximum speed of 802.11b. Both 802.11b and 802.11g networks use the 2.4 GHz radio band, and the two standards are compatible with one another.

A new variant of 802.11g, called MIMO, came to market just as we went to press. MIMO stands for Multiple Input Multiple Output, and it essentially uses two 802.11g radio systems working in tandem to deliver connection speeds up to 108 mbps. MIMO access points use two or more antennas to provide a broader coverage area than standard 802.11g access points. Figure 4-4 shows a typical MIMO access point.

Figure 4-4: The Linksys WRT-54G wireless router uses three antennas for better coverage. (Photo courtesy of Linksys)

MIMO devices are backwards-compatible with 802.11b and 802.11g devices, so you don't have to toss out all of your old equipment if you upgrade to MIMO; however, if you want to take full advantage of MIMO's increased speed, you'll need a MIMO-capable device at both ends of the wireless connection. If your laptop is equipped with a built-in 802.11g wireless adapter, you'll get better range using a MIMO access point or wireless router, but you won't see an increase in performance. Also, each manufacturer implements MIMO in a slightly different way, so it is a good idea to use the same brand of equipment across your entire network.

Wireless Architecture

Each device that will connect to the wireless network must have a *wireless network card*, also called a wireless adapter card, installed. Wireless adapters are available in a variety of form factors, including PCI cards for desktops, PC cards for portable computers, and external USB adapters for use with any USB-equipped computer.

"a" versus "g"

802.11a networks operate at 54 mbps. Because 802.11a uses a different set of radio frequencies in the 5 GHz radio band, it is not compatible with 802.11b or 802.11g products. 802.11a also has a much shorter range than 802.11b and g networks. Given their higher price, shorter range, and lack of compatibility with other WiFi devices, I don't recommend 802.11a products for use on a home network.

802.11g is just as fast as 802.11a but costs less and works with legacy 802.11b equipment; however, 802.11a has a few advantages that justify the higher cost. 802.11a's shorter range means that you need more access points to cover a given area. While this may seem like a disadvantage, there will be fewer wireless clients sharing each access point, resulting in higher overall performance for each client.

Because it operates in a different radio band, 802.11a is immune from interference caused by 2.4 GHz cordless phones and microwave ovens, but this will change as new 5.8 GHz cordless telephones become more popular.

The new generation 802.11g MIMO products offer better performance at a lower cost than 802.11a. Unless you're really concerned with interference from 2.4 GHz devices, MIMO is a better choice for home use.

Cross-Reference

Wireless adapters are covered in detail in Chapter 7.

Wireless networks can operate in one of two modes. The first, called *ad hoc mode*, allows wireless devices to communicate directly with one another. Figure 4-5 shows how ad hoc mode works.

Ad hoc mode is most useful for setting up on-the-fly network connections between portable devices. It is often used in business meetings to allow participants to exchange files with one other. Ad hoc mode is best suited for use on very small networks of two to three computers.

The majority of wireless LANs use *infrastructure mode*, where a central device called a wireless *access point* (or AP for short) manages the traffic on the wireless network. There are several types of AP units available for home use, including models with built-in firewalls and Ethernet switches, as you'll see in Chapter 5. The access point acts as an intermediary between the wireless network and a wired LAN, as shown in Figure 4-6.

In many ways, the AP performs the same function on a wireless LAN as a switch does on an Ethernet network. The AP manages the flow of traffic among the devices on the wireless network, and it also directs the traffic between the wired and wireless networks. Most APs are connected to an existing Ethernet network, so wireless devices can communicate with any other device on the wired or wireless networks.

Cross-Reference

See Chapter 7 for details on the finer points of wireless architecture.

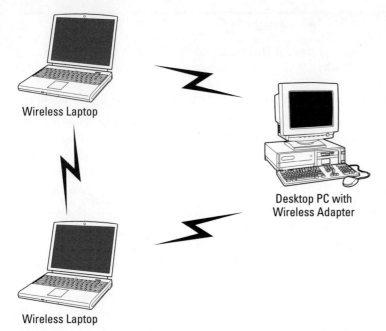

Figure 4-5: Computers operating in ad hoc mode communicate directly with one another.

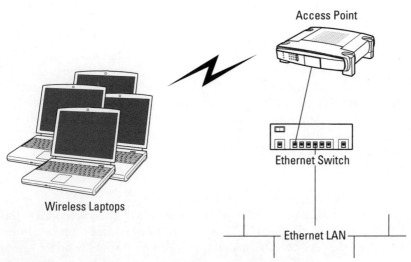

Figure 4-6: An infrastructure mode wireless LAN uses an access point to connect wireless devices to an Ethernet LAN.

Wireless Coverage Area

Wireless LANs use microwave radio signals to communicate. Similar to all radio signals, microwave signals become weaker as the distance between the receiver and transmitter increases. As the signal gets weaker, the wireless connection gets slower. When you reach the edge of the AP's coverage area, you'll lose the signal—and your network connection—entirely.

If you read the box for any wireless product, you'll probably find a manufacturer-provided figure for the range of the AP. Most AP makers claim an indoor range of 300' or so, which would seem to be more than enough for all but the largest houses. Too bad it isn't true.

The problem is that the figures quoted on the box are a theoretical maximum, achievable only in a wide-open space with no obstacles and no outside interference from things like cordless phones and microwave ovens. In the real world, you can expect to get a circle of full-speed coverage about 30' to 50' around the AP. Concrete walls, metal wall studs, and even the ordinary wiring inside your home's walls can reduce that figure even farther.

The short range of most APs may be a problem, or it might not, depending on your needs. If you plan to use your laptop computer in a relatively confined area—the kitchen and den, for example—you can place the AP in the center of that area so that you have the best-possible coverage on those areas. AP Placement for MIMO networks is somewhat less critical than for 802.11b and 802.11g networks, but it's still a good idea to place the AP in a central location if possible.

If your home is large or has multiple stories, you may need to add a second access point to provide coverage in more than one area of the house. Figure 4-7 shows how you can use two access points to cover both floors of a two-story home (with one PC outside the wireless coverage area connected via wire to the main switch in the basement).

Wireless Security

If you look closely at Figure 4-7, you'll notice that the coverage area from the two APs extends outside the boundaries of the house. In some cases, the circle of coverage will extend outside in front of your home, perhaps in the driveway or even out to the curb.

Under these circumstances, anyone with a wireless-equipped laptop computer can simply park in front of your home, turn on his or her laptop, and connect to your network. Once on the network, the interloper may be able to access files on your computer. This is not a good thing.

I have good and bad news to report on this front. The good news is that virtually all wireless equipment sold today includes a feature called Wired Equivalent Privacy, or WEP, and many include a newer, enhanced security feature called WiFi Protected Access, or WPA. If you enable WPA on your wireless equipment, it is nearly impossible for someone to tap into your home network without your permission. WEP and WPA use data encryption techniques to scramble the signal between the AP and each wireless device. WEP has a well-publicized security problem that makes it much less secure than WPA, but it is still far better than no security at all.

The bad news is that despite widespread publicity about the lack of security on wireless networks, the majority of home users choose not to enable the security features on their networks. Part of the blame goes to the equipment makers, who leave WEP or WPA turned off by default. If you are at all concerned about securing your home network, I urge you to use WPA or WEP if at all possible.

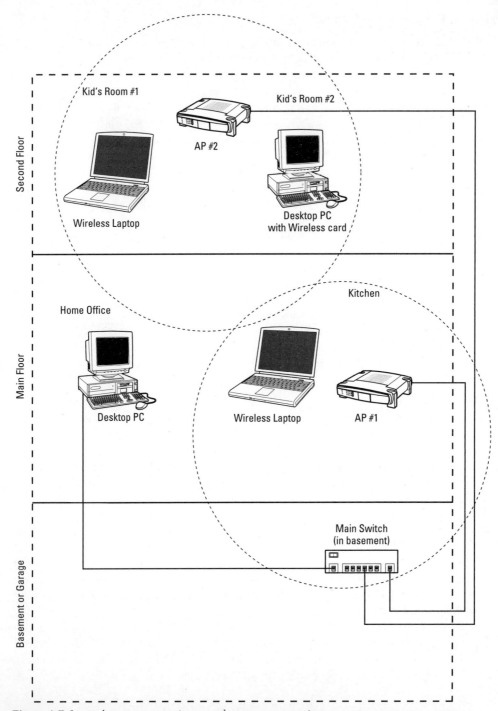

Figure 4-7: Larger homes may require more than one access point.

Cross-Reference
Security for wireless networks is covered in more detail in Chapter 7.

HomePlug

HomePlug is an interesting networking technology that uses your home's AC power wiring to carry data. The first-generation power line networking products were very disappointing, but HomePlug really works. HomePlug operates at speeds up to 14 mbps, depending on the distance between the devices and the quality of your home's wiring. The best part about HomePlug (and the reason I prefer it over the similar phone line networking technology) is that every power outlet in your home becomes a potential network outlet.

Figure 4-8 shows an Ethernet LAN with an additional PC connected using HomePlug.

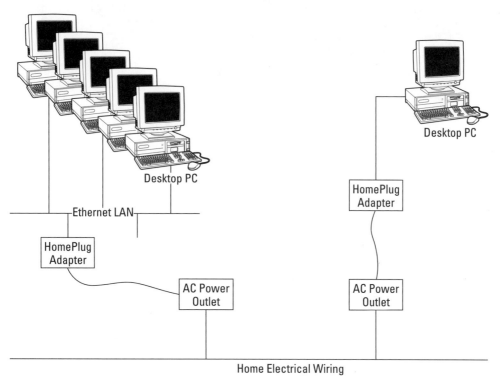

Figure 4-8: A HomePlug network uses your home's electrical wiring to carry data.

Several manufacturers offer a variety of HomePlug-compatible equipment that includes USB-connected adapters and Ethernet bridges. In Figure 4-8, the Ethernet bridge connects the Ethernet LAN to the HomePlug power line network, and a USB adapter connects the lone desktop PC to the power line network. You can get a closer look at these devices in Figure 4-9.

Figure 4-9: A HomePlug Ethernet Bridge (left) connects an existing Ethernet LAN or Ethernet-equipped PC to a HomePlug network. The HomePlug USB adapter (right) plugs into any power outlet and connects to a laptop or desktop PC via a USB cable.

It is possible to build an entire network using HomePlug technology, but it is most useful as an extension of an existing Ethernet or WiFi network. Because of HomePlug's relatively limited bandwidth, I recommend it as a problem-solver technology, to be used when wireless won't reach and Ethernet is too difficult to install.

Summary

By this point, you should have a good idea of the pros and cons of each of the major home networking technologies. The key points in this chapter are as follows:

- Ethernet is still the price/performance leader.
- Wireless LANs can approach Ethernet speeds but offer greater convenience and flexibility.

▨ Security is a major concern for wireless LANs, and you should plan to employ WEP or WPA on your own network.

▨ HomePlug is a simple, effective alternative when wireless won't reach and Ethernet is too difficult to install.

In this chapter, I explained the difference between wired and wireless networks so that you can choose what's best for your needs. In Chapter 5, I'll take you on a virtual shopping trip so you can buy the best products to build your own LAN.

Chapter 5

Getting the Right Stuff

N ow that you understand the basic principles behind a home network, it's time to explore all your options. In this chapter, I provide a brief overview of each of the major types of devices you may need to build your network:

- Network adapters for desktops and laptops

- Ethernet switches

- Routers and firewalls

- Wireless access points

- Print servers

Shopping for networking equipment can be a shot in the dark. You can try just about everything else in the store before you buy it, but the network equipment aisle in most computer and electronics stores is usually a long row of shrink-wrapped boxes.

Before you go shopping, visit several manufacturers' Web sites and see if they offer downloadable user manuals for their products. You can often learn a lot more from the manual than you will from the outside of the box.

Choosing a Network Adapter

Each computer on your network will need a network adapter. As you may recall from Chapters 1 and 4, the network adapter provides a wired or wireless connection between each individual computer and the rest of the network. If you're lucky, your computer came with a factory-installed Ethernet or wireless adapter. If not, you'll have to choose and purchase the correct type of adapter for your computer and network.

Note for Mac Users

All current-model Macs come equipped with an Ethernet connection, and all Macs can be ordered with a built-in wireless adapter as well. Apple calls their wireless adapters by the trade name AirPort, but they are fully compatible with 802.11b and 802.11g WiFi networks.

There are no fewer than eight types of network adapters available, so the choices can be a bit overwhelming. Table 5-1 will help you sort out your options. The adapters are divided between desktop and laptop types, and the sections following the table provide details on each type.

Table 5-1   Network Adapter Types

Adapter Type	Pros	Cons
Desktop PCI or built-in Ethernet	Inexpensive, very high performance. Preinstalled on many desktop PCs.	Installation requires opening the PC's case; not an option if your computer has no free expansion slots.
Desktop USB Ethernet	Easy, no-tools installation.	USB 1.1 products are slower than PCI cards. USB 2.0 products are very fast but require newer USB 2.0 ports on your computer.
Desktop PCI Wireless	No external wires.	Installation requires opening the PC case, and you'll need a free PCI slot. Antenna location (on the back of your PC) isn't optimal.
Desktop USB Wireless	Easy, no-tools installation. Long USB cable lets you adjust the antenna position to obtain the best signal.	USB 1.1 limits speed on 802.11a and 802.11g networks; use a USB 2.0 device if possible.
Laptop built-in Ethernet	High performance, no additional parts to carry with you. Available as an option on many newer laptops.	None
Laptop CardBus Ethernet	High performance and easy installation.	One more thing to take with you on the road. Cards with external "dongles" are fragile. Some models occupy both card slots.
Laptop USB Ethernet	Small and inexpensive, does not tie up one of your CardBus slots.	More stuff to carry. USB 1.1 limits speed; use USB 2.0 if possible.
Laptop built-in wireless	Best choice, no installation required, and you can't lose it!	None

Adapter Type	Pros	Cons
Laptop CardBus Wireless	High performance, easy to upgrade.	Protruding antenna is easy to break.
Laptop USB wireless	Small and inexpensive, does not tie up one of your CardBus slots	More stuff to carry. USB 1.1 limits speed on faster 802.11a and 802.11g networks. Use USB 2.0 if possible. One-piece products are neat but fragile.

Did I say there were eight types? Although there are 10 in the table, the laptop and desktop USB adapters are the same products. There are actually more than 10 types because wireless adapters are available for 802.11a, 802.11b, and 802.11g wireless networks. Some manufacturers also offer 802.11a/b/g *combo cards* that work with any type of wireless network. I'll cover those cards in detail later in this chapter.

In the next two sections, I'll explain the options available for Ethernet and wireless networks for laptop and desktop computers.

Desktop Ethernet Adapters

The majority of desktop PCs ship from the factory with an Ethernet adapter installed. If your desktop PC came with a factory-installed Ethernet adapter, you can skip this section. If you're not sure whether your PC has an Ethernet adapter, check the manufacturer's specifications, or simply look for an Ethernet connector on the rear of your PC. The connector looks like an oversized telephone jack (you can see one on the card in Figure 5-1), and it will have eight gold connectors inside the jack (telephone jacks have only two or four connectors.)

If your PC doesn't have an Ethernet adapter, you'll need to install one, and you have two options. You can install an expansion card inside the computer, or you can use an external USB adapter.

PCI ETHERNET ADAPTERS

Virtually all desktop computers have expansion slots called *PCI slots*, and PCI Ethernet adapters are your best choice for a desktop PC. They are relatively inexpensive and provide the best performance. Figure 5-1 shows a typical desktop Ethernet adapter.

Because they install entirely inside your computer, there are no additional cables other than the cable that connects the PC to the network. Your PC must have an empty PCI expansion card slot, and you'll need to open the PC's case to install the card.

Note

If you are nervous about installing a PCI card, you may want to have it professionally installed. But keep in mind that you'll need to unplug all the cables from your PC and drag the computer into the store to get the card installed. If this is too much trouble and you don't feel comfortable opening up your PC, you should consider a USB Ethernet adapter instead.

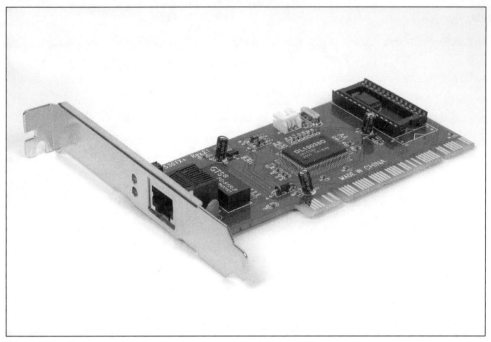

Figure 5-1: This 10/100 Ethernet adapter installs in a PCI card slot. The two lights beside the Ethernet connector are useful for troubleshooting.

PCI cards are typically very easy to install. You'll need a screwdriver, a flashlight, and a little patience. Most expansion cards come with detailed installation instructions. In most cases, the most difficult part of the job is opening and closing the PC's case. Be sure to unplug the computer's power cord and read all the instructions (for both the computer and the expansion card) before you begin.

USB ETHERNET ADAPTERS

If you're squeamish about opening up your PC, or if your computer doesn't have any empty expansion slots, you'll need an external USB Ethernet adapter. USB devices are extremely easy to install; they simply plug into a USB connector on the front or back of your computer.

There are two types of USB connections: USB 1.1 and USB 2.0. USB 1.1 operates at a maximum speed of 12 megabits per second (mbps). Although this is fast enough to keep up with a 10 mbps Ethernet connection, it is far too slow for 100 mbps networks. USB 2.0 operates at speeds up to 480 mbps, or 40 times the speed of USB 1.1, so it is a much better choice for external Ethernet adapters.

USB 2.0 was designed to be backward-compatible with USB 1.1, and both use the same connectors. Because the connectors are identical, you can't tell one from the other just by looking at the connectors. If you're not sure which type you have, check the manufacturer's Web site for your computer. In general, most computers built in 2003 and after have USB 2.0; most computers built before then have USB 1.1.

Tip

Most desktop PCs have at least two USB connectors, and some have as many as five. USB is the industry standard for connecting external devices such as printers, scanners, pointing devices, keyboards, and digital cameras, so it's possible that all of your USB ports are already spoken for.

If you need more USB ports, you can purchase an inexpensive USB hub. The hub plugs into one of your existing ports and provides four or more additional USB connectors. You may have to disconnect a device from your computer to make room for the hub, but you can plug that device into one of the hub ports instead. Hubs come in two types[md]powered and unpowered. Powered hubs can supply power to devices that draw their power from the USB connection, such as mouse devices, keyboards, and most Ethernet adapters. Unpowered hubs are typically used with devices that have their own power supply, such as scanners, printers, and external storage devices.

If your PC came with USB 1.1 and you need more ports, you may want to consider installing a USB 2.0 PCI adapter card inside your PC instead of adding a hub to your system. These cards are very inexpensive (often less than the cost of a USB 1.1 hub) and provide four or five USB 2.0 connectors that you can use with other USB devices.

USB Ethernet adapters come in all shapes and sizes. Some are barely larger than the USB plug itself; others are the size of a matchbox. Figure 5-2 shows a typical USB adapter suitable for use with desktop PCs.

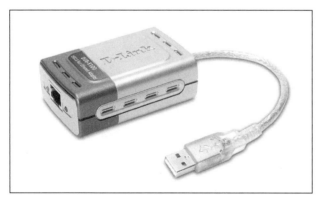

Figure 5-2: This compact USB 2.0 Ethernet adapter adds 10/100 Ethernet to any USB-equipped PC.

The larger, sturdier, matchbox-sized USB adapters are a better choice for use on desktop computers. The smaller, one-piece units sold for use with laptops will work on a desktop PC, but they are much more fragile.

Desktop Wireless Adapters

Many people think of wireless networks as a "laptop thing." Much of the popularity of wireless networks is due to the go-anywhere nature of wireless networks, but that same flexibility applies to desktop PCs as well.

You can't pick up your desktop PC and carry it around the house, but a wireless network lets you put your PC wherever you like, without having to worry about getting an Ethernet cable to the PC.

There are two types of wireless adapters for desktop PCs[md]internal PCI cards and external USB adapters. (See the preceding section on desktop Ethernet adapters to decide which is better for you.) Either way, you'll need to make sure that you choose an adapter that uses the same standards (802.11b, 802.11g, or 802.11a) as your wireless network.

PCI WIRELESS ADAPTERS

PCI wireless adapters install in a PCI expansion slot inside your PC; USB adapters simply plug into a USB port on your computer. Figure 5-3 shows a typical PCI wireless card.

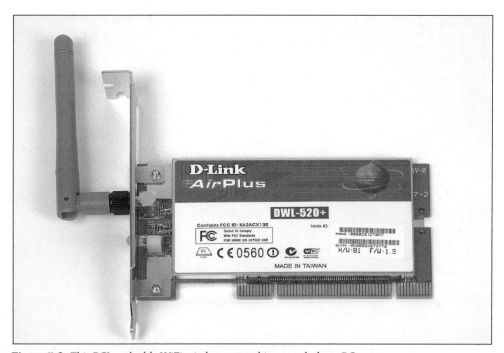

Figure 5-3: This PCI card adds WiFi wireless networking to a desktop PC.

If you read the section on PCI Ethernet adapters, you know that they are my first choice for desktop PCs. However, I'm not a big fan of PCI wireless adapters. My major gripe with these cards has to do with the position of the antenna, located on the back of the card. After you've installed the card and put your PC back under your desk, you may find that the antenna is in a less-than-optimal position to receive the signal from the access point. If this happens, there's not much you can do to correct the situation, short of moving the PC, the access point, or both.

Some manufacturers offer antenna cable extension kits to solve this problem, but these kits add yet another cable to that rat's nest of wires behind your PC. If you have an extra USB port, you'll probably be happier with a USB adapter.

USB WIRELESS ADAPTERS FOR DESKTOPS

If you need to add a wireless connection to a desktop PC, consider using a USB external adapter instead of a PCI card. If your computer has USB 1.1 ports, you'll be better off installing a USB 2.0 PCI adapter and using a USB wireless adapter—and you'll have the added benefit of having faster USB 2.0 ports to use with other devices. Any USB wireless adapter can operate with either desktop or laptop computers, but some specific models are better suited to desktop use. One-piece USB adapters have a USB connector directly attached. They are very compact but are best suited for use with laptops. For desktops, I recommend a USB adapter with a detachable cable, like the one shown in Figure 5-4.

Figure 5-4: This wireless USB adapter comes with a long USB cable, so you can position the adapter for the best signal reception.

The adapter in Figure 5-4 comes with a 6' USB cable, so you can position the wireless adapter up and away from your computer. Most adapters of this type also include a piece of Velcro or double-sided tape, so you can stick the adapter to the back of your desk.

Laptop Ethernet Adapters

Most laptop computers come with an Ethernet connection as standard equipment. That's great if you're buying a new computer, but if you own an older laptop—or a newer model that didn't come with built-in Ethernet—you'll need to purchase and install an Ethernet adapter to connect your laptop to your wired LAN.

There are literally hundreds of types and models of Ethernet adapters to choose from, including external USB adapters and internal CardBus adapters.

Tip

Just because your laptop has an Ethernet connector on the back, don't assume that it actually works! I've seen several laptops from reputable manufacturers that came from the factory with an Ethernet connector on the outside of the computer—but no Ethernet hardware on the inside.

Apparently, it is easier for manufacturers to simply put the connector on all versions of a particular model, even on those that don't include built-in Ethernet.

CARDBUS ETHERNET ADAPTERS

Virtually all laptops have at least one (and more often two) expansion slots. Most laptops built since 1996 have CardBus slots; older laptops have PC Card (also known as PCMCIA) slots. The two technologies are similar, and CardBus is essentially an updated, faster version of PC Card technology. PC Card devices will operate in CardBus slots, but CardBus cards do not work in older PC Card–based computers. From here on, I'll use the term *CardBus* to cover both technologies.

Tip

Have an expansion card but don't know which type it is? PC and CardBus cards share identical form factors and connector types, so it can be hard to tell one from the other. Here's the trick: CardBus cards have a copper shielding strip across the connector end of the card (like the one in Figure 5-5); PC Cards don't.

The CardBus standard is based on the PCI expansion card technology used in desktop computers. Similar to their desktop counterparts, CardBus devices can communicate with the host computer at very high speeds. CardBus cards are compact and easy to store. Unlike desktop PCI cards, CardBus cards are *hot pluggable*, meaning that you can install and remove them at any time, without first turning off the computer's power.

Some older CardBus and PC Card Ethernet adapters put the Ethernet connector at the end of a short cable attached to the card with a fragile connector. These cards work fine, but they are notoriously easy to break. Most laptop Ethernet adapters now use a molded plastic connector, like the card shown in Figure 5-5.

Figure 5-5: This CardBus 10/100 Ethernet card features a built-in Ethernet jack with link and activity indicator lights.

The only drawback to the external connector design is that it requires that the card be placed in the upper of the laptop's two expansion slots. If you place the card in the lower slot, the connector blocks access to the upper slot.

CardBus adapters are your best choice for adding Ethernet to a laptop. Unlike external USB adapters, there is no cable to attach. Most CardBus cards have a power-saving feature that turns the card off when no cable is attached, so you can leave the card in your computer all the time without having to worry about increased power consumption. This, in turn, reduces the possibility of your leaving the card behind in a hotel room.

USB ETHERNET ADAPTERS FOR LAPTOPS

USB Ethernet adapters have become very popular in the past year or so, despite the fact that USB 1.1 is far too slow to take full advantage of a Fast Ethernet connection. I have two theories about why this is so:

- Many people think that USB devices are easier to install than CardBus devices.

- Buyers don't realize that a USB 1.1 adapter can't take full advantage of Fast Ethernet, or they simply don't care about the speed.

I can certainly understand the first theory. Early PC Card devices (and PCMCIA cards, the predecessor to the PC Card standard) were, to put it politely, cranky. Fortunately, Windows XP fixed many of the compatibility issues that plagued earlier devices.

The speed issue may or not be a concern to many users. If you'll just be surfing the Internet and doing e-mail over your connection, then a USB 1.1 adapter is already much faster than your Internet connection. But if you plan to use your USB-connected computer for heavy-duty file sharing or head-to-head gaming, you should make sure you get a USB 2.0 adapter—if your laptop has USB 2.0 ports. If not, you should consider a CardBus adapter instead.

USB adapters come in two basic form factors. The larger, matchbook-sized units are more appropriate for use with desktop PCs (or with the increasing number of laptops that aren't used as portable PCs), and I discussed these products in the desktop USB section earlier in this chapter.

If you're like most people who travel with a laptop PC, you like to keep things as small as possible. Several network equipment manufacturers offer tiny USB Ethernet adapters, as you can see in Figure 5-6.

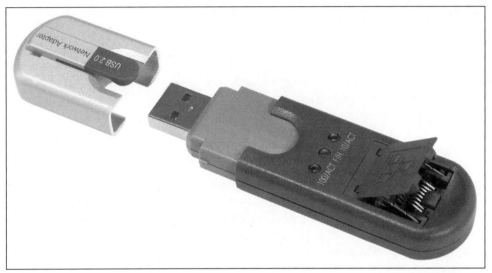

Figure 5-6: This tiny USB 2.0 Ethernet adapter is less than 4 inches long and less than an inch thick. The plastic cap on the left protects the USB plug during storage.

Miniature network adapters are great products that provide fast connectivity in a small package with a low price. The only thing that keeps me from categorically recommending them is that they are very fragile. One accidental yank on your Ethernet cable will almost certainly break the connector—so be careful!

Laptop Wireless Adapters

The wireless networking revolution began with laptop computers, so it's not surprising that there are dozens of wireless laptop adapters on the market. Choosing the right adapter for your network can be a chore because of the sheer number of choices involved.

First, you must decide if you want an internal CardBus (or PC Card) adapter or an external USB adapter. After you've made that choice, you'll need to choose an adapter that is compatible with your wireless access point. For example, if you plan to install an 802.11a network, you'll need to purchase compatible 802.11a cards.

The vast majority of wireless network products sold today are 802.11b- and 802.11g-compatible. The older, slower 802.11b products are adequate for home Internet access, where the cable modem or DSL modem is the slowest link in the network.

If you're planning to use your network for file sharing, 802.11g is the way to go. The faster 802.11g products offer nearly five times the speed of 802.11b products for a modest increase in price. 802.11g networks are backward-compatible with 802.11b adapters, so if you bring home an 802.11b-equipped laptop from your office, it will still work on your 802.11g network.

CARDBUS WIRELESS ADAPTERS

CardBus adapters are the simplest, easiest way to connect a laptop to a wireless LAN. Most manufacturers offer a variety of CardBus (and PC Card) wireless adapters to provide compatibility with 802.11a, 802.11b, and 802.11g wireless LANs. Before you purchase a wireless card, you should make sure that it is compatible with your home wireless network. If you plan to use the same card at home and at the office, make sure that you purchase a card that is compatible with both.

Tip

Most wireless equipment manufacturers offer *tri-mode* cards that will operate with any of the three major wireless standards. These cards don't cost much more than a single-mode 802.11g or 802.11a card, and they are worth the extra money if you frequently travel with your computer. They're also a good choice if you have an 802.11a network at the office and an 802.11g network at home.

CardBus wireless adapters look very much like the CardBus Ethernet adapter shown in Figure 5-5, except that wireless adapters have a small plastic antenna in place of the Ethernet connector.

Windows XP was the first release of Windows to include direct support for wireless networking. In many cases, you can simply plug in a card and use the wireless connection with little or no installation of drivers or additional software.

Some manufacturers include their own configuration software designed to make it easy to move your laptop among several wireless networks. I'll discuss this software in detail in Chapter 7.

USB WIRELESS ADAPTERS FOR LAPTOPS

As I mentioned in the section on desktop wireless adapters, there are two basic classes of USB wireless adapters. The larger, cable-connected adapters are best suited for use with desktop PCs. The smaller, one-piece products like the one shown in Figure 5-7 are a better choice for portable computers.

As you can see, the adapter in Figure 5-7 is very small, and the pop-up antenna folds flat when you're not using the card. Most recent USB wireless adapters are USB 2.0–compatible, so they are more than fast enough for use on 802.11g and 802.11a networks.

The only drawback to these tiny USB adapters is that they stick out the back of your laptop when in use. They look cool, work fine, and are a great choice for subcompact laptops with no CardBus slots—but the sturdier CardBus adapters are a better choice for most users.

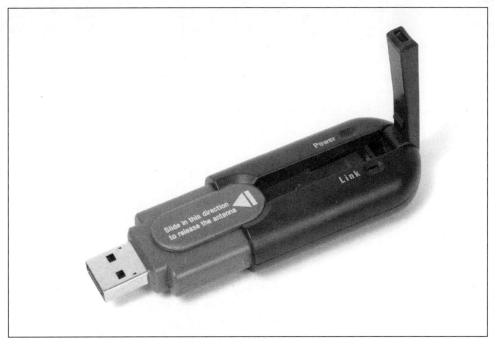

Figure 5-7: This tiny USB wireless adapter features a pop-up antenna that folds flat for storage and travel.

Choosing an Ethernet Switch

I cover Ethernet switches as part of my beat at *PC Magazine*. I always have a hard time convincing my editors that we really need to cover switches because—and I'm the first to admit it—they're boring. How much can you say about a box with a bunch of Ethernet jacks and a few flashing lights, anyway? And how much difference is there between any two of them?

The switch is the focal point of your network. Every single packet of data traveling on your network must pass through the switch on the way to its destination. While there aren't a lot of differentiating factors to help you choose a switch for your home, there are some subtle differences that you need to know.

The first and most obvious factor is the number of ports. You can buy switches made for home use with as few as 4 or as many as 16 ports. My advice is to add up the number of ports you need to start out and buy a switch with at least 50 percent more ports. I can almost guarantee that you'll need them at some point in the future. If you buy a switch that is too small, you'll have to replace it with a larger one (or add a second switch) anyway.

Tip

Some switches made for commercial use are designed to be mounted in an equipment rack, so they have all of the connectors on the front. This is an awkward arrangement for a home switch, unless you're planning to mount the switch in a wiring closet or on a wall. Also, most rack-mount units have noisy ventilation fans.

Virtually all 10/100 switches are *autosensing*, meaning that each port automatically adjusts itself for 10 or 100 mbps operation, depending on the device connected to that port. This is an important feature if you plan to have a mix of 10 and 100 mbps devices on your LAN.

Figure 5-8 shows the front and rear views of a 16-port switch.

Figure 5-8: This 16-port switch is a little large for most home networks, but it has plenty of room to grow.

As you can see, the switch in Figure 5-8 has all the connectors on the rear and a corresponding set of lights on the front. The lights indicate the status, operating speed, and traffic flow on each port. Although you don't need to watch the lights in normal operation, they are an invaluable troubleshooting tool.

Most switches include an uplink feature that connects two or more switches together. This is a useful feature to have when you need several network connections in more than one room, or when you run out of ports and need to add another switch to the network.

Higher-end switches designed for business applications often have one or more Gigabit Ethernet connections, usually on the uplink port. This feature allows you to use a 1000 mbps Gigabit Ethernet connection to connect two or more 10/100 switches together using CAT6 Ethernet cable. This is a great setup for users who plan to move lots of large files around their home LAN.

Choosing a Wireless Access Point

The access point will be the heart of your wireless network, so it is important to choose the right one.

There are two basic classes of access points: standalone access points and wireless routers. The standalone units are simple, inexpensive products designed to add wireless access to an existing Ethernet LAN. Wireless routers combine an access point, router, and a small Ethernet switch into a single, compact unit, and they are your best value if you are building a new network from scratch.

This section deals with standalone APs, but most of the information presented in this section also applies to wireless routers (covered in the next section), so stick with me here, even if you're planning to buy a wireless router.

Why Use a Standalone Access Point?

An access point essentially acts as a wireless switch; it monitors and controls all of the traffic on the wireless LAN. The AP also manages the flow of information between the wired and wireless LANs.

Standalone access points can be used to add coverage to an existing Ethernet LAN, as shown in Figure 5-9, or they can be used to enhance the coverage area of an existing wireless LAN, as in Figure 5-10.

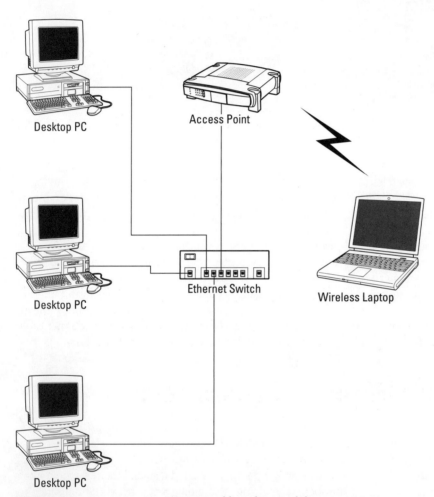

Figure 5-9: You can use an access point to add wireless capability to an existing Ethernet LAN.

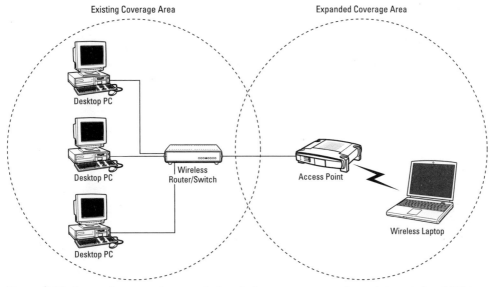

Figure 5-10: A second access point extends the wireless coverage area of an existing wireless LAN.

Figure 5-9 shows an access point added to an existing Ethernet LAN. The AP connects to the existing switch with an Ethernet cable, making it easy to locate the AP where it will provide the largest coverage area.

Which Standard Should You Choose?

Just a year ago, choosing a wireless standard was simple—there was only one. The arrival of 802.11g, 802.11a, and the upcoming 802.11n (see below) products gives you more choices, but it also makes your decision more difficult. (For a discussion of the differences among the three standards, see *Wireless Networks* in Chapter 4.)

To sum up what I said in Chapter 4, 802.11g is currently the most popular choice for home wireless networking. It offers the best combination of speed and compatibility at a reasonable price. As we went to press, there is little or no interoperability between 802.11g MIMO from different manufacturers. The IEEE standards committee is working on a new standard to be called 802.11n, which will hopefully result in a unified, MIMO-based standard. In the meantime, I really like the 802.11g MIMO products, but you'll need to purchase all of your wireless equipment from a single manufacturer.

802.11a networks offer better protection from interference, but 802.11a products are more expensive than 802.11g products. If you can't decide which to choose, several manufacturers offer tri-mode APs that support all three standards.

The diagram in Figure 5-10 shows a standalone AP being used to increase the coverage area of an existing wireless LAN. This is often necessary in larger homes or in buildings where the AP's signal coverage is blocked by steel-reinforced walls.

As a rule, access points are very small, compact units with a single Ethernet connection, a power cord connection, and an antenna. Figure 5-11 shows a typical access point.

Figure 5-11: This access point is about the size of a paperback book.

If you've been following our coverage of wireless products in *PC Magazine* over the past few years, you probably know that some early wireless products were very difficult to configure. The new generation wireless products are just the opposite. Virtually all APs offer browser-based config-uration, so you can configure and manage the AP using a Web browser. Figure 5-12 shows the main configuration screen for a D-Link access point.

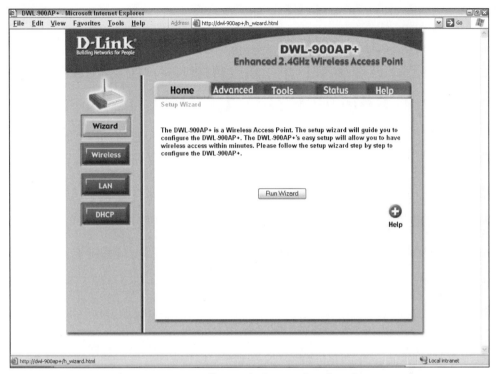

Figure 5-12: Most wireless access points offer simple, browser-based configuration.

Wireless LAN Security

As the number of wireless LANs has exploded, security has emerged as a major concern. Many early wireless LAN products had few or no security features, so anyone with a wireless network card could connect to virtually any wireless network. This was a major issue for corporate users, and many corporations banned the use of wireless networks because of the security threat.

As mentioned in Chapter 4, many wireless LAN products include a security feature called Wired Equivalency Privacy, or WEP. The WEP standard uses data encryption to scramble the data transmitted over the wireless network, so users must have the proper descrambler code (called a *WEP key*) to use the wireless connection. Although WEP is effective, it can easily be broken by a determined hacker. The bigger problem with WEP, however, is that the majority of home LAN users never bother to enable the security features in the first place.

An improved security feature called WiFi Protected Access (WPA) provides user authentication (ID and password) features and an improved form of data encryption. Most importantly, Microsoft and Apple have added WPA support directly into Windows XP and OS X, making WPA easier to deploy and less intrusive to use than WEP.

To use WPA, all of the wireless devices on your LAN must be WPA compliant. While most network equipment makers have embraced WPA, there are still a large number of devices on store shelves that do not support WPA.

Cross-Reference

For more detail on wireless network security, see Chapters 7 and 13.

Choosing a Router/Firewall

Before I get into specifics about routers, I need to clear up some nomenclature. Strictly speaking, a *router* is a device that monitors and forwards data traffic between two or more networks. The most common use for a home router is to operate as a gateway between the local network (LAN) and a wide area network, namely the Internet. Most routers sold for home use include a firewall to protect your LAN from hackers and intruders.

So far, I've used three terms—router, gateway, and firewall—to describe a little box that connects your LAN to the Internet. In large corporate networks, those three terms describe separate and distinct devices. In the home market, they are almost always rolled up into one single device.

Now you understand why some manufacturers (and many writers!) can't seem to decide on one single term to describe home routers. I call them routers throughout most of this book, but you may see any or all three of the terms used to describe the same thing.

To further confuse the issue, many home routers include an Ethernet switch, a wireless access point, or both. These all-in-one boxes don't have a name, so you'll see manufacturers calling them things like (as Dave Barry would say, "I'm not making this up"!) "Wireless Access Point Router with Four-Port Switch." Now that I have that off my chest, let's move on.

How Routers Work

Despite their small size and simple operation, routers are very complex devices. A router is essentially a small computer running a single program. The program is called *firmware* and is almost always stored in rewritable flash memory so that it can be updated from time to time.

Tip

You should check your router manufacturer's Web site periodically to see if there is a new firmware release for your router. New firmware features typically address newly discovered security issues, and they can also add important new features and make performance improvements.

The router's firmware contains code to monitor and control the flow of information between your LAN and the Internet. Virtually all small routers use a technique called *Network Address Translation*, or NAT, to provide shared Internet access for all the computers on the LAN. At the simplest level, a router is a black box with two connections; one connection goes to your LAN and the other to your cable or DSL modem, as shown in Figure 5-13.

As you saw in Chapter 3, most ISPs provide a single public IP address for a broadband Internet connection. And as you know by now, each computer on the LAN must have a unique IP address. NAT routers include a Dynamic Host Configuration Protocol (DHCP) to provide a pool of private IP addresses for the computers on the LAN. The NAT code in the router keeps track of all data coming from and going to the Internet.

Figure 5-13: You can think of a router as a black box that connects your LAN to the Internet.

When a user on the LAN connects to a Web server, for example, the NAT router knows that all traffic to and from that Web server should go to that particular user. All of this takes place in a manner that is completely invisible to the user.

NAT routers provide a natural firewall between the LAN and the Internet. Any unsolicited traffic arriving at the router is simply ignored.

All-in-One Routers

If you're building a new LAN from scratch, an all-in-one unit that combines a router, Ethernet switch, and wireless access point is your best value. It is also the most compact and simplest to install, since all of the cables will connect to a single, centrally located unit. Figure 5-14 shows a typical all-in-one router.

Figure 5-14: This router includes a wireless access point with two antennas as well as a four-port Ethernet switch.

Given the complexity of all-in-one devices, you might think that you would need a great deal of technical knowledge to install one. Fortunately, this is not the case. Virtually all routers incorporate a browser-based setup wizard that literally walks you through the basic steps needed to get the router up and running. I'll cover router installation in detail in Chapter 6, but the screen in Figure 5-15 will give you an idea of what to expect.

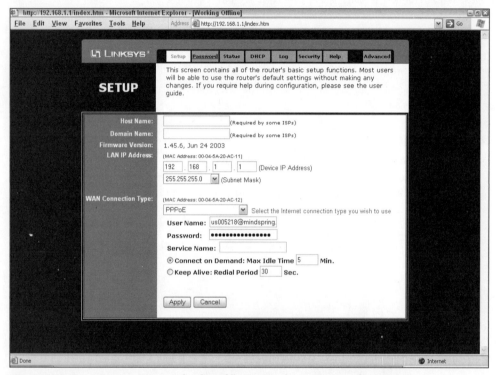

Figure 5-15: In many cases, you need only to fill out a single screen to configure your router.

Choosing a Print Server

If you are like many home users, your printer is located next to your PC. If you're fortunate, you have enough room on or near your desk to accommodate your computer, keyboard, monitor, mouse, and printer. If you're crowded for space, you can use a print server to connect your printer to your home network, so you can get that printer off your desk.

Ethernet print servers require an Ethernet cable to connect them to the network, while wireless print servers use your home's wireless LAN. Obviously, wireless print servers allow you more freedom to place your printer wherever you like. There are several types of print servers, so you need to choose the correct one for your network (Ethernet or wireless) and printer connection (USB or parallel).

Tip

Many all-in-one routers include a built-in print server. This is great if you want to put your printer near your router. But my guess is that you'll already have enough cables and clutter near your router, and you'll probably want to put the printer somewhere else.

Wireless print servers are a good choice for slower printers that are primarily used to print text, but an Ethernet print server is a better choice for color photo printers. The photo-printing process transfers a huge amount of data between the printing PC and the printer, and the data transfer may cause a noticeable slowdown on your entire wireless network.

Most printers come with both parallel and USB ports. Parallel cables are a holdover from the original 1981 IBM PC. They are bulky and slow, and fortunately are being phased out. If your printer has both USB and parallel connectors, be sure to get a USB print server so you can take advantage of the faster USB connection. I cover shared printers in detail in Chapter 11.

Summary

At this point, you should be ready to break out the checkbook and head for the computer store. Here are a few key points to keep in mind on your shopping spree:

- You'll need a network card for each PC on your LAN.
- Buy an Ethernet switch with a few more ports than you need today—you'll need them later.
- You may need two wireless APs to cover your entire home.
- Combo router/switch/AP products are a good value.
- Make sure you know what type of connection (USB or parallel) your printer needs.

So now you're ready to go LAN shopping. When you get back from the computer store, the next chapters will walk you through the process of installing all your new stuff.

Part III

Installing Your LAN

Chapter 6

Installing an Ethernet LAN

I t's time to get your hands dirty! Installing an Ethernet network can be hard work, but it can also be very rewarding. A well-planned network will serve you for many years to come—if you plan ahead now.

This chapter shows you how to plan and install your network cabling, Ethernet switch, and network adapters. Topics include the following:

- Installing your Ethernet cables
- Installing your Ethernet switch
- Installing network adapters

Apart from running the cables, Ethernet networks are usually easy to install. Almost all networking products sold today have true plug-and-play operation to help get your network up and running as quickly as possible.

Installing Ethernet Cables

The first step in building a LAN is installing the cables. Depending on the complexity of your LAN and the location of your computers, this can be the simplest or the most difficult part of your home LAN installation. The degree of difficulty is a complex equation involving the number and location of computers on your LAN, the type of construction used in your home, and your local fire and building codes.

If you're still with me, I'm going to assume that all those disclaimers didn't scare you off and you're ready to install your LAN cables.

Cabling Caveats

Cable installation can be dangerous work, full of unforeseen hazards. For example, you might think it's a piece of cake to drill a hole through a wall—and most of the time it is. But it is nearly impossible to tell what is inside the wall, and it is possible to drill into a water pipe, an electrical cable, or a gas line.

You may also need to climb ladders, navigate unpleasant basement or attic crawl spaces, or perform other hazardous duty to run cables to your computers. Before you decide to install your own network cables, you should consider hiring a professional cable installer to do the work for you. Most electrical contractors, alarm installers, and custom stereo installers will be glad to give you an estimate, usually free of cost or obligation. It may cost less than you'd expect to have your cables installed by a professional.

On the other hand, there is a certain amount of satisfaction to be had from a job well done. If you decide to do it yourself, please read all instructions thoroughly, make sure you're adhering to local building codes, and be careful—especially when working around existing electrical wiring and plumbing.

Planning Your Network

Before you break out your work gloves, power drill, and wire cutters, take a few minutes to draw out a rough plan of your home. Think about where you need to have network connections right now, and also consider locations (like a younger child's room) where you might need a network connection in the future. Then think about the fact that all of those cables need to connect to an Ethernet switch at the other end of the cable.

Your initial inclination may be to run all of the cables to a central location in your home, perhaps in the room where your primary computer resides. But unless you enjoy watching the flashing green lights on your Ethernet switch, there's no need to run all those cables into your home office, den, or living room. The cables invariably end up in a tangle behind your desk.

Your best bet is to run the cables to one easily accessible location in your home. This is called *home run* wiring because each wire runs back to a single "home" location. Your home location can be just about anywhere in the house, but remember that you'll need an AC outlet to provide power for the Ethernet switch. Some good home locations are the garage, basement, utility room, closets, or other nonliving space inside, above, or below the house. Ethernet cable is cheap, so don't compromise your LAN design by trying to make the cables as short as possible. Instead, maximize your LAN design by making it as flexible as possible. If you need more than one Ethernet connection in a room, you can use a small, inexpensive switch to connect several devices using a single Ethernet cable.

Figure 6-1 shows the right and wrong way to plan your LAN cabling.

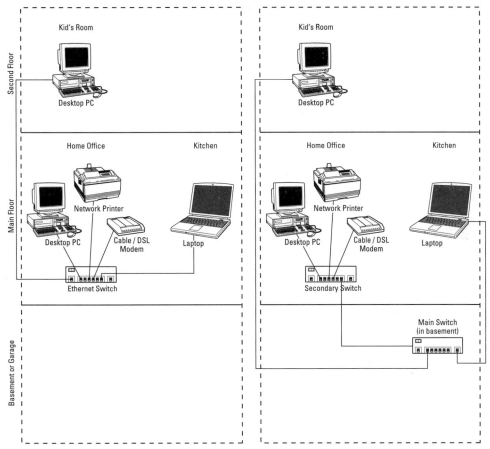

Figure 6-1: You can avoid cable clutter (left) by routing all of your Ethernet cables to a convenient location (right).

The diagram on the left side of Figure 6-1 shows all of the Ethernet cables in the house running back to a single location in the home office. This layout will work fine, but you will end up with a tangle of cables coming into the Ethernet switch. It is easier and neater to run the majority of the cables into a central location outside of the main living area. The diagram on the right side of Figure 6-1 shows most of the cables running to an Ethernet switch located in the basement. This layout requires only a single cable into the home office.

Cable System Components

Thanks to the tremendous popularity of Ethernet cable, you have a wide variety of cables (in several colors), connectors, wall plates, and patch cables to choose from when designing your home LAN. Most computer retailers (including large chain stores such as Best Buy and Circuit City) carry

Ethernet cables in several lengths (usually up to 100') and in one or two neutral colors. If you need to run more than a few cables, or if you need to run very long cables, you can purchase cable in bulk spools of 250' and 500'. You'll need some inexpensive tools to attach the connectors to the cables (described in the next section), but bulk cable is much less expensive.

Ethernet cable contains four pairs of wires. Each pair is twisted together to provide shielding from electrical interference. Figure 6-2 shows a close-up of an Ethernet cable.

Ethernet devices like computers, routers, and switches connect together using eight-pin modular plugs and jacks called *RJ-45* connectors. Typically, the equipment end of the cable contains a female jack, and the cable itself has a male plug. Figure 6-3 shows a picture of an RJ-45 plug.

RJ-45 plugs and jacks look and work very much like the RJ11 telephone jacks used in most homes, but RJ-45 jacks are larger than RJ11 jacks. Each RJ-45 plug has a small plastic protrusion called a *tang* that snaps into place when you plug a cable into a jack. To release the cable, you press down on the tang while pulling out on the cable.

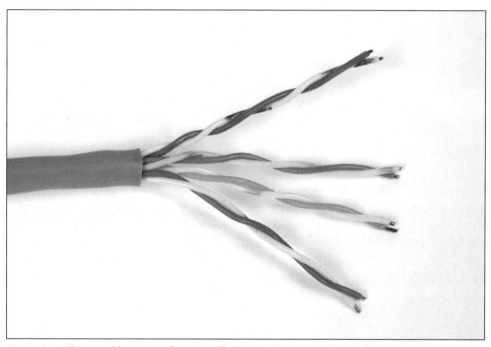

Figure 6-2: Ethernet cable contains four pairs of color-coded wires. Each pair of wires is twisted together.

Figure 6-3: The RJ-45 connector used for Ethernet cable has eight tiny copper pins embedded into a clear plastic connector.

Preassembled cables are very convenient to use; you just run them from the switch to each computer and plug them in. They are best suited for short-run applications where the computers are fairly close to the switch. They are also a good choice for installations where you can route the cable without the cable passing through a hole in the wall. Because the connector is much larger than the wire itself, premade cables require a larger hole to pass through a wall. If preassembled cables won't work for your installation, you can purchase Ethernet cable in bulk and install your own connectors, as explained in the next section.

ESSENTIAL INSTALLATION TOOLS

If you decide to make your own cables, you'll need some special tools like the ones shown in Figure 6-4.

The cable stapler in Figure 6-4 isn't essential, but it is handy for securing cable to baseboards, in attics and basements, and to the outside of a wood house. Cable staplers use special round-top staples that hold the cable securely without damaging the wires inside the cable. An ordinary staple gun with square staples won't work and will damage the wire.

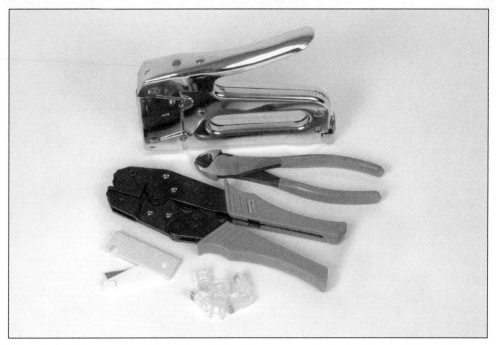

Figure 6-4: These are a few of the tools you'll need for a neat, professional cable installation. They are (from top to bottom) a cable stapler, a wire cutter, an RJ-45 connector crimper, and a cable stripper. You'll also need a supply of RJ-45 connectors.

The RJ-45 crimping tool is used to attach RJ-45 connectors to Ethernet cable. Crimping tools are very simple to use and cost from $35 to $75, depending on the quality of the tool. If you've never used one of these before, I strongly suggest that you make a few test cables to get the hang of it. The exact operating instructions vary from one brand of crimping tool to another, but the basic steps are as follows:

1. Cut the cable to the desired length.

2. Use the cable stripper or a sharp knife to remove about 1" of the outer insulating jacket from the cable, being careful not to nick or cut the individual wires.

3. Separate the individual wires into the correct order for the connector. From left to right (as seen from the top of the connector with the end of the cable facing away from you), the order is as follows:

   1. Orange/White

   2. Orange

   3. Green/White

4. Blue

   5. Blue/White

   6. Green

   7. Brown/White

   8. Brown

4. Using the wire cutters, trim the wires so that they extend about 5/8" beyond the end of the plastic jacket.

5. Place the connector over the wires, making sure that the wires remain in the proper order from left to right. Make sure that each wire is inserted all the way into the tip of the connector, and double-check the order of the wires.

6. Insert the connector into the crimping tool and squeeze the handle.

This process sounds much more complex than it actually is. After you've done it a few times, it takes about five minutes per connector. Of course, when your friends find out that you have a crimping tool and know how to use it, you'll get plenty of practice.

Tip

If you ever have problems with your network, you may need to know which LAN cable is which. As you install each cable, number both ends of the cable so that you'll be able to tell the cables apart easily later. Make a list of the cables and their destinations, and keep the list near your Ethernet switch.

HOW THE PROS DO IT

If you want a professional-looking cable installation, consider using modular in-wall or surface-mount wall jacks. These products are widely available at computer stores, home improvement stores, and electrical supply outlets. One of the best features of these products is that a single wall plate can hold as many as six connections for a mix of cable types including Ethernet, telephone, cable TV, and even stereo speakers. Figure 6-5 shows a modular wall plate and modular surface-mount jack. These particular jacks are made by Leviton; several other manufacturers offer similar products.

The wall plate on the left side of Figure 6-5 is a great choice when you're able to run cables inside the wall. I'm a big fan of modular jacks, and I installed them in my own home a few years ago. The best thing about these jacks is their flexibility. If you have an existing telephone jack in the wall, you can pull an Ethernet cable into the same outlet box and use one of these dual jacks for both the telephone and the Ethernet cables. In addition to the wall jacks, you'll need to purchase a short Ethernet cable to go from the wall jack to each computer. If you can't run cables inside the wall, you can use surface-mount jacks such as the one on the right side of Figure 6-5.

Figure 6-5: A modular wall plate (left) fits into a standard outlet box and holds two jacks for Ethernet, telephone, TV, or speaker cables. The jacks (center) simply snap into the openings on the plate. The surface-mount jack (right) works the same way but can be mounted on any flat surface.

If you use modular jacks at the computer end of each cable, you can avoid buying (and learning to use) a crimping tool. Here's how:

1. Buy a premade cable and a jack for each computer on the LAN.

2. Run each cable from the switch location to a wall jack.

3. Cut off the connector at the computer end of the cable, and attach the cable to the wall jack.

4. Use a short Ethernet cable to connect the wall jack to the computer.

5. Plug the switch end of the cable into the Ethernet switch.

This approach will cost a little more money, but you'll have a professional, nicely finished installation.

The Leviton jacks are exceptionally easy to install, and you don't need any special skills or tools to install them. The rear side of each jack has a slot for each wire in the cable. Figure 6-6 shows the rear side of an Ethernet and telephone jack.

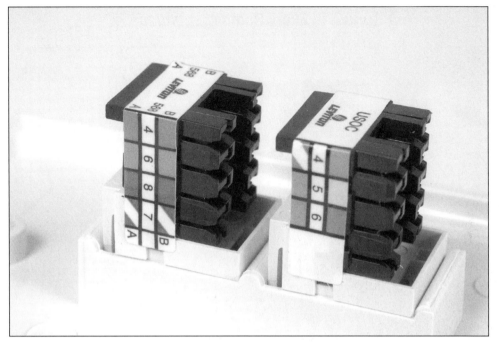

Figure 6-6: The color-coded, numbered wire slots on this in-wall jack make cable installation simple and nearly foolproof.

To connect a jack to the cable, strip back a few inches of the outer insulation from the cable, place each wire into the appropriate numbered, color-coded slot, and press the wire into place with the provided plastic tool. You don't even have to strip the individual wires; a small blade at the bottom of each wire slot cuts into the insulation as you press down on the wire.

A Switch in Every Room

So you've run an Ethernet cable to every conceivable place in your home, and a few months later you find that you need two or more connections in one particular room. As I mentioned earlier, you can always add a secondary switch to provide multiple Ethernet connections over a single home run cable.

3Com's NJ100 Network Jack is a clever product that lets you replace any in-wall Ethernet jack with a four-port 10/00 switch.

Continued

A Switch in Every Room *(Continued)*

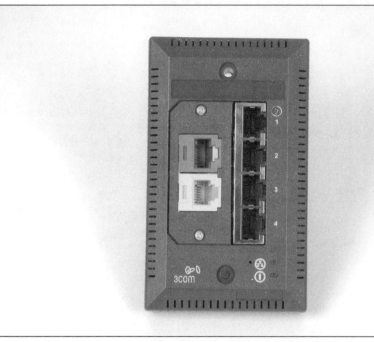

3Com's NJ100 packs a four-port switch and two telephone jacks into a single wall plate.

Photo used by permission of 3Com Corporation. 3Com and the 3Com logo are registered trademarks of 3Com Corporation.

The existing Ethernet cable plugs into the back of the NJ100. The front faceplate has four 10/100 Ethernet jacks, so you can connect up to four Ethernet devices to the NJ100. The two connectors on the left side of the NJ100 are optional and can be used for telephone, DSL, or other applications. The NJ100 comes in black (shown here) and white.

Installing Your Network Hardware

The next major step in the LAN-building process is to install the Ethernet switch or a combination router/switch. You'll also need to install a network adapter in each computer that will connect to the LAN.

Note

The instructions in the next section apply equally to Ethernet switches and combination router/switch units. I'll cover router configuration in detail in Chapter 9.

Installing an Ethernet Switch

Ethernet switches are extremely simple to install. In most cases, you can simply plug in the cables coming from each computer, connect the power cord, and you're finished. 10/100 Ethernet switches automatically detect the speed of each port to suit the device connected to the port. This means you can connect a mix of 10 and 100 megabit per second (mbps) devices to the switch without making any adjustments.

If you numbered your Ethernet cables as you installed them, make sure you connect the cables to the correct numbered port.

MOUNTING THE SWITCH

Small Ethernet switches are designed to sit on a desk or tabletop. But the weight of the attached Ethernet cables is often enough to cause the switch to tip backward or even to slide off the desk. Most small switches come with brackets and screws so that you can mount the switch on a wall or other flat surface.

MULTIPLE SWITCH NETWORKS

Virtually all Ethernet switches allow you to expand your network using additional switches. To connect two switches together, you connect a port on the one switch to a special uplink port on the other switch. There are two types of uplink ports, as you can see in Figure 6-7.

Figure 6-7: Larger switches (left) have a switch-selectable uplink port; smaller switches (right) often have a separate uplink connectors.

Some switches, like the one on the left side of Figure 6-7, use one port (usually the highest-numbered port) as an uplink port. The push-button switch to the right of the connector tells the switch if a computer or another switch is connected to the port. Other switches, such as the one on the right side of Figure 6-7, have an extra connector marked Uplink (the rightmost port). You can use this connector to uplink another switch, but if you do, you cannot use the last port on the switch.

Note

There are two types of Ethernet connections—*device ports* and *switch ports*. Device ports are the ports found on computers, print servers, and other network devices. Switch ports are the ports on an Ethernet switch. Device ports normally connect to switch ports. If you need to connect a device port to another device port or if you want to connect a switch port to another switch port, you normally need a special cable called a *crossover* cable.

The uplink ports on an Ethernet switch are actually wired as device ports, eliminating the need for a crossover cable. Remember that you must connect the uplink port on one switch to a normal port on the other switch. You cannot connect two uplink ports to one another.

Installing Network Adapters

Each PC that will connect to your Ethernet network must have an Ethernet adapter. Most computers currently on the market include a built-in Ethernet adapter. If your computer doesn't have an Ethernet adapter, you'll need to purchase and install one. See Chapter 5 to help you select the best Ethernet adapter for your needs.

Because there are so many brands and types of Ethernet adapters, it is impossible for me to give detailed installation instructions for each one. The best advice I can offer is to read all of the printed material packaged with your adapter before you install or connect the adapter.

CONFIGURING YOUR NETWORK ADAPTER (WINDOWS XP)

Windows XP contains built-in support for many popular Ethernet adapters. If your adapter is supported by Windows, you won't need to install any drivers. Other adapter cards may require that you install a driver from a CD before you physically install the Ethernet card in your computer. If so, you'll need to run the provided driver installation program before you install the adapter. In most cases, you run an installation program from the floppy disk or CD-ROM provided with the adapter and follow the instructions on the screen.

After the installation process is complete, you should see a new device in the Network Connections control panel. To see this device, open the Windows control panel and double-click Network Connections. You will see a screen like the one in Figure 6-8.

The Network Connections control panel display shows all the ways your computer can connect to a network. Active connections (such as the 1394 and Local Area Connections in the example) appear in blue; inactive connections display in gray. If a connection is active but disconnected (as your PC should be at this point), a red X appears on the right side of the connection icon.

To test your Ethernet adapter installation, follow these steps:

1. Install the adapter and drivers according to the manufacturer's instructions.

2. Turn on the power to the Ethernet switch or router.

3. Make sure that all the cables are connected to the switch or router.

4. Connect the Ethernet cable to the PC. The red X should disappear.

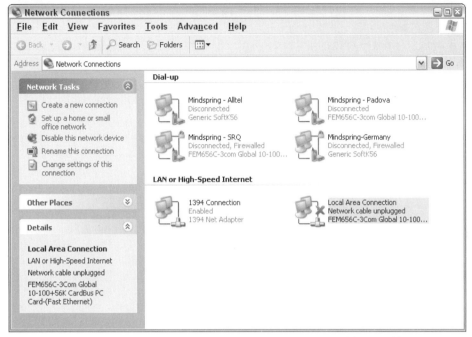

Figure 6-8: The Network Connections control panel display shows all of the possible network connections for your computer, including dial-up (top), local network (middle), and virtual private network connections.

If the red X is still present after you connect the cable, you may have a wiring problem. Double-check the wiring of the cable and jacks to make sure that the wires are connected in the correct order. If possible, connect the problem PC to a different Ethernet cable to isolate the problem. If your LAN adapter has indicator lights, check the link and activity lights to see if they are lit. If the link light is out, you most likely have a cabling problem. If the link light is on but the activity light doesn't blink, you may have a software or driver problem.

CONFIGURING YOUR NETWORK ADAPTER (MAC OS X)

All current-model Mac computers (and the majority of Macs built in the past five years) have a built-in Ethernet adapter. In most cases, you can simply connect an Ethernet cable from your Mac to the LAN, and the Mac's automatic Ethernet configuration will take care of the details for you.

You can check (and, if necessary, change) your Mac's Ethernet network settings using the Network settings dialog in the System Preferences. Figure 6-9 shows the main Network dialog box.

As you can see in Figure 6-9, if your Ethernet connection is active and connected to a LAN with automatic addressing (as will be the case if you are using a router or firewall on your LAN), the configuration is totally automatic.

Figure 6-9: The Network dialog box shows the status of your Mac's network connections at a glance. In this example, both the Ethernet and AirPort wireless connections are active.

Note

If both the Ethernet and AirPort connections are active, the Mac will use the Ethernet connection instead of the AirPort. If you unplug the Ethernet cable, the Mac will automatically switch to the AirPort connection. This is a handy feature if you use your Mac laptop in multiple locations, such as a wired connection in your office and a wireless connection in your home.

If your LAN doesn't provide automatic IP addressing or if you want to manually override the automatic settings provided by your router, you can easily do so by clicking on the configure button in the Network dialog box. Figure 6-10 shows the Network preferences settings for the Ethernet connection.

To change the IP settings for your Ethernet connection, click the Configure IPv4 pull-down menu and select Manually; then fill in the IP address, subnet mask, and router address (also called the gateway address) for this computer. Remember that if you choose to use manual addressing, each computer on the LAN must have a unique IP address.

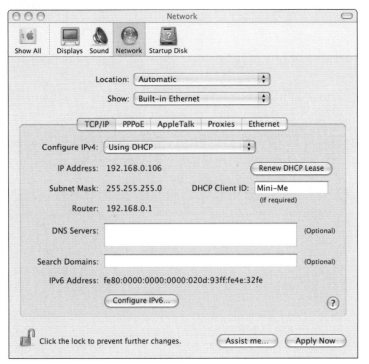

Figure 6-10: The Network dialog allows you to change the settings for your Mac's Ethernet connection. In this example, the Ethernet connection is set for automatic configuration, and you can see the IP address automatically assigned by the router.

Summary

Here are several parting thoughts to keep in mind when planning your home network:

- The shortest cable route isn't always the best.
- You don't need a lot of special tools to install a LAN, but a crimper can be a big help.
- Be careful when working around wiring.
- You may need to use two or more switches on your LAN.

After you've completed all the tasks in this chapter, you're only a few steps away from having a functioning home network. The remaining steps are common to both wired and wireless LANs, and I'll cover them in Chapter 8. If you're not installing any wireless equipment, you can skip Chapter 7 and move on to Chapter 8 to finish setting up your network.

Chapter 7

Installing a
Wireless LAN

Before you begin to install your wireless network, you should have a good understanding of the capabilities and limitations of your wireless network hardware. In this chapter, I'll guide you through the process of installing and configuring your wireless network.

In this chapter, you'll see how to:

- Determine the best location for your wireless access point

- Install and configure wireless adapters in desktop and notebook computers

- Secure your wireless LAN against intruders

Before You Install . . .

You've read the book up to this point, you've gone out and bought everything you need, and you're ready to get started. For most people—I included—your first inclination is to put the wireless access point or router where it is most convenient, hook it up, and leave it at that.

You can certainly do this, and your network may even work as well as you had hoped. But sometimes the most convenient location for your access point isn't the best location. Walls, wiring, and seemingly innocent nearby objects (including fish tanks, cordless phone base stations, and filing cabinets) can interfere with the signal path between the AP and your wireless laptops. Wireless networks use radio waves to communicate, and those radio waves are subject to the laws of physics. If there is a large metal (or water-filled) object between your AP and your favorite Web-surfing couch, the radio signal simply can't get through. If this happens, you will experience slow, intermittent, or no connection between the laptop and the AP. Unless you absolutely must install your AP in a given location, it is well worth the time and effort to determine the best location for your AP.

To do this, you need to perform what network professionals call a *site survey*. The survey will help you identify possible problem spots in your wireless coverage area so that you can place your AP in the best-possible location. The *Surveying Your Wireless LAN* section later in this chapter provides detailed instructions for conducting the survey.

After you've determined the best place to put your AP, you'll need to decide how to connect the AP to the rest of your equipment. If you are adding a standalone AP to an existing Ethernet LAN, you'll need to run an Ethernet cable from the AP to your existing network switch. If you're installing a combination router/firewall/AP device that will connect to a cable or DSL modem, you can either run an Ethernet cable from the modem to the router, or you can move the modem so that it is close to the router.

Tip

DSL modems are easy to move because they can usually plug into any telephone jack in your home. Cable modems aren't so easy to move. You might think that you could just plug your cable modem into any cable TV outlet in your home, and in some cases, you can. But your modem may or may not work if you move it.

Before you uproot your entire computing universe, check to make sure that your cable modem will still function if you move it to a new location. If not, you may need to get the cable company to come out and move the modem for you. Your cable company may charge extra for this service.

Because you'll need to install at least one wireless client adapter to perform your site survey, I'll cover that topic first. In the following sections of this chapter, I'll guide you through installing and configuring the rest of your wireless network.

Installing Wireless Adapters

Each wireless computer on your wireless network must have a wireless adapter installed. As you learned in Chapter 4, wireless adapters are available in a variety of form factors, including PCI cards for desktop PCs, CardBus and PC Cards for laptop PCs, and USB adapters for both desktops and laptops.

Mac users can skip this section because virtually all Macs use the same wireless card—Apple's own AirPort Extreme card.

There are hundreds of wireless adapters on the market today, so it simply isn't possible to give you detailed installation instructions for each one. But having installed dozens of wireless adapters myself, I can give you some helpful hints and tips that may save you some aggravation or a call to the vendor's tech support hotline. The number one tip I can give you for all of these adapters is to READ THE INSTRUCTIONS packed with your card!

Note

Many wireless adapters come with driver software that must be installed before you install the hardware. If you install the adapter first, the computer will not have the proper drivers installed. The adapter won't work, and you won't be happy.

In the following sections, I'll describe the basic installation steps required for each type of adapter (PCI, USB, and CardBus). You'll also need to configure the software for your wireless adapter; these steps are the same for all wireless adapters.

PCI Wireless Adapters

PCI wireless adapters used in desktop computers can be difficult to install. You'll need to open your PC's case, identify an available PCI card slot, install the card, and put the case back together. This type of PC surgery is second nature to those of us who work with PCs every day, but if you're squeamish about opening up your computer, you may want to opt for professional installation.

Tip

Some PCs are exceptionally easy to work on; others are a nightmare. The easy ones have a door on one side of the case that slides off to reveal the PCI card slots. Others, like one of my own PCs, must be partially disassembled in order to install a PCI card.

Most computer stores and computer service departments will install your PCI adapter for a nominal fee, but you'll need to disconnect your computer and haul it in to the shop.

To install a wireless PCI card in your computer, follow these steps:

1. Read the instructions packed with your card. Most cards require that you install driver software from a CD packed with the card. Some cards require that you install the software before you install the card; others require that the CD be in the drive after you install the card.

2. Install the software if necessary and then shut down your computer.

3. Disconnect the AC power cord from your computer. If you need to move the computer to remove the case, you may have to disconnect the remaining cables.

4. Remove the case or access door from your computer. Figure 7-1 shows a typical desktop PC with the access door removed.

5. Locate an empty PCI card slot. Figure 7-2 shows two empty PCI card slots.

6. Remove the blank cover from the rear of the PCI slot.

Tip

When you are installing a PCI card, be very careful not to drop the retaining screw inside the computer. If you do (and it's easy enough to do), make sure you retrieve the screw before you turn the computer back on. If the screw lands in the wrong spot, it can do severe and permanent damage to your PC.

Figure 7-1: A typical desktop PC with the access door removed.

7. Insert the card into the empty slot. Make sure the card is fully seated in the slot. You may have to push down firmly on the card, but you shouldn't have to force it.

8. Replace the screw you removed in Step 4.

Figure 7-2: This computer has two empty PCI slots, seen in the center of the picture.

9. Close the case and reconnect the cables.

10. Orient the antenna so that is vertical. See Figure 7-3.

11. Install the driver software (if necessary), and configure the wireless adapter to operate with your wireless network. I'll cover this step in detail in the *Configuring Your Wireless Adapter* section.

Tip

It is important to keep the antenna clear of adjacent cables as much as possible. You can turn the antenna up or down as necessary; it works just as well in either direction. You may find it convenient to move one or more of your computer's existing PCI cards to make room for the antenna. If you do, Windows will reinstall any drivers for the cards you move. If you see a number of Windows Plug and Play screens when you restart your computer, don't panic—just follow the prompts and wait for the drivers to reinstall.

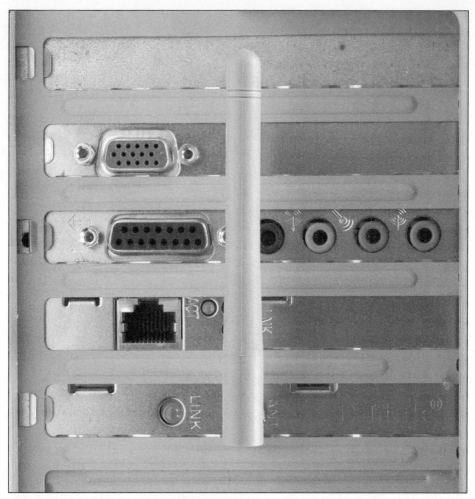

Figure 7-3: The antenna should be vertical to the floor.

CardBus, PC Card, and USB Wireless Adapters

CardBus and PC Card adapters are the simplest of all cards to install; you simply plug the card into a vacant slot on your laptop and follow the prompts on the screen.

USB wireless adapters are a good alternative to PCI cards for desktop PCs because they are so simple to install. Some USB adapters include a long cable, so you can position the adapter (and its antenna) away from that jumble of wires behind your PC. Many USB wireless adapters come with a small piece of double-stick tape or Velcro, so you can attach the adapter to the back of your desk. Other USB adapters have no cable at all and are designed to plug directly into the USB port on a laptop computer.

To install a wireless adapter in your computer, follow these steps:

1. Read the instructions packed with your adapter. Most wireless adapters require that you install driver software from a CD packed with the card before you install the adapter; others install the software after you install the adapter. You may need to reboot the system after you install the driver.

2. For PC Card and CardBus adapters, plug the card into an unused card slot on your laptop. For USB adapters, plug the adapter into an unused USB port on your computer or USB hub. Windows will recognize the adapter and install the proper driver as shown in the next section, *Configuring Your Wireless Adapter*.

Tip

Many USB devices such as printers and mouse devices don't require any driver software because the necessary drivers are built into Windows XP. Many computer users think that *all* USB devices will install with no additional drivers, but this is not true.

Because wireless USB adapters appeared on the market after the initial Windows XP release, you may need to install the drivers before you connect the wireless adapter to your computer.

Configuring Your Wireless Adapter

Even if your computer came from the factory with a wireless adapter already installed, you may need to configure your computer's wireless adapter before you can connect to your wireless LAN. I know that many computer users flinch when they hear the word "configuration," but the process is usually very simple and takes only a minute or two.

WINDOWS XP CONFIGURATION

Windows XP contains built-in driver support for many wireless adapters. This feature, called *Wireless Zero Configuration*, or WZC, makes it possible to install many wireless adapters simply by plugging the adapter into the computer. When Windows recognizes a WZC-compatible adapter, it automatically installs the drivers and attempts to obtain a wireless network connection with no intervention from the user.

Tip

The network equipment marketplace is very competitive, so many wireless-equipment and notebook computer makers include additional software to give their product a competitive advantage over other products. This software typically replaces the wireless configuration software that is built into Windows XP, but it works in much the same way.

Before you install your wireless adapter, check the instructions to see if you need to install the additional software before you connect or install the network adapter. Some products, such as the one shown in the example that follows, may require that you insert the installation CD after you install the card into the laptop.

For this example, I'll install a wireless adapter card that requires the CD to complete the installation. The basic steps to install this card are as follows:

1. Power up your computer. If you are using a USB, PC Card, or CardBus adapter, connect the adapter to your computer.

2. The Found New Hardware Wizard appears, as shown in Figure 7-4. Notice the instruction to insert an installation CD if one is included.

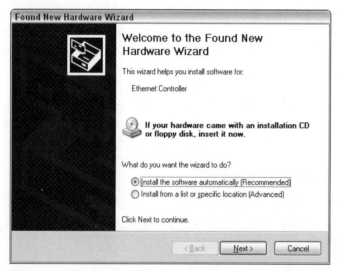

Figure 7-4: The Windows Found New Hardware Wizard appears when you first insert a new adapter card.

3. Unless your installation instructions specify otherwise, select Install the Software Automatically, and click the Next button. Windows searches for the appropriate driver for your wireless adapter. If the proper drivers are already installed on your computer, Windows will automatically use those drivers. If not, Windows will prompt you for the location of the driver software.

4. In most cases, Windows will locate the correct driver to use with no further intervention from you. If Windows finds more than one possible driver, you may be prompted to choose the proper driver, as shown in Figure 7-5. Examine the drivers closely, using the horizontal scroll bar to see all the details if necessary. Choose the appropriate driver from the list and click Next.

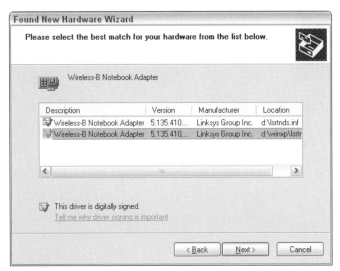

Figure 7-5: In this example, Windows found two possible drivers and needs to know which one to use.

5. Windows installs the driver software. This normally takes only a few seconds. When the drivers are installed, you'll see the final screen from the Found New Hardware Wizard, as shown in Figure 7-6.

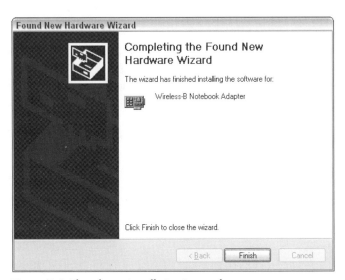

Figure 7-6: The adapter installation is complete.

At this point, your wireless adapter is installed and should be functioning correctly. Of course, you won't know if it is actually working until you install your wireless access point—the next step in the installation process. If you need to install more than one wireless adapter, you may want to install the AP next and make sure everything is working, and then go back and install the rest of the wireless adapters.

MAC OS X CONFIGURATION

Apple was one of the first computer makers to embrace wireless technology, so Apple has had plenty of time to work the kinks out of wireless technology. OS X makes wireless network configuration as simple as possible. In most cases, you can simply select the AirPort connection in the network control panel and click the Connect button. You'll see the AirPort status display shown in Figure 7-7.

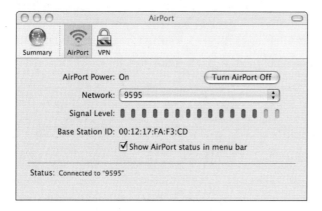

If you've never used the AirPort connection before, you'll need to click the button marked Turn AirPort On to enable the wireless connection. Once you turn the AirPort on, the bar graph in the middle of the window will indicate the relative strength of the wireless connection to your access point. If you like, you can check the box marked Show AirPort status in menu bar. The AirPort status indicator will appear in the status bar at the top of the screen. This is a handy feature for laptop users who frequently need to check or reconfigure their wireless connection in different locations.

Installing Your Access Point

Now that you've installed at least one wireless client adapter, it's time to install and configure your access point or wireless router. There are four basic steps in this section, and you may be able to skip one of them:

1. Survey your wireless LAN to make sure you have good wireless communication between the AP and the clients.

2. Connect your AP or wireless router to the rest of the LAN.

3. Configure your AP and wireless clients.

4. Secure your wireless LAN.

Surveying Your Wireless LAN

Many people think they don't need to do a survey, because their wireless AP is rated for several hundred feet indoors. But you're unlikely to get that "several hundred feet" range in your own home unless you live in a big, open space—such as an airplane hangar.

Here in the real world, the actual maximum range of a typical AP in a typical home is about 100 feet—or even less. There are all sorts of things that can conspire to reduce the range of your AP, including wiring and metal studs inside interior walls, refrigerators, filing cabinets, and other large metal objects, fish tanks, microwave ovens, 2.4 GHz cordless telephones, and even your neighbor's wireless LAN!

If you plan to use your portable computer in very close proximity to your wireless AP, you can probably skip the survey and simply install the AP in the most convenient location. As a general rule, if you can see the AP, you can connect to the AP. For more suggestions on positioning your AP, see the "Where to Put the AP" sidebar later in this section.

To perform your site survey, you'll need a laptop with a wireless network adapter, and a wireless AP or combination AP/router. Don't have a laptop? If you plan to link several desktop PCs with a wireless network, you still may want to do a site survey first. Instead of moving your desktop PC from room to room, you can simply move the AP to several locations and check the wireless signal quality on each of your wireless desktop PCs. Of course, you'll need to install the wireless adapters in the desktop PCs before you perform the survey.

Note

This example uses a Windows PC. Mac users should perform steps 1 and 2, then open the airport status screen shown in Figure 7-7, and follow the instructions beginning at step 7 below.

To perform the survey, follow these steps:

1. Decide where you would prefer to place the AP and then put the AP in that location.

2. Plug the AP into a power source so that you can establish a connection to the AP to make sure that your wireless adapter is working correctly. The AP does not need to be connected to your network or broadband modem for this test.

3. Within view of the AP, turn on your wireless client PC. After the system starts up, you should see a message on the lower right-hand corner of the screen, as shown in Figure 7-8. If you don't see this message, your machine is not within range of the AP.

Figure 7-8: This message appears when your computer discovers a new wireless network.

4. Click the notification balloon. If the balloon has disappeared, right-click the network icon (it looks like two computer screens, one in front of the other), and select View Available Wireless Networks. You will see the wireless network connection dialog box, shown in Figure 7-9.

Figure 7-9: This dialog box makes sure that you understand that you are about to connect your computer to an unsecured network.

5. You should see the name of your wireless network on the screen, under the list of available wireless networks. Select your wireless network, check the box marked Allow Me to Connec, and click the Connect button.

Note

If one of your neighbors has a wireless network, you may see more than one network in the list of wireless networks.

6. Right-click on the network icon on the taskbar, and select Status from the pop-up menu. You'll see a display like the one shown in Figure 7-10.

7. Move your computer around the house while monitoring the speed and signal strength indicators on the wireless connection status screen. Be sure to test the signal strength and connection speed at the locations where you are most likely to use your computer. Keep in mind that the signal strength indicator isn't as important as the link speed.

8. If you have one or more desktop computers on your wireless network, check the signal strength and connection speed on each desktop.

9. If you are satisfied with the coverage area, signal strength, and link speed, you're finished with the survey, and you can move on to the next section. If not, move the AP to another location and repeat the survey.

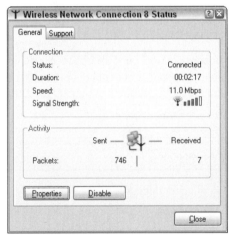

Figure 7-10: The wireless network connection status display shows the speed and signal strength of your wireless connection.

Connecting and Configuring the Access Point

After you've determined the best location for your AP, you're ready to connect the AP to the rest of your network. If you are adding a wireless AP to an existing Ethernet network, you'll need to connect an Ethernet cable from the AP to an unused port on your Ethernet switch. If you are installing a combination AP/router, you'll also need to connect an Ethernet cable from your cable or DSL modem to the router.

Where to Put the AP

If you encounter problems finding a spot for your AP, some of the tips here may help.

- Many access points can be mounted on a wall. While an AP isn't the most attractive thing you can hang on your wall, you may find that you'll get better coverage from your AP by mounting it up high, clear of your furniture and other obstructions.

- If you don't want to wall-mount your AP, you can also place it on a high shelf, or on top of a tall piece of furniture.

- The best place to put your wireless router is as close as possible to the center of the area that you want to cover.

- The weakest signal area is located directly above and below the AP. Keep this in mind if you live in a multistory home.

- Keep your AP's antenna(s) vertical if possible.

- Don't put your AP near large metal objects like metal filing cabinets and desks.

- Try to keep your AP as far as possible from microwave ovens and 2.4 GHz telephone base units. These products operate intermittently but can cause severe interference when they are in use.

- Avoid large, water-filled objects like fish tanks and water heaters.

- Keep the AP away from exterior walls. If you want your wireless LAN to cover part of the outside area of your home, place the AP close to a window.

Note

The examples in this section show how to configure a standalone access point. If you are installing a combination AP/router device, the procedure will be similar to the example shown here but will include one or two additional steps. I'll cover those additional steps in Chapter 9, so you may want to read both chapters before you install your wireless AP/router.

Virtually all wireless access points feature a browser-based configuration wizard. To configure the router, you start your Web browser, enter the IP address of the access point, and answer a few questions. The D-Link AP in the following example uses this approach.

Some access points come with a configuration program on a CD-ROM. To configure these products, you install the configuration program, which walks you through the steps required to configure your AP.

In either case, the steps required are very similar. The following example shows the steps required to configure a D-Link access point using the Web browser interface.

Before you can configure the AP, you must establish a connection from your PC's Web browser to the AP's browser interface. In most cases, the AP will come with specific instructions to help you determine the IP address of the AP. Many manufacturers include a small "locator" program that locates new AP devices and allows you to set the IP address for the AP. After you've determined the IP address of the access point, you'll need to start your browser and enter the IP address of the AP in the address bar, as shown in Figure 7-11.

As you can see in Figure 7-11, the browser interface has a button marked Run Wizard that starts the setup wizard. The wizard walks you through the configuration. Figure 7-12 shows the first step in the Setup Wizard.

The first step is to set a password for your AP, as shown in Figure 7-13. I strongly recommend that you change the password from the factory's default setting. If you leave the AP set with the default password, it is very easy for someone to break into your wireless network and change your network settings. Use a password with a mix of alphabetic and numeric characters.

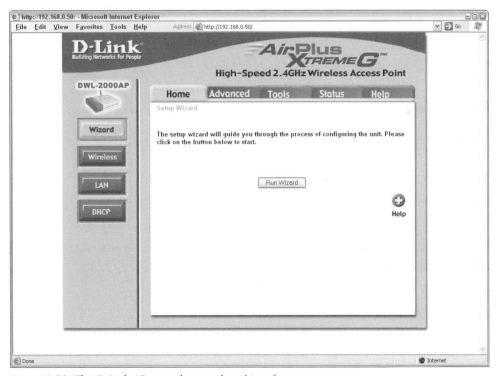

Figure 7-11: This D-Link AP uses a browser-based interface.

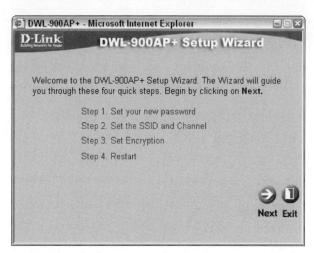

Figure 7-12: The first screen in the D-Link Setup Wizard tells you what you'll do in the following steps.

Figure 7-13: Change the password to something other than the default setting.

The next step is to set a name (called a service set identified or SSID) and a channel number for your AP, as shown in Figure 7-14. The SSID name can be anything you like. For security reasons, I suggest that you not use your family name or house address as part of the SSID.

You can set your AP to one of 11 channels. Virtually all APs come from the factory set to operate on channel 6. If you experience interference from a nearby AP at a neighbor's home, set your AP to channel 1 or channel 11. If you are planning to install a second AP in your home, set one AP for channel 1 or 6 and the other for 6 or 11. Do not set both APs to the use the same channel.

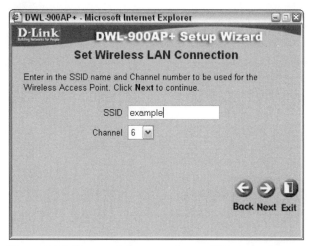

Figure 7-14: This screen lets you select an SSID name and a channel number for your AP.

Next, you can enable your AP's encryption security feature. For the time being, I recommend that you leave encryption turned off until you have installed and configured all of the wireless PCs on your network. I'll cover encryption at the end of this chapter. Figure 7-15 shows the encryption settings screen for the D-Link router.

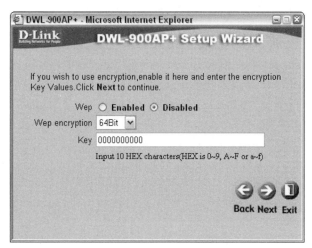

Figure 7-15: This screen lets you enable the data encryption feature on your AP.

The final step (shown in Figure 7-16) is to accept the settings you have just changed and apply them to the AP. In most cases, the AP will need to reset itself, and you will momentarily lose the connection between the AP and your wireless PC. If you changed the SSID setting, you will need to reconfigure your wireless PCs to use the new SSID setting. If this happens, you will see the "One or more wireless networks are available" message that you saw in Figure 7-8. Click on the message, select the new network name from the list, and click Connect.

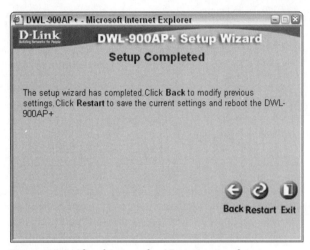

Figure 7-16: After this step, the AP resets using the new settings you just entered.

If everything went according to plan, your AP is now configured and operating properly, and you have at least one wireless PC installed and configured to operate with the wireless network. The next step from here depends on your network configuration:

- If you have more wireless clients to install, this is a good time to install and configure each of them.

- If you are installing a separate router or a combination AP/router, go on to Chapters 8 and 9, and then come back here and enable the encryption feature on your wireless LAN.

Securing Your Wireless LAN

Wireless networks are very convenient, but they pose a problem for security-conscious users.

Because wireless signals can penetrate through walls and floors, it is possible for anyone with a wireless laptop to connect to your network. After connected, they can poke around in your shared files, introduce virus or Trojan horse programs onto your network, or send malicious e-mails or spam.

Shortly after the introduction of 802.11b wireless networks, the equipment manufacturers realized that they had a major security problem on their hands. The industry responded by introducing two different types of data encryption for wireless networks—Wired Equivalent Privacy and WiFi Protected Access.

The Wired Equivalent Privacy (WEP) encrypts data using a shared password called an *encryption key*. The AP and each client PC must be configured to use the same key. Although WEP uses relatively strong 128-bit data encryption, researchers (and crackers) have found a way to crack the WEP encryption. As a result, the WiFi organization introduced a newer, stronger form of encryption called WiFi Protected Access, or WPA—which is in turn based on the IEEE 802.1X authentication protocol.

WPA ENCRYPTION

WPA is similar to WEP, but WPA combines encryption with user authentication. Instead of using a shared encryption key, WPA first requires users to identify themselves with a password, called a shared key. If the user passes the authentication test, the AP sends the user a unique key that is valid for a limited period of time, usually 15 minutes or less. The data connection between the user's PC and the AP is encrypted using the temporary key. When the key expires, the AP and the PC agree on a new key, and the data exchange is encrypted using the new key.

Tip

The only downside to WPA is that many older APs, routers, and PCs don't support it. If you have a mix of old and new devices on your wireless LAN, you may need to use WEP encryption instead.

Before you can begin using WPA, you'll need to configure your AP and your client PCs. This step should be done from a wired PC if possible. After you set the AP for WPA encryption, your wireless clients won't be able to connect to the LAN (or to the router's management screen) until you enter the WPA password on your wireless clients.

To configure WPA, connect to your AP's management screen, and locate the WPA settings. Figure 7-17 shows the WPA settings screen for a Linksys router.

If your router or AP offers more than one type of security mode, choose the one marked "Pre-Shared Key," often abbreviated as "PSK." The shared key itself can be any combination of letters, numbers, and punctuation marks. As with any password, avoid using obvious or common words. The best password is easy for you to remember but difficult for someone else to guess. I've found it helpful to use two disconnected words separated by a hyphen or period. In most cases, you should leave the key update interval set for 15 minutes (shown as 900 seconds on many routers.)

Figure 7-17: The Wireless Security screen for a Linksys router.

After you've configured your AP or router to use WPA, you'll need to enter the WPA shared key on each of your wireless computers. When your wireless PC or Mac attempts to connect the wireless LAN, you'll be prompted to enter the shared key, as shown in Figure 7-18. (Mac users will see a similar screen.)

Figure 7-18: Windows XP requires you to enter your WPA key twice to make sure you typed it correctly.

You'll need to repeat this step for each wireless computer on your LAN.

WEP ENCRYPTION

While WEP isn't as secure as WPA, it is still reasonably secure and is much better than no protection at all. Virtually all APs provide WEP encryption, and WEP is very easy to configure. In the following example, I show you how to configure WEP on a typical AP and on a Windows XP client PC.

Keep in mind that once you have enabled WEP on your AP, you will need to configure each client PC on your wireless LAN to use the same WEP encryption key.

To begin, connect to your AP's management screen, and locate the WEP settings screen. In the example shown in Figure 7-19, the WEP information is located on the same screen as the SSID and channel settings. It is not necessary to change the SSID or channel to enable WEP.

To enable WEP, select the Enabled radio button. If your router or AP offers multiple levels of encryption, choose the one with the strongest encryption. In this example, the AP supports 40-, 64-, and 128-bit encryption, and I have selected 128 bit.

Most APs allow you to enter the WEP key as a string of hexadecimal numbers or as a string of readable (ASCII) text. Unless you have a thing for hex numbers, choose the ASCII setting, and enter a string of text to use as the encryption key. Although I've used a readable phrase (mumbo-jumbo) in the example, you should use a random string of numbers and letters for your key. Whatever key you choose, be sure to write it down in a safe place; you'll need to enter the key into each of your client PCs.

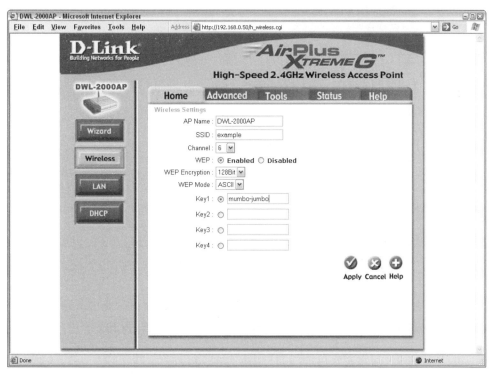

Figure 7-19: The WEP settings screen for a D-Link router.

Tip

Some APs—like the D-Link unit in the example—allow you to enter more than one key. You can switch among the four keys at any time by returning to the WEP settings screen and choosing a different key. The Windows XP client remembers four keys for each AP and will automatically locate the correct key when the key is changed.

After you've enabled WEP on the access point, you need to configure the WEP key on each of your wireless client PCs. The first time you attempt to connect to the wireless LAN after you enable WEP, you'll see a screen like the one in Figure 7-20. Carefully enter the key in each of the two boxes, and click the Connect button. If you change the key on the AP, you will need to re-enter the key on each of the client PCs.

Figure 7-20: You can't connect to a WEP-enabled network without the correct key.

Summary

Your wireless network is now complete. Now you can surf the Internet from anywhere in the house. (Just remember what I said back in Chapter 4 about surfing by the pool.) To sum up, here are the key things you should take away from this chapter:

- A wireless network survey can help you get the most out of your wireless network.

- The best place to put your wireless AP isn't always the most convenient.

- WEP or WPA security is essential for keeping intruders out of your wireless LAN.

At this point, you've installed all of the hardware necessary to create a LAN. In Chapter 8, I'll show you how to configure your computers for operation on a network. Fortunately, Windows XP and Mac OS X practically configure themselves, so your network is almost complete!

Chapter 8

Configuring Your Network

After you've purchased and installed your networking hardware, you are just one important step away from having a working LAN: You must install and configure the networking software for each computer on your LAN.

This step isn't as complicated as you might think. Windows XP and Mac OS X come with all the software you need to share files, printers, and an Internet connection on the LAN, and most of that software is already installed on your computers. In this chapter, I show you how to configure the software to make your LAN spring to life. You'll learn about:

■ How Windows networking works

■ How Mac OS X Networking Works

■ Running the Windows XP Network Setup Wizard

■ How Windows IP addressing works

How Windows Networking Works

Before you can configure your PCs or laptops for networking, you need to understand the role of each machine on your LAN. As you learned in Chapter 3, Windows XP includes built-in peer-to-peer networking features. Any computer on the LAN can share files, printers, and an Internet connection with any other computer. Computers that provide resources for others to use are called *servers*, and computers that utilize those resources are called *clients*.

On a peer-to-peer network, any computer can be a client, and any computer can be a server. It is even is possible for a computer to be both a client and a server at the same time. Figure 8-1 shows several computers sharing resources on a LAN.

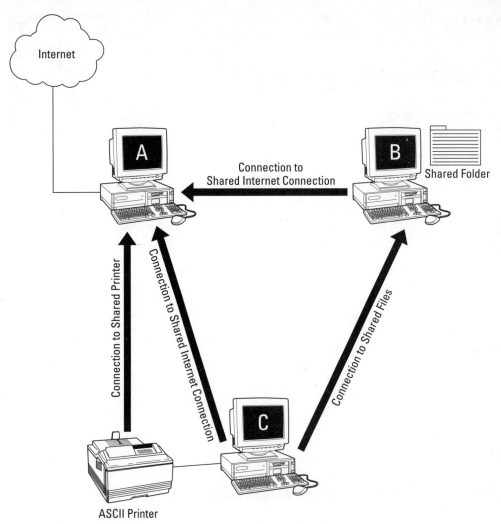

Figure 8-1: In this example, computer A is sharing an Internet connection, computer B is sharing files, and computer C has a shared printer.

In the example shown in Figure 8-1, the computer at the top left of the diagram has an Internet connection, the computer at the top right has a shared file folder, and the computer at the bottom has a shared printer. Each of the computers in this network is operating as a server, and each is also operating as a client to the other two computers on the network. For example, computer C is acting as a printer server for computer A, and computer A is acting as an Internet connection server for computer C.

All of this sharing looks very complicated, but it really isn't. The client and server features are built into Windows XP, so you don't have to install any additional software to use these features. But before you can use your home network, you'll need to decide which computer (if any) will be the

Internet Connection Sharing (ICS) server, and you'll need to spend a few minutes configuring each PC. You'll also need to create a user ID and password for each user on your network.

Finally, you'll need to configure all your computers with the same *workgroup name*. Windows uses this name to organize large numbers of computers into smaller, more manageable groups. Most home networks don't have enough computers to warrant separating them into several groups, but all of the computers on your network should have the same workgroup name.

Configuring Your Network

For your computers to communicate with one another over the network, each computer must be configured for network operation. Table 8-1 shows a checklist of network configuration tasks.

Table 8-1   Network Configuration Tasks

Task	Purpose
Configure network adapter with unique IP address	Essential for any IP network
Install second network adapter for shared connection (ICS server PC only)	Provides connection for a shared broadband connection on the ICS server. If you will be sharing a dial-up connection, you don't need the second network adapter.
Install Microsoft Network Client software	Allows a computer to use network shared files and printers
Install file and printer sharing software	Allows a computer to share files and printers with other computers on the network
Assign a unique computer name	Makes sure that each computer can be uniquely identified with a "human-friendly" name
Assign each computer to the same workgroup	Ensures that each computer can use files and printers shared by other computers on the LAN
Install Internet Connection Sharing software (ICS server PC only)	Allows one computer to share its Internet connection with other computers
Configure IP routing settings	Ensures that all computers on the LAN can connect to the Internet, either through an ICS server or a router/firewall

If this sounds like a lot of work, you're right. If you were to perform each of these tasks manually, you'd spend 15 to 20 minutes configuring each PC on your network. Fortunately, you can accomplish all these tasks at one time by using the Network Setup Wizard. In this section, I walk you through the Network Setup Wizard and explain what each step does.

Note

If you plan to use Microsoft's Internet Connection Sharing (and not an external router/firewall) to share your Internet connection, you should run the Network Setup Wizard on the ICS server PC first and then run the wizard on the rest of your PCs.

To start the Network Setup Wizard, click the Start button; then select All Programs → Accessories → Communications → Network Setup Wizard. The wizard displays the screen shown in Figure 8-2.

Figure 8-2: The Network Setup Wizard is the easiest way to configure your computers for network operation.

The first screen contains introductory information that you, as an informed reader of this book, already know. Click Next to move on to the next screen, shown in Figure 8-3.

The Before You Continue. screen makes sure that you have installed all of the hardware for your network. If you haven't, the wizard won't be able to continue. Click Next to move on to the next screen, shown in Figure 8-4.

This is one of the most important steps in the configuration process. If you select the top button (This computer connects directly to the Internet), the computer will be configured as an ICS server. You should select this choice only if you plan to use Internet Connection Sharing and this is the one computer on the network that will provide the shared connection for the other computers to use.

Select the middle button if your network uses a router/firewall, or if the computer you are configuring will connect to the Internet through an ICS server located on another computer.

Figure 8-3: This screen makes sure that you've already installed the necessary hardware.

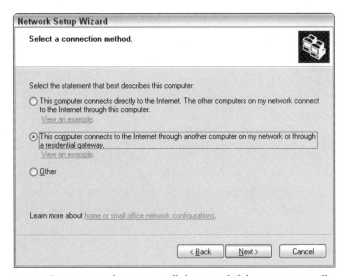

Figure 8-4: You use this step to tell the wizard if this computer will be an ICS server.

The bottom button is used only in unusual circumstances. Select this button only if:

▨ Your network is directly connected to the Internet with no firewall or router.

▨ Your computer is connected directly to the Internet but not to a LAN.

▨ You have multiple computers on a LAN but no Internet connection.

After you have made your selection, click Next to move on to the next screen.

If your computer has more than one network adapter, or if it has a network adapter and a dial-up modem, you'll see the screen in Figure 8-5. You use this screen and the next screen to tell the wizard which network connection to use. If your computer has only a single connection, you'll see the screen in Figure 8-7.

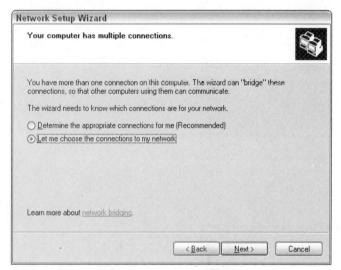

Figure 8-5: If your computer has more than one LAN connection, you'll need to tell the wizard which one to use.

Tip

The wizard will offer to automatically select the correct network connection for you, but it often selects the wrong connection. For example, when I ran the wizard on my laptop to take the screenshots for this chapter, the wizard decided that I wanted to use my computer's FireWire connection as my main network connection. It takes only a few extra seconds to manually select the correct connection; doing so may save you from having to run the wizard a second time.

Select the Let Me Choose the Connections button, and click Next. A screen similar to the one shown in Figure 8-6 appears.

If one of your network adapters is connected directly to the Internet (through a cable or DSL modem, for example), be sure to uncheck the checkbox to the left of the connection's name. Choose the correct network connection from the list by clicking on the connection's name. The connection should be highlighted as shown in Figure 8-6. Click Next to move on to the next step (see Figure 8-7).

Network Setup Wizard

Select the connections to bridge.

Select the check box for each connection that connects this computer to your other network computers.

Clear the check box for connections that connect this computer directly to the Internet.

Connections:

☑	1394 Connection	1394 Net Adapter
☑	Local Area Connection	FEM656C-3Com Global 10-100+56K CardBus PC Card-(Fast E

Learn more about network bridging.

< <u>B</u>ack   <u>N</u>ext >   Cancel

Figure 8-6: This screen lets you choose the correct connection to your LAN.

Network Setup Wizard

Give this computer a description and name.

<u>C</u>omputer description: Les' Laptop

Examples: Family Room Computer or Monica's Computer

Co<u>m</u>puter name: TWEETY

Examples: FAMILY or MONICA

The current computer name is TWEETY.

Learn more about computer names and descriptions.

< <u>B</u>ack   <u>N</u>ext >   Cancel

Figure 8-7: Give each computer a unique name.

In this step, the wizard asks you to name your computer. Try to give your computers memorable names so you'll know which one is which later on. The Computer Description is optional and can be any text you like. Users on the network will see the description when they connect to shared files and printers, so make the description easy to decipher.

Enter the computer's name and description, and click Next to go to the next step, shown in Figure 8-8.

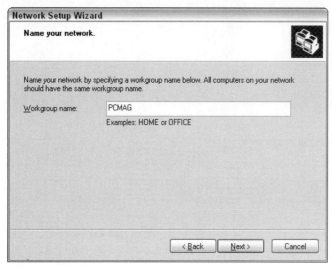

Figure 8-8: Enter the same workgroup name for each computer on the network.

This step lets you set the workgroup name for your computer. It is very important that all of your computers have the same workgroup name. Double-check your typing to make sure you've entered the correct name and then click Next to move to the final step, shown in Figure 8-9.

Figure 8-9: This is the last chance to change your settings.

At this point, the wizard has all the information it needs to configure your computer for network operation. The screen in Figure 8-9 reviews the information you've entered, so you can go back and make changes if necessary. When you click the Next button, the wizard applies the changes you've entered; if you need to make additional changes after you click the Next button, you'll need to run the wizard again. Double-check your changes, and click Next.

The actual installation and configuration process takes anywhere from a few seconds to a few minutes, depending on the options you've selected. The wizard displays an animated screen while it copies files and configures your network software. When the configuration changes are complete, the wizard displays the screen shown in Figure 8-10.

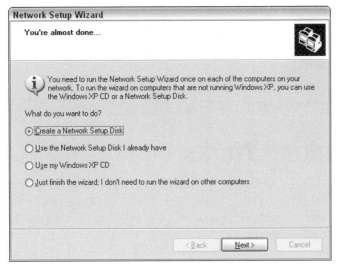

Figure 8-10: You can save the settings from the Network Setup Wizard and use them on another computer.

At this point, your computer is configured and almost ready to go. If you will be configuring additional computers, you can save the configuration settings you just used onto a floppy disk or a flash memory drive. If you choose to create a network setup disk, the Network Setup Wizard will create a disk containing a copy of the Network Setup Wizard and all of your network settings (with the exception of the computer name). You can take the floppy disk to any other computer on the LAN (including Windows 95, 98, and Me systems) and then run the Network Setup Wizard from the floppy disk.

If you choose to create a setup disk, the wizard will take you through three additional screens to create the disk. After the disk is created, the wizard displays a final screen, shown in Figure 8-11.

In almost all cases, you'll need to restart your computer for the configuration changes to take effect. Keep in mind that you won't be able to share files or printers until you've run the Network Setup Wizard on all the computers on the network.

Figure 8-11: The last step in the Network Setup Wizard.

How OS X Networking Works

Before the release of OS X Version 10.2, networked Macs were an island unto themselves. Earlier versions of the Mac OS included excellent networking features based on Apple's own AppleTalk protocol. But with a few exceptions (mostly involving third-party add-on software), it was very difficult to share files between Macs and PCs, even on the same LAN.

OS X version 10.2 and later now provides the ability for Macs and PCs to painlessly share files and printers. Mac clients can access files and printers attached to Windows PCs, and vice-versa. I'll explain file and printer sharing in detail in Chapters 10 and 11; in this section, I'll tell you what you need to do to enable file and printer sharing on your Mac.

File and printer sharing on Macs works in much the same way as it does on Windows PCs. Any Mac on the network can act as a client, a server, or both. Macs acting as servers provide shared file space and printer connections that can be used by other Macs or PCs on the LAN. A computer that uses one or more of the shared services is acting as a client.

Sharing Files and Printers with Other Macs

If your home LAN is an all-Mac network with no Windows PCs, you can share files and printers among the Macs on your LAN with just a few clicks. Click the Apple menu and select System Preferences; then click the Sharing icon. You'll see a display like the one in Figure 8-12.

As you can see from the example in Figure 8-12, there are separate checkboxes for file and printer sharing. Choose the appropriate checkboxes to turn on file and/or printer sharing, and close the preferences window. I'll explain how to use shared files and printers in Chapter 10.

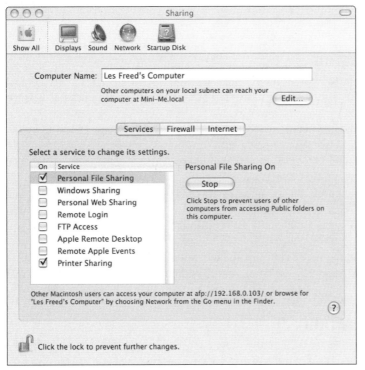

Figure 8-12: Personal File Sharing and Printer Sharing are turned off by default. The Sharing Preferences screen lets you turn these features on.

Sharing Files and Printers with PCs

Macs can use shared files stored on Windows PCs, and Macs can also share files so that they can be used from a Windows PC on your LAN. If you want to be able to use files stored on a Windows PC or use a printer that is connected to a PC, you don't need to change any settings on your Mac.

If you want to share files on your Mac so that a Windows user on your LAN can access the files, you'll need to enable Windows Sharing on your Mac. The Windows Sharing checkbox is located just below the Personal File Sharing checkbox in the Sharing Preferences shown earlier in Figure 8-12. The Windows Sharing setting controls both file and printer sharing with Windows PCs.

Windows IP Addressing Basics

By now, you know that each computer on your LAN must have a unique IP address. If you are using a router/firewall or Microsoft's Internet Connection Sharing, the Network Setup Wizard has already set your computer to use automatic IP addressing. Automatic addressing spares you from the tedium of manually entering an IP address, router address, and DNS server address for each computer on your LAN.

Automatic IP Addressing

As you saw in Chapter 3, external router/firewall devices and Microsoft's ICS both contain DHCP servers that provide a pool of IP addresses that client PCs can use for automatic IP address configuration.

If you don't have a router and you're not using ICS, your network doesn't have a DHCP server, so you might think that you'll need to manually configure an IP address for each computer. Fortunately, Windows XP contains a feature called *Automatic Private IP Addressing* that automatically assigns and manages addresses on networks that don't have a DHCP server.

You don't have to do anything special to use automatic addressing. When your computer first starts up, it will try to contact a DHCP server on the LAN. If a DHCP server is located, the computer requests and receives an IP address from the DCHP server. If no DHCP server responds within 60 seconds, the computer attempts to use the alternate IP address settings (described later in this section). If there is no alternate IP address configuration, the computer creates its own IP address from a pool of addresses reserved by Microsoft. These addresses are in the range between 169.254.0.1 and 169.254.255.254.

Alternate IP Configuration

If you frequently move your portable computer between two locations, you should know about the *Alternate IP Configuration* feature. This feature lets you set your computer to use an automatic IP address at one location while using a fixed address at another location.

I use this feature all the time. My home network has a DHCP server for automatic addressing, but my office network uses fixed IP addresses. Without this feature, I'd have to change my IP address settings every time I moved the computer. The Alternate IP Configuration screen is fairly well hidden, but the following steps show you how to get there.

You first need to select the correct network connection. To do this, follow these steps:

1. Click Start and then open the Control Panel. Select the Network Connections icon. (If your Control Panel is set to Category View, select the Network and Internet Connections icon and then select the Network Connections icon at the bottom of the screen.)

2. Right-click on the connection you want to change, and select Properties. You should see the Connection Properties screen, as shown in Figure 8-13.

3. You want to change the TCP/IP address settings, so click the Internet Protocol item, as shown in Figure 8-13, and then click the Properties button. This takes you to the TCP/IP properties screen shown in Figure 8-14.

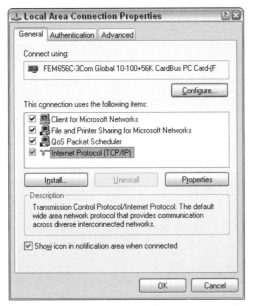

Figure 8-13: The Connection Properties screen lets you change some of the more obscure network connection settings.

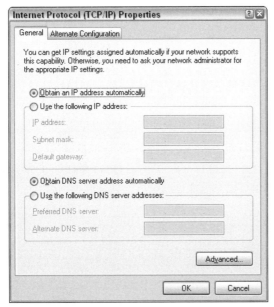

Figure 8-14: This computer is configured for automatic IP addressing.

4. As you can see from Figure 8-14, the example computer is configured for automatic IP addressing. To set the alternate IP address configuration, click the Alternate Configuration tab at the top of the screen to see the screen in Figure 8-15.

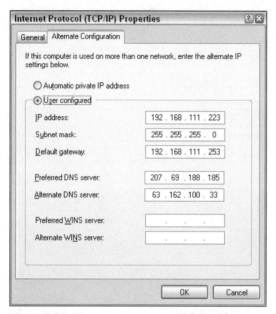

Figure 8-15: Now you can set a manual IP address to use at the office.

5. Enter the IP address information for your alternate location and click OK. Note that you may need to ask your office network administrator for the correct IP address information to use.

After you've configured the alternate IP address information, you can move your laptop back and forth between home and office without having to change settings. When you set up your computer at the office, remember that Windows XP will try to locate a DHCP server for one minute before it attempts to use the Alternate Configuration. The computer will not be able to connect to the network during that time.

Summary

At this point, your home network is installed, configured, and ready to use. In the next section of the book, I'll show you how to use your new network.

The key points in this chapter are as follows:

- You can use the Network Setup Wizard to help configure your network.

- The wizard can save the settings you select for one computer and use those settings to configure additional computers.

- Most router/firewalls and the Windows ICS server act as DHCP servers for automatic address configuration.

- You can use Windows Automatic Private IP Addressing on networks with no DHCP server.

- The Alternate IP Configuration is handy for moving a portable computer between two networks where one network uses a static IP address.

So now you've installed the hardware and configured the software. It's time to actually start using your home network. In the next few chapters, I'll discuss how to actually use your new LAN, beginning with Internet Sharing in the next chapter.

Part IV

Using Your LAN

Chapter 9

Sharing Internet Access

If you've never used a network before, you're in for a treat. After you've properly installed and configured your home network, you'll be able to enjoy Internet access from any computer in your home. If you have a cable or DSL broadband connection, you'll be able to surf the Net, download files, and check your e-mail at high speed, without waiting for a connection (or for someone else to get off the Internet-connected computer). And if you don't have a high-speed connection, you'll be able to get on the Internet from any computer in the house, even if someone else in your home is online at the same time. In this chapter, you'll see how to:

- Set up automatic IP configuration on your network

- Prepare your networked Macs and PCs for Internet access

- Install routers from Linksys and D-Link

As you saw in Chapter 2, you can share an Internet connection on your LAN using a hardware router or with a software-based connection-sharing program like Microsoft's Internet Connection Sharing (ICS). These products are typically very easy to install, and most router products provide nearly automatic Internet connection sharing right out of the box. But in some cases, you'll need to configure your router to work properly with your cable, DSL, or dial-up connection. You may also need to reconfigure some of your client PCs to enable them use the shared connection. This chapter gives you the technical background you need to configure a router.

Note

Most of the material in this chapter explains how to configure a hardware router. If you're using Microsoft Internet Connection Sharing, you should be aware that Microsoft ICS systems typically don't require any configuration, but the IP addressing concepts covered in the first section of this chapter also apply to ICS, so it's worth a read.

How IP Addressing Works

As you know by now, each PC on your LAN must have a unique IP address. These addresses should be in one of the public nonroutable IP address ranges specifically reserved for private LANs. Most routers come preconfigured to use LAN addresses in the 192.168.x.x address range. A few manufacturers use the 10.1.x.x address space, which provides a much larger range of addresses. Unless you plan to have more than 65,000 computers on your local LAN, either one will work just fine.

Your Internet connection (cable, DSL, or dial-up modem) also has a unique IP address assigned by your Internet Service Provider. In most cases, your Internet connection's IP address is assigned by your ISP when you connect to the Internet. Your router manages the traffic flow between your LAN and the Internet using a technique called Network Address Translation (NAT).

In addition to a unique IP address, all of the computers on a LAN need to know how to communicate with the Internet. Specifically, they need to know the address of the local router (called the *gateway* address) and the address of one or more Domain Name Service (DNS) servers.

All NAT routers also contain a DHCP server that manages and assigns IP addresses for the computers on the LAN. When each computer on the LAN first starts up, it queries the LAN, looking for a DHCP server. The DHCP server answers the PC's query and provides the PC with the information it needs to communicate with the LAN. Table 9-1 shows the information provided by most DHCP servers.

Table 9-1   DHCP Server Information

Item	Purpose
IP address and network mask	Address assigned to computer by the DHCP server
Gateway address	Address of the Internet gateway on the local LAN
DNS server address	Address of the nearest DNS server

As you saw in Chapter 3, home routers operate as both a DHCP client and as a DHCP server. The router may also act as a DNS server for the PCs on the LAN. Figure 9-1 shows how the router, client PCs, and your ISP work together to provide DHCP and DNS services for the client PCs on your LAN.

Here's the explanation for the steps shown in Figure 9-1.

1. When your router first powers up, it sends a DHCP request to the ISP.

2. The DHCP server at the ISP responds to the request, sending back an IP address, the address of the gateway router at the ISP, and the address of one or more DNS servers. The router assigns the IP address to the router's WAN interface, and it stores the gateway and DNS server addresses in its memory.

3. When a PC on the LAN powers up, it sends a DHCP request out on the LAN.

4. The local router responds to the DHCP request and sends the PC an IP address, the address of the router, and the address of one or more DNS servers. The PC uses these settings to communicate with the LAN and the Internet.

Note

It's important to remember that the local router's address is the LAN's gateway address. The WAN gateway address is used only by the router to communicate with the Internet.

DHCP is a great feature to have on home networks because it lets you add new PCs to the LAN by simply plugging them in. Although this example shows a wired Ethernet connection, DHCP also operates over WiFi wireless connections.

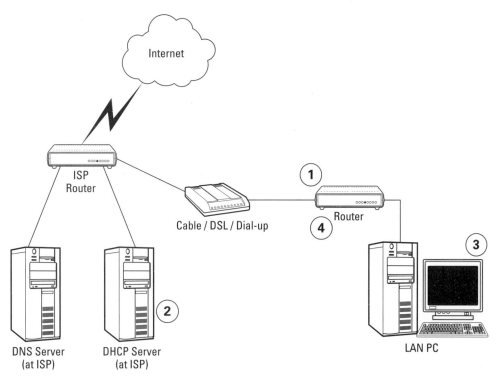

Figure 9-1: A typical home router operates as a DHCP client to obtain a public IP address from the ISP, and it also operates as a DHCP server for the client PCs on the LAN.

Note

Some routers use DHCP to pass on the address of the ISP's DNS server; other routers set themselves up as the DNS server. The latter technique is called a *DNS proxy*, so called because the local router accepts and responds to DNS requests on behalf of the ISP's DNS server.

Some routers store recent DNS requests in a *cache* so that they can respond to repeated DNS requests for the same address without passing the request on to the ISP's DNS server. This feature speeds up Internet access when your ISP's DNS server is slow to respond or is simply overloaded with requests.

Configuring Your Router

Before you can use your networked computers to connect to the Internet, you may need to manually configure your router. I say *may* because most home routers can automatically configure themselves to work with most cable modem connections. If you are using a DSL modem or if your cable modem provider requires that you enter a user name and password to access its service, you will need to configure your router with the proper user authentication information. You'll also need to manually configure your router if your broadband provider supplies you with a fixed (also called *static*) IP address.

Fortunately, most home routers are very easy to configure. Virtually all routers on the market today use a browser-based configuration interface, and you usually need to fill in a few forms on the screen.

In order to connect to the browser interface on your router, you'll need to know the factory-set IP address of the router, and you'll need to make sure that the computer you use to do the configuration is set for automatic IP addressing. If you just installed a network adapter in your computer, or if you've never used the network adapter before, chances are very good that it is already configured for automatic operation. If you aren't sure about your computer's IP configuration settings, see the *IP Addressing Basics* section in Chapter 8.

Note

These examples assume that you have installed, connected, and configured your network equipment, as I explained in the previous chapters. In particular, it assumes that your router contains a DHCP server, and that the DHCP server is enabled by default. If your router does not contain a DHCP server or if it is turned off by default, you will need to manually configure the IP address for at least one of the computers on your network. Consult your router's instructions for details.

Checking Your PC's IP Configuration

Before you can configure your router, you should make sure that your computers can communicate with the router. The steps in this section will make sure that your router and computer are connected and communicating with one another.

WINDOWS USERS FOLLOW THESE STEPS:

1. Turn on the router and any additional network equipment such as Ethernet switches and wireless APs.

2. Turn on one of the computers connected to the LAN. If you have both wired and wireless LAN clients, perform the initial setup from one of the wired PCs. If the computer was already on when you turned on the router, you do not need to restart the computer.

3. Check the PC's IP settings to see if the computer obtained an IP address from the router. To do this, click Start → Control Panel → Network Connections. (If your Control Panel is set to Category View, select the Network and Internet Connections icon, and then select the Network Connections icon at the bottom of the screen.) Right-click the network connection, click Status in the pop-up menu, and select the Support tab. You should see a display like the one in Figure 9-2.

Figure 9-2: This Connection Status screen shows that our example PC received an address from a DHCP server.

4. Your Connection Status display should look very much like the one in Figure 9-2. If it doesn't (or if your computer was already on when you turned on the router), click the Repair button on the Status display. If the computer was able to obtain an address from the router's DHCP server, you'll see a message like the one in Figure 9-3.

5. If your PC can't obtain an IP address or if you see a message saying that the repair operation failed, check the cable between your PC and the router. Make sure it is plugged in tight, and that the "link" lights on the router and the PC are lit.

Figure 9-3: If your PC's DHCP request was successful, you'll see this screen.

6. You now have a working IP connection between your PC and the router. Write down the Default Gateway address shown on the Connection Status screen. This is the IP address of your router.

7. Start your Web browser. If your usual Internet start page appears, your router is already configured to connect to the Internet, and you don't need to configure your router (although you might want to read the section titled "Configuring Your Router" in case you ever need to change the connection settings).

8. If your start page does not appear or if you see a dialog box asking if you want to use a dial-up connection, your PC's network connection isn't configured properly, or there's no physical connection between your PC and the router.

MAC OS X USERS FOLLOW THESE STEPS:

1. Turn on the router and any additional network equipment such as Ethernet switches and wireless APs.

2. Turn on one of the computers connected to the LAN. If you have both wired and wireless LAN clients, perform the initial setup from one of the wired Macs. If the computer was already on when you turned on the router, you do not need to restart the computer.

3. Check the Mac's IP settings to see if the computer obtained an IP address from the router. To do this, open the System Preferences from the Apple Menu; then click the Network icon. You will see a display like the one in Figure 9-4.

Figure 9-4: The example Mac has both an Ethernet and an AirPort connection. The Ethernet connection has successfully obtained an IP address from the router on the LAN.

4. If your Mac and your router are connected and working correctly, you should see a display similar to the one in Figure 9-4. A green dot will appear on the left side of the status window, indicating that the Ethernet cable is properly connected, and the Ethernet status will show the IP address the Mac obtained from the router.

5. If you see a red dot, you have a cable problem. Check both ends of the cable to make sure they are plugged in tight, ensure your router is powered on, and try again. If you see a green dot but no IP address, click the Configure button near the bottom of the window. You will see a display like the one in Figure 9-5.

6. You now have a working IP connection between your Mac and the router. Write down the Default Gateway address shown on the Connection Status screen. This is the IP address of your router.

7. Start your Web browser. If your usual Internet start page appears, your router is already configured to connect to the Internet, and you don't need to configure your router (although you might want to read the next two sections in case you ever need to change the connection settings).

8. If your start page does not appear, your router isn't configured correctly.

Figure 9-5: This screen shows detailed IP address information for your Mac.

Configuring Your Router

After you've established a connection between your computer and your LAN router, you may need to configure the router to work with your Internet connection. The following two examples show the steps required to configure two different routers (one from Linksys and one from D-Link Systems) for several different types of ISP service. Each manufacturer's menus are different, but the concepts and terminology used are the same for virtually all routers.

Note

The following examples show how to configure routers from D-Link and Linksys. I chose these two companies because, together, they account for a very large share of the home networking market. Other companies, including 3Com, Microsoft, NETGEAR, SMC Networks, and Siemens—among others—offer similar and equally capable products.

Configuring a Linksys Router

Like many of its competitors, Linksys makes a large variety of networking equipment. Most Linksys products use a similar browser-based configuration menu. The router shown in this example is a combination router/firewall with a built-in Ethernet switch. Linksys makes several versions of this router, including models with wired and wireless (802.11x) connections. The configuration menus for all models are nearly identical, although there are some small differences between models.

To configure a Linksys router, follow these steps:

1. Perform the steps outlined in *Checking Your Computer's IP Configuration* in the previous section.

2. Open your Internet browser and choose File → Open. In the dialog box that opens, enter the Default Gateway IP address you wrote down in Step 6 in the preceding lists.

3. The first screen you'll see is the Setup screen shown in Figure 9-6. This screen controls the WAN and LAN settings for the router. There are only five items you can change on this screen.

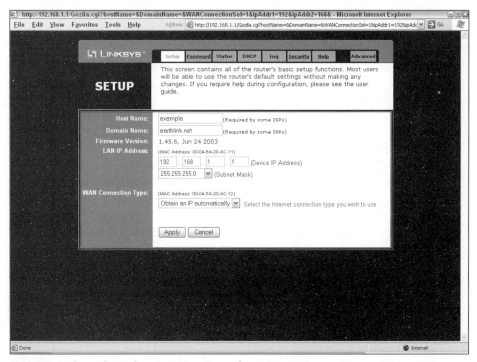

Figure 9-6: This is the Linksys router's main configuration screen.

4. The Host Name and Domain Name are not typically required by most ISPs, and you can almost always leave them blank.

5. The LAN IP address has a default setting of 192.168.1.1. There is no reason to change this unless it conflicts with another device on your LAN. The Subnet Mask should remain at the default setting of 255.255.255.0 unless you plan to have more than 253 computers on your local network.

6. The WAN Connection Type is the most important setting on this screen. The default setting is Obtain an IP Automatically, which is the correct choice if you are using a cable or DSL modem and your ISP does not require you to enter a user name and password when you connect to the Internet. If you are using such a modem, leave this setting as it is, click the Apply button, and go to Step 11.

7. If your cable or DSL provider requires you to enter a user name and password, select PPPoE from the WAN Connection Type pull-down menu. Some additional items appear on the screen, as shown in Figure 9-7.

8. Enter your user name and password in the spaces provided. You don't need to enter the Service Name type unless instructed to do so by your ISP. Leave the Connect on Demand and Keep Alive settings as they are, click Apply, and go to Step 11.

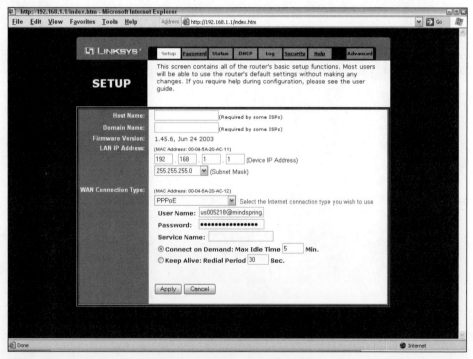

Figure 9-7: When you select the PPPoE connection type, several new menu options appear on the screen.

If your ISP provides you with a static (fixed) IP address, select Static IP from the WAN Connection Type menu. Several additional items appear on the screen, as shown in Figure 9-8.

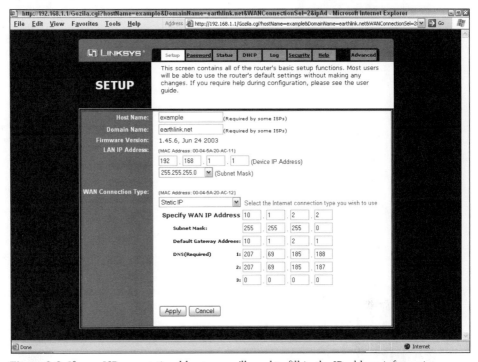

Figure 9-8: If your ISP uses static addresses, you'll need to fill in the IP address information manually.

9. Most routers, including this example router, offer the option to either connect to the ISP as needed (see "Connect on Demand" in Figure 9-6) or to stay connected all the time. In most cases, you'll want to check the Keep Alive box so that the router doesn't have to re-connect to the ISP each time you fire up your Web browser.

10. Enter the IP address information provided by your ISP. Your ISP may provide you with one to three DNS server addresses; enter as many as you have, and leave the others set at 0.0.0.0. Click the Apply button.

11. Your router should now be connected to the Internet. To double-check your router's settings, click the Status tab at the top of the Linksys menu screen. You'll see a status display like the one in Figure 9-9.

12. The exact configuration of the status screen varies depending on the type of Internet connection. If you are using PPPoE or automatic (also called *dynamic*) IP addressing, you should see the ISP-assigned IP address and DNS server settings in the WAN section of the display.

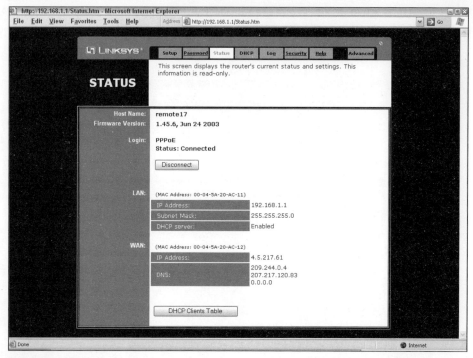

Figure 9-9: The Linksys status screen shows the current status of the LAN and WAN settings. The router in this example is connected to DSL modem using PPPoE.

Configuring a D-Link Router

D-Link makes a large variety of home and commercial networking equipment. Although most Linksys products use the single-screen configuration menu shown in the preceding example, most D-Link products use a multiscreen Setup Wizard to walk users through the initial configuration process.

To configure a D-Link router, perform the steps outlined in the preceding section, *Checking Your PC's IP Configuration*, and then continue with Step 1 as follows:

1. Open your Internet browser and choose File → Open. Enter the Default Gateway address you wrote down earlier. The router asks you for a user name and password. Check your user's manual for the correct login information.

2. After you enter the password, the main D-Link configuration screen appears. Click the Setup Wizard button. The wizard appears in a new window, as shown in Figure 9-10. Click Next to continue.

Note

Some pop-up ad blocker programs may block the Setup Wizard screen. If you don't see the Setup Wizard, turn off your pop-up blocker program.

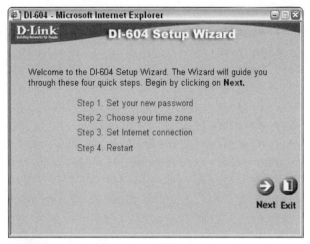

Figure 9-10: The first Setup Wizard screen simply explains
what you'll be doing in the following steps.

3. The first step in the wizard, shown in Figure 9-11, asks you to set a new password for your
   router. Write the password down and keep it in a safe place; if you lose the password, you'll
   need to reset the router, and you'll lose all your configuration settings. Click Next to continue.

Figure 9-11: Enter a new password here, and be sure to keep
the password in a safe place.

4. Select the correct time zone from the pull-down menu as shown in Figure 9-12.

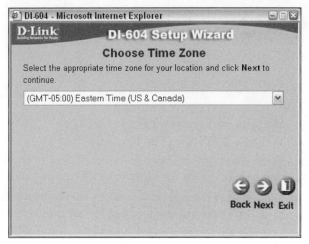

Figure 9-12: The router needs to know what time zone it is in so that it can set its internal clock.

Note

At this point, you may be wondering why the router needs to know what time zone it is in. This router—like most D-Link routers—has an internal clock that is set automatically from an Internet time server. The time server tells the router what the time is in Greenwich Mean Time (GMT), but the router needs to convert GMT to local time.

So why does the router need a clock? Some router features—such as the error log, firewall filters, and time-of-day parental controls—need to know the correct local time.

5. Click the Next button. The router attempts to determine what type of Internet connection you have. When it has determined the correct connection type, you'll see the screen shown in Figure 9-13. If the router is successfully able to determine the connection type, it will pre-select that connection for you.

6. Confirm the connection type and click the Next button. Note that the PPTP connection type is used only by a few European ISPs and is not used in North America.

7. If you selected Dynamic IP Address, you'll see the screen shown in Figure 9-14. In most cases, you can simply leave this screen at the default settings and click Next.

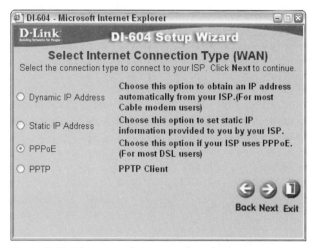

Figure 9-13: This screen lets you confirm the Internet connection type.

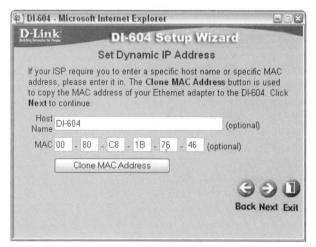

Figure 9-14: This screen allows you to "clone" the MAC address of your cable modem.

Note

Some cable modem ISPs require that you enter a specific computer host name to verify that you are an authorized user of their service.

A very few ISPs log the Ethernet Media Access Control (MAC) address of the first computer that you connect to the cable modem. Subsequent connections must come from the same MAC address. In theory, the MAC address is unique to each Ethernet device on the planet. The Clone MAC Address button copies your PC's MAC address into the router; as far as your ISP knows, the connection is in fact coming from your PC.

8. If you need to use the Host Name or MAC address features, enter the information into the space provided, click Next and then go on to Step 12.

9. If you are using a static IP address, the screen in Figure 9-15 appears.

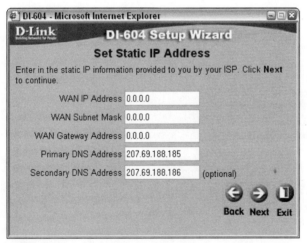

Figure 9-15: You use this screen to enter your cable or DSL modem's static IP address.

10. Enter the IP, subnet mask, gateway, and DNS server addresses provided by your ISP. Click Next and go to Step 12.

11. If your ISP uses PPPoE authentication, you need to enter your user name and password, as shown in Figure 9-16.

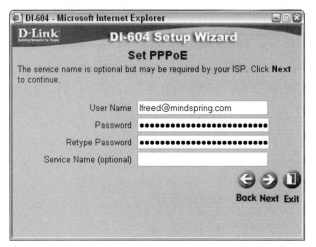

Figure 9-16: For PPPoE connections, enter your user name and password.

12. Enter your user name and password. The service name setting is rarely used in North America. Click Next.

13. The Setup Completed screen appears, as shown in Figure 9-17.

Figure 9-17: The Setup Wizard is complete, and your router is almost ready to go.

14. Your router configuration is nearly complete. The changes you just made will not take effect until you click the Restart button. Click Restart and wait about 10 seconds for the router to restart. Click the Status tab at the top of the main configuration screen. You will see a display like the one in Figure 9-18.

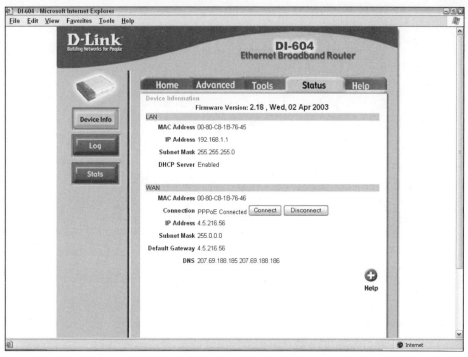

Figure 9-18: This screen shows the status of the current WAN connection.

15. If you are using a dynamic IP or PPPoE connection, you should see the IP, gateway, and DNS server addresses assigned by your ISP in the lower portion of the status screen.

What's Next?

After you've configured your router, there are a few things left on your to-do list.

If you have multiple PCs on your network, you'll need to check the IP configuration on each PC. You can do this quickly by performing Step 3 under *Checking Your PC's IP Configuration* at the beginning of this chapter.

If your network includes one or more wireless access points, make sure that you enable WEP or WPA security for each AP and device on the network. (See Chapter 7 for more information on WEP and WPA.)

You may want to explore the network protection and Internet filtering options that your router provides. You should also perform a security audit of each PC on your network. I'll cover these topics in detail in Chapter 13.

As you use your network and Internet connection, you may find that some application programs will not work through a firewall. In particular, some instant messaging programs and multiplayer games may require that you make some changes to your router's firewall settings. Most programs that encounter such a problem will let you know that they can't work through a firewall, and many will offer suggestions on how to fix it.

Summary

This chapter showed you that you don't need an electrical engineering degree to install and configure a router. The key points in this chapter are as follows:

- Each PC on your LAN needs to know how to communicate with the local router.

- Most routers provide automatic IP configuration using a DHCP server.

- The majority of routers are very easy to configure.

- Most DSL and some cable modem providers use PPPoE to authenticate users as they connect to the Internet.

Congratulations! If all went well (and I hope it did!), you now have a fully working, Internet-connected home LAN. At this point, you should be able to connect to the Internet from any PC on your network.

In Chapter 10, I'll show you how to use your new LAN to share files with other computers on the network.

Chapter 10

Sharing Files on Your LAN

Network file sharing is one of the most useful—and most often overlooked—aspects of home networking. In this chapter, I show you how to:

■ Share Mac and Windows files and folders on your network

■ Use shared files from another computer

■ Map a drive (on Windows XP systems)

How File Sharing Works

Windows XP and Mac OS X include simple file sharing features that make it very easy to share files on your network. You can use file sharing to share any type of file, including documents, music, and photo files, with any computer on your network.

The ability to share files with other computers and to use files shared on other computers is built into Windows XP and Mac OS X. You don't need to purchase or install any additional software. As you may recall from Chapter 3, the type of network where any computer can be a server, a client, or both at the same time is called peer networking. Figure 10-1 shows an example of a peer network with three computers.

The example in Figure 10-1 is based on my own home network. My main desktop PC is named Marvin, and it is where I do most of my work. Elmer is another desktop PC with two very large hard drives, and it is where I store my work in progress, as well as archived copies of all my books, magazine articles, and other documents. My laptop is named Tweety. When I need a screenshot for an example, I almost always use the laptop, rather than interrupting my writing on Marvin. Because the laptop has a relatively small (and almost always full) hard drive, I save the screenshot files directly onto Elmer's capacious hard drive.

I have a large cache of MP3 files (legal ones, ripped from my CD collection!) stored on Marvin so that I can listen to music while I work without having to shuffle CDs all day long. Occasionally, I need to work on Elmer. Rather than cranking up the volume on Marvin so that I can hear it across the room, I use the MP3 player on Elmer to play the MP3 files located on Marvin's hard drive.

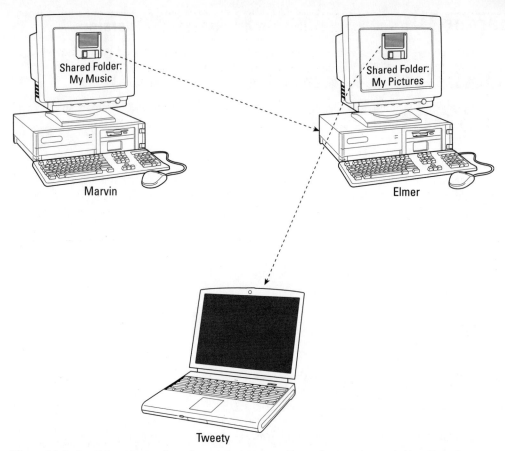

Figure 10-1: Any PC or Mac can be a client and any PC or Mac can be a server—or both at the same time.

The beauty of file sharing is that you can get to your files no matter where they are physically located. In the sections that follow, I'll show you how to share files and how to use shared files located on another computer.

Windows File Sharing

Windows 2000, XP Home, XP Professional, and XP Media Center Edition all provide the ability to share files with other Windows and Mac computers on the same LAN. Windows 2000, XP Professional, and XP Media Center edition offer more advanced networking features than XP Home Edition (see the following sidebar for details), but the basic networking features in all versions of Windows XP operate in the same way.

Older versions of Windows (Windows Me, 98, 95, and Windows for Workgroups v.3.11) also include file sharing features. Windows XP is compatible with these older versions of Windows, but the method used to share files and to access shared files in these versions is different from that in Windows XP. If you are using one of these older versions of Windows, consult your Windows user's manual or the built-in help file for specific how-to information.

File Sharing with Windows XP Professional Version

Windows XP Professional includes a much more sophisticated file sharing system than Windows XP Home Edition. The additional file sharing features in XP Professional allow users (and network administrators) to carefully control access to shared files on a user-by-user basis.

Because this book is targeted at the home market, I will not discuss Windows XP Professional file sharing in detail. The Windows XP Help system includes detailed information on XP Professional's additional features under the topic Access Control.

The advanced file sharing features in Windows XP Professional are turned off by default. You can check to see how your copy of Windows XP is configured by opening My Computer and clicking → Tools → Folder Options. Click the General tab and then scroll down to the last item in the Advanced Settings list. If the Use Simple File Sharing box is checked, your system is set to use a simpler form of file sharing, identical to the file sharing in Windows XP Home Edition.

You can use two methods to share files on your computer: You can share one or more folders, or you can share an entire disk drive.

Sharing a Folder

Before other users can access files on your computer, you must first tell Windows which files you want to share.

Windows XP automatically creates a folder called Shared Documents on every computer. This folder makes it easy to share files with other users. To share a file (or a folder full of files), you simply drag the file or folder into the Shared Documents folder. Any files placed into the Shared Documents folder will be available for sharing on the network. You can see the contents of the folder by selecting My Computer → Shared Documents. The Shared Documents folder contains several subfolders, as shown in Figure 10-2.

The Shared Pictures, Shared Music, and Shared Video folders are automatically created by Windows XP to help you organize your shared files. Other application programs may create additional folders inside the Shared Documents: folder. In the preceding example, Adobe Acrobat has created a folder named Adobe PDF 6.0.

Although the Shared Documents folder is convenient to use, it requires you to rethink the way you store files on your computer. Most users—myself included—keep their documents organized within the My Documents folder. To share a file using the Shared Documents folder, you must drag (or copy) the file out of the My Documents folder and into the appropriate folder inside the Shared Documents folder.

If you frequently share a large number of files on the network, you may find it easier to simply share the entire My Documents folder—or any other folder on your computer. To share a folder with other users, select the folder in Windows Explorer, right-click on the folder, and select Sharing and Security from the pop-up menu. You will see a Sharing and Security display like the one in Figure 10-3.

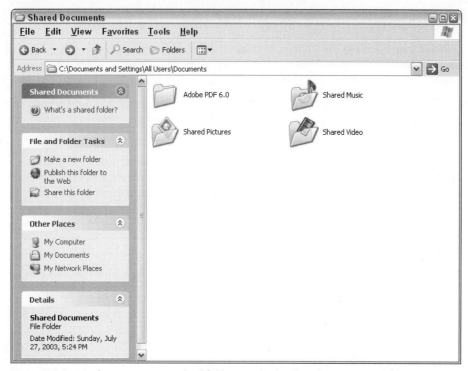

Figure 10-2: Windows creates several subfolders inside the Shared Documents folder.

Note

Some (mostly older) programs store their data files in the Program Files subfolder rather than in the My Documents folder. If you need to share data files created with such a program, you'll need to share that program's data folder separate from the My Documents folder.

As you can see from Figure 10-3, Windows assigns a share name to each shared folder on your computer. Windows simply copies the folder's name into the share name, but you may change the name if you want.

By default, other users on the network may delete or modify shared files on your computer. If you do not want other users to be able to change your files, uncheck the Allow Network Users to Change My Files setting and then click OK.

Figure 10-3: The Sharing and Security properties display lets you control your shared files.

Sharing a Drive

If you frequently work on multiple computers in your home, you may find it easier to simply share the entire drive on your computer rather than just share a few folders. To share an entire drive, open My Computer, right-click the drive, and select Sharing and Security from the pop-up menu. You'll see a warning dialog box like the one in Figure 10-4.

Be Careful What You Share!

It is important to remember that when you share a folder, all of the files and subfolders within the shared folder are also shared. For example, if you share the My Documents folder, all of the files and folders in the My Documents folder will be available to all of the other computers on the LAN. If you have private or confidential files stored in the folder, those files will be available to everyone—which is probably not what you want.

Before you begin sharing your files, you may want to take a few minutes to organize your files into separate folders and share only the appropriate folders. For example, you may want to create separate folders for your digital photos, MP3 files, and personal files. You could then share the photos and MP3 folders so that everyone can use those files but not share the personal files folder.

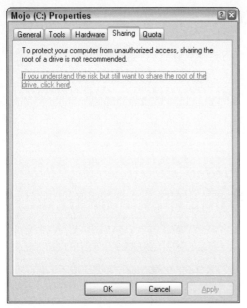

Figure 10-4: Windows doesn't really want to let you share a drive.

As you can see, Windows XP tries to discourage you from sharing the entire drive. When you share the entire drive on the network, another user (or an intruder, if you don't have a firewall) has carte blanche to snoop, delete, and modify files on your hard drive. Another user may mistakenly (or maliciously) modify critical system files on your computer, making your computer unstable or even unusable. You should only use this feature if you understand the risks involved, and you absolutely must have strong firewall protection to keep Internet hackers from messing with your system.

Caution

How real is the threat from hackers? Very. During some research for a *PC Magazine* article, I set up an experiment. I added a second IP address to my cable modem, and I set up a Windows PC directly connected to the cable modem. I also installed a packet sniffer program, a special piece of software that monitors and logs all the traffic on the IP network.

Within 15 minutes of firing up my test PC, the computer was bombarded with all sort of malicious traffic. Intruders attempted to delete files and install Trojan horse programs on the test PC. Within 24 hours, the system was receiving so much traffic—almost all of it malicious—that I was afraid that my cable service provider would notice the traffic increase and cut my service off, so I shut the system down.

The moral of the story is that the threat from hackers isn't just media hype—it is very real. If you don't have a firewall and up-to-date antivirus software on your PC, you are a sitting duck. See Chapter 13 for more information on protecting your system from the bad guys.

If I haven't scared you off yet, you've clicked the disclaimer and are ready to share your drive on the LAN. The options for sharing a drive are identical to those for sharing a folder, as you can see in Figure 10-5.

Figure 10-5: Sharing a drive isn't much different from sharing a folder.

Give your shared drive a name (Windows defaults to using the drive's volume name), decide if you want other users to be able to change your files, and click OK.

Accessing Shared Drives and Folders

There are several ways to connect to and use shared drives and folders on your network. The simplest and fastest way is to use the My Network Places folder. This folder contains icons that represent each shared folder on your network. You can click any of the icons in the My Network Places display, shown in Figure 10-6, and browse through the files, just as you would with files on a local hard drive.

If you want to see only the resources shared by a specific computer, you can click View workgroup computers on the left side of the My Network Places screen, and select the individual computer from a list. This is handy when you have a large number of shared folders on your LAN.

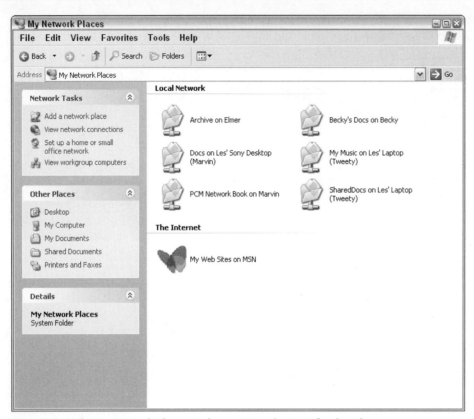

Figure 10-6: The My Network Places window contains shortcuts for shared resources on your network.

You can also access shared files and folders from within many applications. When you open a file using the File → Open command in certain applications, the My Network Places icon also appears in the Open dialog box. If the application program isn't designed to work with networked files, you won't see the My Network Places icon. The example in Figure 10-7 shows the Open dialog box from Microsoft Word.

To open a networked file in a network-aware application, use the normal File → Open command, and click the My Network Places icon on the left side of the File Open dialog box. A list of network resources will appear in the dialog box, and you can choose a file to open.

Controlling Automatic Discovery

Windows XP Home automatically includes new additions to network folders, drives, and printers in the My Network Places display. This is convenient on small networks but can become an annoyance on larger networks. Fortunately, it is simple to turn this feature on and off.

Open My Computer and select Folder Options from the Tools menu. Click the View tab, and you'll see a display like the one in Figure 10-8.

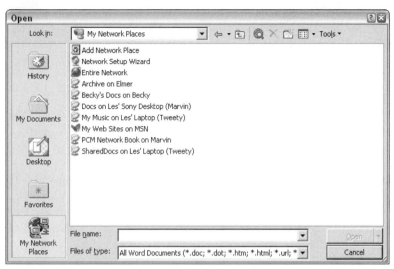

Figure 10-7: Many applications include My Network Places in the Open dialog box, making it easy to open files located on other computers.

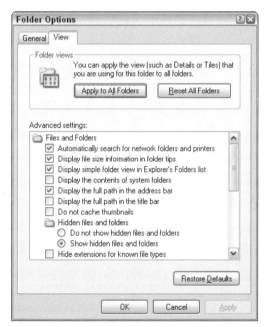

Figure 10-8: You can use the Folder Options settings to turn off automatic discovery of new network folders and printers.

The first setting under Advanced Settings tells Windows XP whether or not to automatically search for new network resources. If you turn off this setting, you can still add frequently used network resources to the My Network Places display. To do this, click the Add a Network Place icon on the left side of the My Network Places window.

Mapping a Network Drive

If you frequently use a shared resource, you may find it more convenient to map a drive to that resource. When you create a drive mapping, Windows assigns an unused drive letter on your PC to the network resource. After you've created the mapping, you can refer to the shared network resource by the drive letter. You can even tell Windows to automatically recreate the drive mapping the next time you start your computer. This is a handy feature to use if you frequently use an older application program that is not network-aware.

To create a mapped drive, right-click My Computer or My Network Places from the Windows desktop, and select Map Network Drive from the pop-up menu. You can also select Tools → Map Network Drive option from Windows Explorer. You'll see the Map Network Drive display in Figure 10-9.

Figure 10-9: The Map Network Drive dialog box lets you create a new drive mapping from a shared network folder.

Select the drive letter you want to use for the drive mapping, and enter the shared resource name. The resource name must be in the form \\server\share. Most users will find it easier to use the network browser; just click the Browse button, and you'll see a display like the one in Figure 10-10.

The Network Browser display shows all of the shared resources on your network, even if those resources don't appear in the My Network Places display. The example in Figure 10-10 shows two computers in the workgroup named Pcmag—one named Becky and the other named Elmer. I have clicked the plus sign next to Elmer to show all of the resources on that computer, and I have selected the shared folder named Archive.

Figure 10-10: The Network Browser presents a display of all the shared folders and drives on your LAN.

Select a network resource, and click OK. The Map Network Drive dialog box reappears with the Drive and Folder fields filled in, like the example in Figure 10-11.

Figure 10-11: You can automatically reconnect to a share each time you log in to Windows.

If you want to automatically reconnect to this network share the next time you start Windows, check the box marked Reconnect at Logon. The next time you start your computer, Windows will automatically re-establish the drive mapping, using the same drive letter. For example, you could create a mapping on one computer that maps drive P: to the Shared Photos file on another computer. That way, your shared photos will always be available as drive P: This makes it simple to access frequently used files on another computer.

If you frequently access the same shared drive from several different client PCs, you may find it convenient to use the same letter for drive mappings on each client PC. For example, you may want to use "P" for photos, "M" for music, and so on.

Note

Many users think that they should be able to run applications stored on another computer by sharing the entire hard drive or the Program Files folder. Unfortunately, this is usually not the case. Many applications require additional files copied to specific directories when the program is installed, and most programs also require specific settings in the Windows Registry.

Mac OS X File Sharing

As you saw in Chapter 8, Mac OS X computers can share files with other Macs as well as with Windows PCs. There are two separate settings in the Network Preferences that control file sharing—one controls Macintosh file sharing and the other controls Windows Sharing.

MAC-TO-MAC SHARING

To share a file or folder with other Mac users on your network, you must drag the file or folder to one of two places:

- The Shared folder, located in the Users folder on your hard drive
- Your Public folder, located in your home folder

After you have copied the items into one of these two folders, any Mac user on your LAN can open the folder and copy the files to their own computer. If the other user wants to change or delete files in your shared folder, they may need to know the username and password for the user who owns the items.

By default, the Shared folder is set up to allow all users on the network to read, write, and delete files. The Public folder inside of your home folder is set up to allow others to open and copy files, but not to delete, rename, or change files. You can change the sharing privileges of each folder by changing the permission settings for the shared folder(s). To do this, Control-click the shared folder and select Get Info. Click to expand the Ownership & Permissions settings and then expand the Details settings. Figure 10-12 shows the default permissions settings for the Public folder.

Figure 10-12: You can set specific sharing permissions for each folder on your computer.

As you can see from Figure 10-12, OS X allows you to set different permissions for different classes of users. In OS X jargon, the owner is the person who actually owns the files. The owner always has full read and write privileges to his/her own files. The owner can assign rights to other users on a group or individual user basis.

To use a shared file or folder on another Mac on your network, click the Network icon in the Finder. You should see a list of all the available servers on your network, as shown in Figure 10-13. Select the server containing the folder you want to use. Depending on the security settings on the server, you may be prompted to enter your user name and password to gain access to the folder.

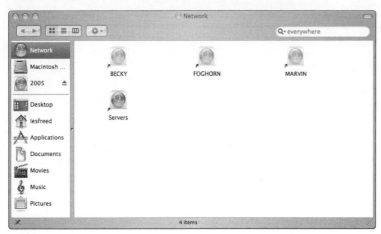

Figure 10-13: The Finder network display shows the available servers on your network.

Note

There may be times when the server you want to use does not appear in the Finder's list of servers. This frequently happens when you have just powered up the server computer, or if you have recently enabled sharing on a computer that was already powered on.

If this happens, use the Connect to Server option from the Finder's Go menu. You will be prompted to enter the name of the server. You must precede the server's name with `afp://` followed by the IP address or name of the server.

When you connect to a shared folder, OS X places an icon on your desktop with the name of the shared folder. The icon for the network folder works much like the icon for that hard drive in your own computer; you can open it and drag and drop files from the folder. If you have the proper permissions, you can also put files into the shared folder, or delete files from the folder.

When you have finished using the shared folder, Control-click on the folder and select Eject to remove the icon from your desktop.

Tip

If you frequently need access to a shared resource on another computer, you may find it convenient to create a desktop alias for the networked folder. To do this, Control-click on the shared folder and select Make alias from the menu. When you double-click on the alias, the corresponding network folder will open without prompting you to enter your user name and password.

MAC-TO-WINDOWS SHARING

Thanks to the addition of Windows networking support in OS X 10.3 and later, cross-platform Mac/PC file sharing is simple. The only hard and fast requirement is that you must enable Windows Sharing in the Sharing preferences screen (see Chapter 8 for details.)

To connect to a shared Windows directory from a Mac, click the Network icon in the Finder, just as you would if you were connecting to a shared folder on another Mac. Look back at Figure 10-13, and I'll point out something you may not have noticed earlier: The three computers at the top of the screen are Windows XP systems. OS X handles all shared folders equally, regardless of the operating system running on the server PC.

Similarly, shared folders on Macs appear in the Windows Network Neighborhood alongside their PC counterparts. To use a shared Mac folder from a Windows PC, just double-click the folder's icon in the Network Neighborhood, or map a drive to the shared folder.

Summary

As you've seen in this chapter, a network gives you the freedom to work with your files, wherever you are in your home. The key points in this chapter are as follows:

- Any computer on your network can share files with other computers.

- Any computer on the network can use those shared files.

- The My Network Places window provides the quickest and easiest way to use shared folders in Windows.

- Mapped drives are convenient for frequently used shared folders on Windows PCs, and desktop aliases save time for Mac users.

File sharing is one of the most useful things you can do with a home network. Now that you have File Sharing 101 under your belt, it's time to move on to printer sharing.

Chapter 11

Sharing Printers

Printer sharing is one of the most useful yet most underutilized aspects of home networking. There are several ways to share printers on your network. In most cases, you don't need to purchase any additional hardware or software. In this chapter, I'll show you how to:

■ Share a printer from Windows XP and Mac OS X computers

■ Share a printer using an external print server

■ Use shared printers on your network

The great thing about printer sharing is that it allows you to use any printer in the house from any computer in the house.

How Network Printing Works

If you want to share a printer on your home network, you have three alternatives:

■ Windows XP and Mac OS X both include built-in printer sharing, so you can share a printer attached to any computer on your network.

■ If you want to connect a printer that is not attached to a computer, you can purchase an external print server. These devices attach almost any printer to a wired or wireless LAN.

■ You can purchase a network-capable printer or add a network printing module to your existing printer, if your printer manufacturer offers one.

Most computers on a home network can use any shared printer connected to the network, regardless of the method used to share the printer. Figure 11-1 shows a network with three shared printers, each using a different type of connection.

The printer at the top left of Figure 11-1 is connected to a Windows XP PC with a USB cable. The printer at the top right is a network-ready laser printer, and the printer at the lower left is a standard printer attached to the network via an external print server. Both computers can use any of the three printers.

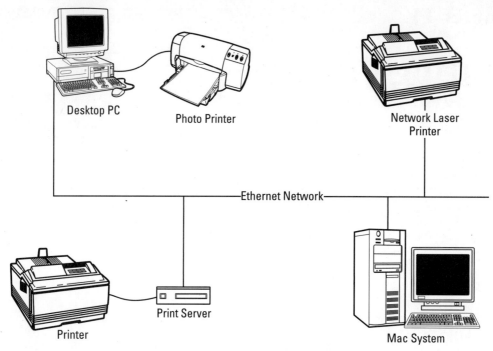

Figure 11-1: The client PC on this network can print to any of three printers.

In this section, I'll explain each of the three printer sharing options so that you can choose the option that works best for you. In the remainder of the chapter, I'll show you how to connect a client computer to a shared printer.

Windows XP Printer Sharing

Windows XP includes a printer sharing feature that allows you to share a printer connected to your computer. This is the simplest, most cost-efficient way to share a printer, but it isn't always the most convenient way for two reasons. First, the attached computer must be turned on for other users to use the shared printer. Second, the printer must be located relatively close to the PC.

To share a printer on the network, follow these steps:

1. Connect the printer to your PC using a USB or parallel printer as appropriate.

2. Install the printer driver and make sure that the printer is working properly.

3. From the Start menu, select Printers and Faxes. If the Printers and Faxes item doesn't appear on your Start menu, open the Control Panel and then select Printers and Faxes. (If your Control Panel is set to Category View, select the Printers and Other Hardware icon; then select the Printers and Faxes icon at the bottom of the list.) You'll see a display containing an icon for each printer and fax device on your computer, like the one in Figure 11-2.

4. Right-click the printer you want to share, and select Sharing from the menu. The display in Figure 11-3 appears.

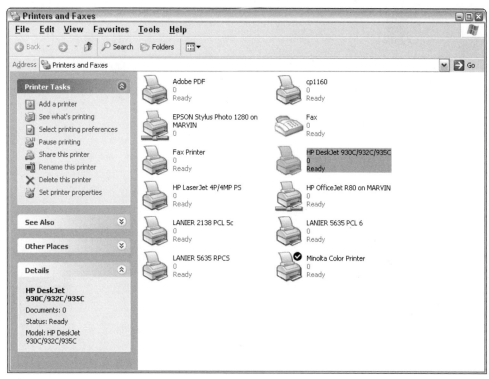

Figure 11-2: The Printers and Faxes window shows all of the output devices on your computer.

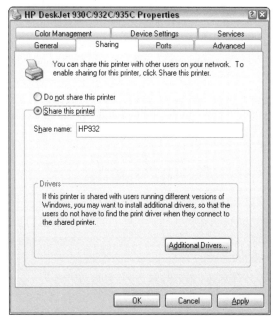

Figure 11-3: Use the Sharing dialog box to set a name for your printer.

5. Click the Share This printer checkbox, and type a name for your printer in the space provided.

6. Click the General tab. You will see the display shown in Figure 11-4.

Figure 11-4: The Location and Comment settings let you add information to identify the printer.

7. Enter a location and comment, if desired. Other network users will see this information when they browse for or connect to a printer.

8. Click OK. Your printer is now ready for use on the network. The printer's icon in the Printers and Faxes display shows a hand beneath the icon, indicating that the printer is shared on the network.

Mac OS X Printer Sharing

You can share any printer attached to your Mac with other Mac and Windows computers on your LAN. To share a printer on the network, follow these steps:

1. Connect the printer to your Mac with a USB cable.

2. Install the printer driver and make sure that the printer is working properly.

3. Open System Preferences and click Sharing.

4. Turn on Windows Sharing (if needed) and Printer Sharing in the Sharing Preferences. (See Figure 11-5.)

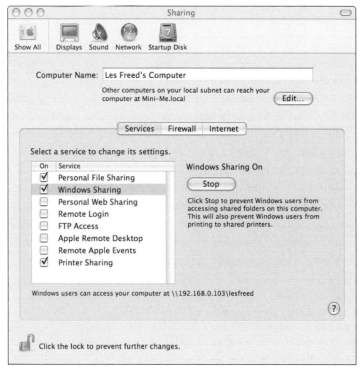

Figure 11-5: The Printer Sharing checkbox shares your printer with other Macs. If you want to use the printer from a Windows PC, make sure you turn on Windows Sharing, too.

  5. Close the Sharing Preferences to save the new settings.

The shared printer is now ready for use from any Mac (or Windows PC, if you turned on Windows Sharing) on the LAN.

Using a Print Server

A print server gives you the freedom to put your printer wherever you want. There are a wide variety of print servers on the market to work with wired and wireless networks. You'll need to purchase a print server with the proper connection type for your printer, either parallel or USB. If your printer has both types of connectors, use the USB connection—it provides better performance than a parallel connection. Some home Internet routers include a built-in parallel or USB print server. If you are shopping for a router and need a printer server, you may want to consider one of these products. But also keep in mind that if you choose a router with a built-in print server, you'll need to locate your printer close to the router—usually within 10'-15'. If you have a mixed Mac and PC network, you may or may not be able to use the shared printer from your Macs. This is due to some driver issues that I'll discuss in the Mac section of this chapter.

Tip

I am a big fan of network print servers, but they have some limitations you need to know about.

Most important: Some printers simply won't work with a print server. This is especially true of combination printer/scanner/fax (often called *multifunction*) devices.

Also, some printer makers "hard code" their printer drivers so that they will only work when connected directly to a USB port. For example, I own an HP photo printer that works with my PCs and Macs, but it won't work through a print server because HP's Mac OS X driver assumes that the printer is connected to the Mac with a USB cable. I solved the problem by installing an inexpensive USB switch box on the printer—a low-tech alternative to printer networking. (The USB switch box is a simple selector switch—available in most office and computer stores—with three connectors. The printer and both PCs connect to the switch, and a button on the top of the switch determines which computer gets to use the printer.)

Finally, many print servers communicate more slowly than a direct USB cable connection. This isn't a problem for everyday printing, but it can affect the speed of photo-quality printers. My advice is to buy your print server from a store with a liberal return policy so you can return it if it doesn't work for you.

The procedure for installing a print server varies widely depending on the make and model of the print server. Most print servers come with a basic setup program on a CD-ROM or floppy disk. This program locates the new print server on your LAN and allows you to set the server's IP address. After you've set the IP address, you use the print server's built-in browser interface to perform the remainder of the server setup. Figure 11-6 shows the browser-based setup screen for a Linksys print server.

Tip

Most print servers come from the factory preconfigured for automatic (DHCP) IP address assignment. This makes the initial configuration simple because the server will automatically obtain an address from your network's DHCP server.

I recommend that you give your print servers permanent addresses. When you configure a client PC to use the shared printer (as you'll see at the end of this chapter), Windows records the IP address of the print server. If the server's address changes (as it will after a power outage), Windows will not be able to locate the print server, and you'll need to manually reconfigure the printer settings with the new IP address.

You can assign a permanent address to your print server using the server's configuration program.

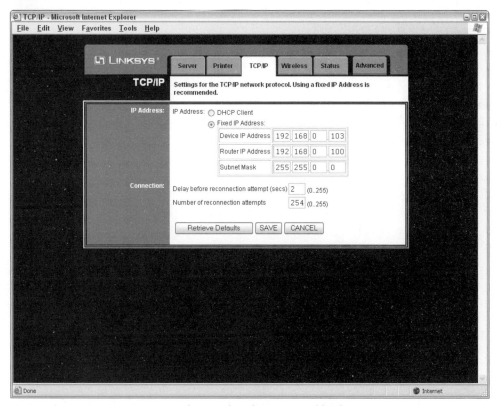

Figure 11-6: Most print servers use a browser-based setup menu like this one.

Most print servers require very little configuration. If you are using a wireless print server, you'll need to connect the print server to a wired Ethernet port to perform the initial configuration, including the IP address and the wireless network's SSID and WEP or WPA security codes, as shown in Figure 11-7. These are the same SSID and WEP or WPA codes that you used to configure your access point. For more information about these settings, see Chapter 7.

After you've connected and configured your print server and printer, the printer is available to all the users on your network.

Note

Many newer printers include a status monitor that shows the status of the ink cartridges and paper supply. These features operate only when the printer is directly connected to a computer; they may not work correctly if the printer is attached to a print server.

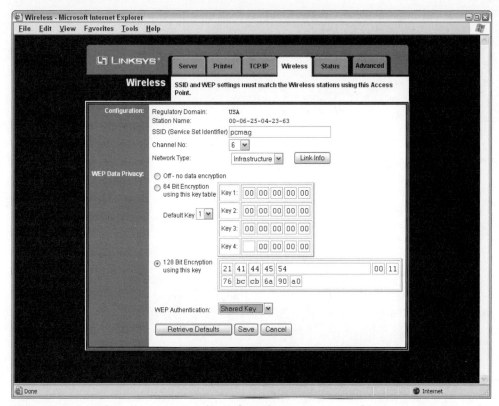

Figure 11-7: A wireless print server must be configured to use your network's security settings.

Using a Network-Ready Printer

Thanks to the growing popularity of home and small-business networks, many printer manufacturers offer models with built-in or add-on print servers. These servers are typically easier to use and provide better performance than third-party print servers.

If you are in the market for a new printer, check the manufacturer's Web site to see if a network-ready model is available. Hewlett-Packard, for example, makes several inkjet and laser printers that can accept one of HP's snap-in modular print servers. Some manufacturers even offer a choice of wired and wireless built-in print servers.

You'll probably save money (and no small amount of grief) by choosing a network-ready printer rather than buying a standalone printer and a third-party print server. Thanks to the resurgence of interest in the Macintosh, many network-ready printers are both Windows and Mac-compatible.

Network-ready printers are easy to install and typically include a browser-based status monitor program so you can check the printer's status. Windows XP includes built-in support for network-ready printers, so you don't usually need to install any additional software (other than the printer driver) to use a network printer with your PC. Mac users may need to download the appropriate printer driver from the printer manufacturer's Web site.

You Want Wireless with That?

Many network printers offer built-in Ethernet networking, but printers with built-in wireless networking are still rare. A new breed of wireless devices, like the D-Link Wireless Ethernet Bridge shown here, let you connect any Ethernet device to a wireless network. As you can see from the picture, a wireless bridge has an antenna to connect to the wireless network and an Ethernet connector to connect to your wired Ethernet device.

D-Link's Wireless Ethernet Bridge brings go-anywhere wireless flexibility to any wired Ethernet device.

The great thing about wireless bridges is that they bring wireless flexibility to devices that are normally tied to a wired network.

I used one of these on my own network to move my noisy color laser printer out of my home office and into a nearby alcove. There was no easy way to get an Ethernet cable into the hallway, so I used the wireless bridge instead.

Wireless bridges work with virtually any Ethernet-connected device, including computers, printers, and home entertainment devices.

Tip

Like most print servers, many network-ready printers come from the factory preconfigured for automatic (DHCP) IP address assignment. As with print servers, I recommend that you give your network printers permanent addresses.

Connecting to a Shared Printer

After you've installed and configured your network printer, you need to add the printer to each PC on your network. In this section, I'll show you how to configure your network Macs and PCs to use shared printers.

Using Shared Printers in Windows XP

The procedure for adding a new printer varies depending on the method used to share the printers. Generally, if you are adding a printer that is shared on another Windows XP computer on your network, Windows will automatically download and install the printer driver for you. If you are adding a network-ready printer or a shared printer using a print server, you may need to have your printer's driver CD or floppy disk handy during the installation.

ADDING A WINDOWS OR MAC SHARED PRINTER

To add a printer shared on another Windows XP or Mac OS X computer on your LAN, follow these steps:

1. From the Start menu, select Printers and Faxes. If the Printers and Faxes item doesn't appear on your Start menu, open the Control Panel and select Printers and Faxes. (If your Control Panel is set to Category View, select the Printers and Other Hardware icon; then select the Printers and Faxes icon at the bottom of the screen.)

2. Click the Add a Printer icon on the left side of the Printers and Faxes display. The Add Printer Wizard starts, as shown in Figure 11-8.

Figure 11-8: The Add Printer Wizard adds new printers to your computer.

3. Click the Next button to move to the next step, shown in Figure 11-9.

Figure 11-9: This screen lets you choose between local and networked printers.

4. Select A Network Printer and click Next. You'll see the screen in Figure 11-10.

Figure 11-10: Save your keystrokes and select the Browse option.

5. Leave Browse for a Printer selected and click Next. The printer browser screen appears, as shown in Figure 11-11.

Figure 11-11: The printer browser displays all of the printers on your network.

6. Select the desired printer from the list and click Next. If the printer is connected to another Windows XP PC, Windows issues a warning, shown in Figure 11-12, about the potential for viruses.

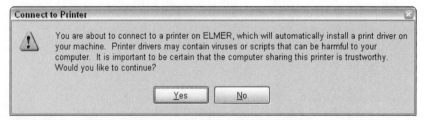

Figure 11-12: Confirm that you really trust the computer sharing the printer.

7. Click Yes. Windows copies and installs the printer driver from the print server PC. This may take a minute, even on a fast network. After a few seconds (or minutes), you'll see the default printer screen, shown in Figure 11-13.

Note

When you connect to a shared printer on another Windows XP PC, Windows will copy the driver from the server PC to your computer. If you are configuring your Windows XP PC to use a shared printer that is connected to a Mac, you will need to manually select the appropriate printer driver for your PC. In many cases, you may need to install the appropriate driver on your PC before you connect to the shared printer.

Figure 11-13: You can make the new printer your default printer.

8. If you want to use the new printer as the default printer on this computer, click Yes. If not, click No. Click the Next button to move on to the final step, shown in Figure 11-14. You can confirm your printer settings or go back to make changes, if desired.

Figure 11-14: You're finished; last chance to double-check your printer selection.

ADDING A SERVER-CONNECTED OR NETWORK PRINTER

The procedure to add a server-connected or network-ready printer is similar to the Windows shared printer procedure outlined in the preceding section, with one critical difference: When you connect to a shared printer connected to another Windows XP PC, Windows automatically downloads and installs the correct printer driver for you. When you add a network printer or a printer connected to a print server, you'll need to identify and install the printer driver yourself.

To add a network-ready or server-connected printer to your PC, follow these steps:

1. From the Start menu, select Printers and Faxes. If the Printers and Faxes item doesn't appear on your Start menu, open the Control Panel and then select Printers and Faxes. (If your Control Panel is set to Category View, select the Printers and Hardware icon; then select the Printers and Faxes icon at the bottom of the screen.)

2. Click the Add a Printer icon on the left side of the Printers and Faxes display. The Add Printer Wizard starts.

3. Click the Next button to move to the next step, shown in Figure 11-15.

4. Select Local Printer Attached to This Computer. I know this seems like the wrong choice, but trust me on this one. The Select a Printer Port screen appears, as shown in Figure 11-16.

Figure 11-15: As far as Windows is concerned, a server-connected printer is a local printer.

Figure 11-16: Windows connects to networked printers using a virtual TCP/IP port instead of a physical cable connection.

5. Click Create a New Port and then select Standard TCP/IP Port from the pull-down menu. The Add Standard Printer Port Wizard starts, as shown in Figure 11-17.

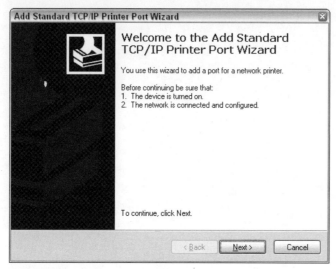

Figure 11-17: Make sure the printer is connected and powered up before proceeding.

6. Click Next to move on to the Add Port screen, shown in Figure 11-18.

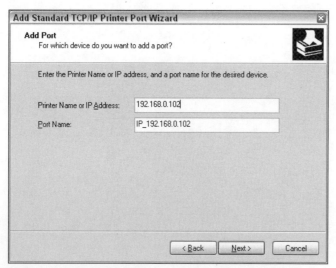

Figure 11-18: As you enter the IP address in the top window, Windows will fill in the port name in the lower window.

7. Enter the IP address of your network printer or print server. Now you know why I suggested that you give your printer a fixed IP address! Windows will attempt to connect to the IP address, and it will also attempt to identify the printer. In most cases, Windows will not be able to determine the proper printer type, and you'll see the somewhat confusing screen shown in Figure 11-19, asking for your help in identifying the device.

8. Leave the setting on Standard, and click Next. The TCP/IP Printer Port Wizard finishes its job, as you can see in Figure 11-20.

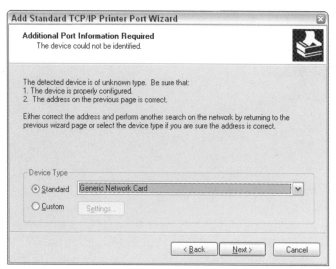

Figure 11-19: Windows can't always recognize networked printers, so you may see this screen during the installation.

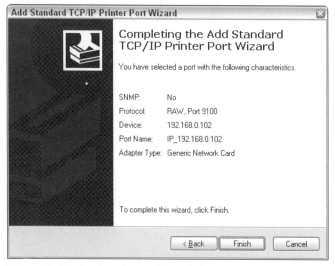

Figure 11-20: Confirm the IP address before you click Finish.

9. Windows returns control back to the Add Printer Wizard. At this point, you must choose the correct driver for your printer using the screen shown in Figure 11-21.

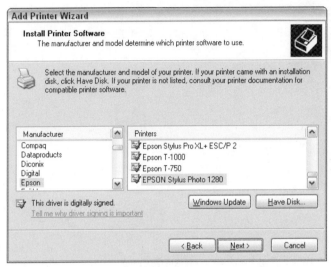

Figure 11-21: Select the correct driver for your printer.

10. Choose your printer from the list of printers. If your printer isn't on the list, you'll need to install the drivers from a floppy disk or CD-ROM. If this is the case, insert the disk and click the Have Disk button. After the correct driver is selected, click the Next button to move on to the Name Your Printer screen (see Figure 11-22).

Tip

In some cases, you may find it necessary to install the printer drivers on the client PC before performing this step. Some printer drivers have their own setup program and cannot be installed using the Add Printer wizard. Consult your printer's driver instructions if you're not sure.

11. Enter a name for your printer, and decide if you want it to be the default printer on this PC. Click Next. The Printer Sharing screen appears (see Figure 11-23).

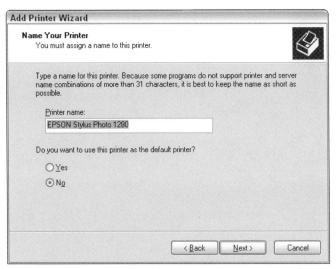

Figure 11-22: Give your printer a meaningful name so that other users will be able to identify it on the network.

Figure 11-23: Because the printer is already shared by the print server, you don't want to share it again!

12. This screen may surprise you because the printer is already shared. Windows is offering to share the printer using Windows print sharing. This is not necessary because the printer is already attached to a network print server. Leave the setting on Do Not Share This Printer and click Next. The Print Test Page screen appears (see Figure 11-24).

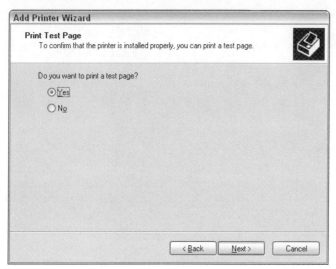

Figure 11-24: You can print a test page to make sure that your PC can communicate with the networked printer.

13. I recommend that you print a test page from this screen. If it works, you'll hear the highly rewarding sound of your first networked print job coming out of the printer. If your test page doesn't print correctly, use the Back button to go back and double-check your settings. Click Next when you're ready to move on, and Windows will tell you you're done, as in Figure 11-25.

Figure 11-25: This is your last chance to change any settings for your new printer.

Your network printer is now installed and ready to use.

Using Shared Printers in Mac OS X

Simple printer sharing is a time-honored Apple tradition, dating back to the earliest (1984) Mac computers and the original Apple LaserWriter printer. OS X makes it easier than ever to connect shared printers to your Mac—with a few caveats.

As I mentioned earlier in this chapter, some Mac printer drivers assume that the printer is connected to one of the Mac's USB ports. This creates a frustrating scenario where you can connect your Mac to a shared printer, but you can't choose the proper printer driver because the driver is hard-coded to only talk to the USB ports.

A similar problem exists when connecting a Mac to printers shared on a Windows XP computer. Some printer makers only provide Windows drivers with their products, making it impossible to use these printers with a Mac. Other makers offer an OS9 driver for older printers, but no OS X version. Unless you want to spend time banging your head against a wall (or your printer), check the printer manufacturer's Web site for an OS X network-compatible driver before you begin.

To connect your Mac to a networked printer, follow these steps:

1. Click the Print & Fax icon in the System Preferences, as shown in Figure 11-26.

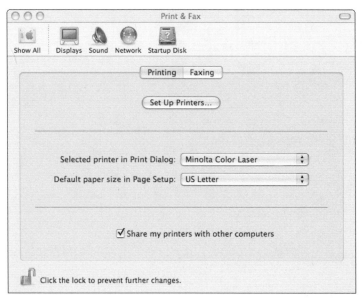

Figure 11-26: To add a new printer, start at the Print & Fax Preferences screen.

2. Click Set up Printers to open the Printer List, as shown in Figure 11-27.

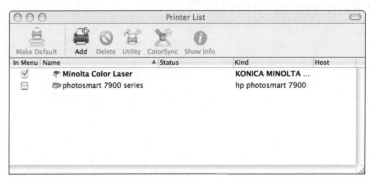

Figure 11-27: The Printer List shows all currently installed printers.

3. Click the Add icon at the top of the Printer List window. You will see the AppleTalk printer list shown in Figure 11-28.

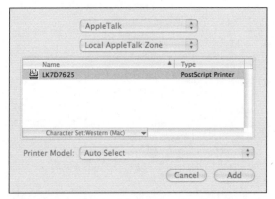

Figure 11-28: The AppleTalk printer list shows any AppleTalk-compatible printers on your LAN.

4. If you want to use an AppleTalk printer, select the printer, click the Add button, and skip to Step 7.

5. If the printer is attached to a Windows XP computer, click the pull-down list at the top of the window and select Windows Printing from the list.

6. Select the name of the computer that is sharing the printer and then click Choose. You'll see a list of available printers, shown in Figure 11-29.

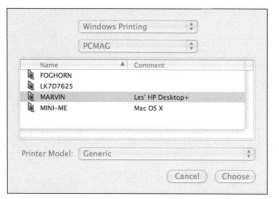

Figure 11-29: The printer I want is connected to the PC named Marvin.

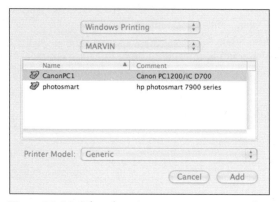

Figure 11-30: Select the printer you want to use and then use the pull-down list to select the appropriate driver.

7. Select the desired printer from the list; then choose the driver from the Printer Model pull-down list. (See Figure 11-30.) Click Add to finish up.

Your printer is now ready for use and you will return to the Printer List (Figure 11-27). If you will be using the new printer as your primary printer, you may want to make it the default printer by clicking the Make Default button in the Printer List.

Summary

Now you know how to share and use printers on your network. As you can see, there's no rocket science involved. Shared printers save time, space, and money.

The key points in this chapter are as follows:

- You can share a printer from any Windows XP or Mac OS X computer.

- Shared network printers work just like any other printer; you don't need to do anything special to use them with your favorite programs.

- If you want to share a printer that isn't connected to a computer, you'll need an external print server.

- By using printer sharing, you may be able to reduce the number of printers in your home.

- Some printers include built-in print servers that simplify connection to a network.

I've been using a home LAN for many years, and I find network printing to be one of the truly indispensable features of my home network.

Coming up, I'll show you how the new wave of home entertainment devices leverages the power of your home LAN and Internet connection to provide you with entertainment options.

Chapter 12

Home Media and Convergence

Media convergence—the marriage of computing and home entertainment technologies—has been the "next big thing" for about 10 years now. After much talk and many false starts (not to mention billions of dollars in investment capital), the first wave of true media convergence devices are in the stores.

In this chapter, I'll introduce you to some new, fun, and innovative products that expand your home LAN beyond computing. These products include:

- The latest media convergence products that let you record, play, and store music, TV programs, movies, and still images on your home entertainment system

- New Media Center PCs specifically designed to integrate your home entertainment and computing worlds in one box

- Products to connect your GameCube, PlayStation2, or Xbox to a LAN

- Video surveillance and videoconferencing systems

Note

My goal in this chapter is to introduce you to some new products that you likely haven't seen before. The examples in this section are intended to give you an overview of the products' features and to give you an idea of the complexity of the products' installation and operation. As such, they are not intended to be a complete how-to guide. Also, keep in mind that most of the products shown in the chapter are just one of many similar products available from several manufacturers.

Home Entertainment Devices

So you've gone out and bought a digital camera, a digital video camcorder, and an MP3 player. You now have tons of digital photos, hours of carefully edited home videos, and hundreds of songs at your disposal—as long as you are in front of the computer. You used to make fun of your parents for keeping all of your family photos jammed into a shoebox. But now you have all of your memories jammed into a hard drive.

In this section, I show you some new and innovative products that can help you free your images, videos, and music files from their hard-drive home. These products harness the speed and power of your home network to let you play music, digital images, and even digital TV and video files on your home entertainment system.

Linksys Wireless Media Adapter

The Linksys Wireless Media Adapter frees your digital photo and audio files from the confines of your PC. The Media Adapter allows you to view digital image files and listen to your MP3 collection on your TV and stereo system, using the files on your network.

Note

The Linksys Media Adapter is just one of several products on the market to provide the same or similar functionality. Some products (like the Gateway Connected DVD Player, discussed later in the chapter) offer MPEG video capability, in addition to still image and MP3 file playback.

Figure 12-1 shows how the Media Adapter fits into your home entertainment system.

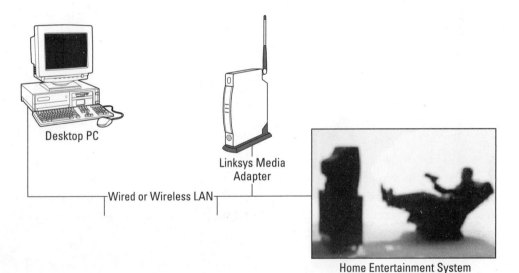

Figure 12-1: The Linksys Wireless Media Adapter connects to your home network and your home entertainment system.

The Media Adapter is fairly small—about the size of this book. There are no controls on the Media Adapter itself other than an on/off switch. You operate the Media Adapter using onscreen displays with the provided remote control, shown in Figure 12-2.

Figure 12-2: The Wireless Media Adapter is controlled via its remote.

The rear panel of the Media Adapter (shown in Figure 12-3) provides connections for your LAN and your home entertainment system, and includes Ethernet, stereo audio, composite video, and S-video connections.

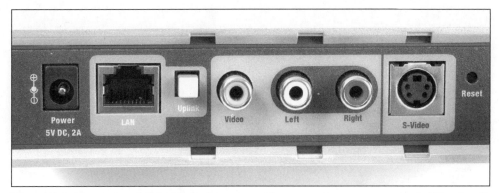

Figure 12-3: The rear panel of the Media Adapter provides connections to your network, TV, and audio system.

INSTALLING THE MEDIA ADAPTER

Installing the Media Adapter takes only a few minutes. You need to connect the audio and video cables to your home entertainment systems. The Media Adapter can connect to your LAN using a wired or wireless connection. If you're using a wired Ethernet connection, you need to connect the Media Adapter to your Ethernet switch. If you're using the wireless link, you'll need to attach the provided antenna to the Media Adapter. Linksys provides all the cables you'll need in the box with the Media Adapter.

After you've hooked up the cables, you need to install the Media Adapter Utility software (provided on a CD-ROM) on your PC. The Utility software consists of two parts. The first is a server program that loads automatically when Windows starts. The server has no user interface, but it installs an icon on the system tray to let you know that the software is running. If you click the icon while the server is running, you'll see the Media Folder Manager, the second part of the program. Figure 12-4 shows the Media Folder Manager display.

The Media Folder Manager program lets you select which files you want to make available to the Media Adapter. In the example in Figure 12-4, I've chosen to share the My Pictures and My Music folders, which are normally located in the My Documents folder on most PCs.

When you first install the Media Adapter, you'll need to tell the Media Adapter how to communicate with the network. You do this using the Media Adapter's remote control and your TV. Pressing the Setup button on the remote brings up the Media Adapter's Setup screen, shown in Figure 12-5.

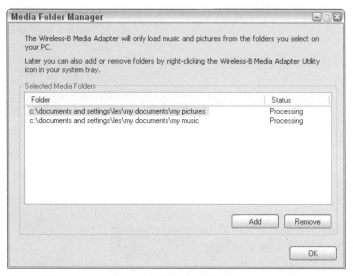

Figure 12-4: You use the Linksys Media Folder Manager to select the files to play on the Media Adapter.

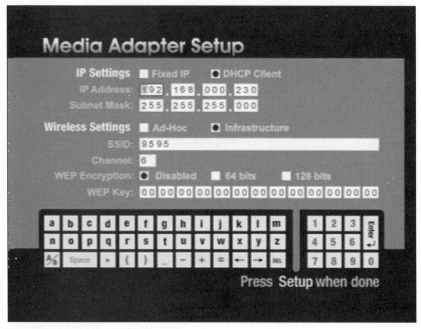

Figure 12-5: You use the Media Adapter's Setup screen and the remote control to configure the Adapter's network settings.

As you can see from Figure 12-5, you don't need to enter much information to configure the Adapter. In fact, if you are using an Ethernet connection and have a DHCP server on your network, you don't need to enter anything at all.

In the example in Figure 12-5, I have configured the Media Adapter to communicate with my wireless network, and I am preparing to enter the WEP encryption key—the most tedious part of the configuration process. The Media Adapter uses the same WEP key as the other wireless devices on your LAN; see Chapter 7 for more information on configuring WEP.

A QUICK TOUR OF THE MEDIA ADAPTER

After you've installed the software and configured the communication settings, you are ready to sit back and enjoy your pictures and music. The Menu button on the remote control brings up the Media Adapter's main menu display on your TV screen, shown in Figure 12-6.

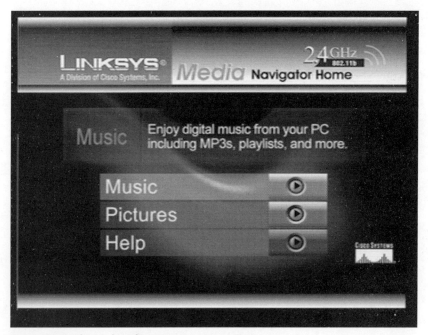

Figure 12-6: The Media Adapter's main menu screen.

At this point, you can listen to music, view your pictures, or get help with using the remote control. Selecting Music from the main menu takes you to the Music Navigator screen, shown in Figure 12-7.

Figure 12-7: The Music Navigator screen lets you choose your music by artist or genre. You can also select a specific folder, use a playlist, or simply play all of the files.

The Media Adapter can identify the artist and genre of each music file on your computer. In the example in Figure 12-8, I've chosen the Artists selection from the Music Navigator, which displays an alphabetical list of all the artists in my music collection.

Note

In these examples, I have used MP3 files that contain artist and title information. Some MP3 files include this information and some don't; it all depends on the software you use to create and manage your MP3 collection. If your files don't contain this information, the Media Adapter will not be able to organize the tracks by artist or genre.

After you've selected an artist, genre, or playlist, the Media Adapter plays your selections in the order you've chosen. As each song plays, the on-screen display updates to show information about the current track, as shown in Figure 12-9.

Figure 12-8: The Artists display shows all the artists in your music collection.

Figure 12-9: The Now Playing screen displays information about the current title, artist, and album.

The Pictures Navigator is similar to the Music Navigator. Figure 12-10 shows the main Pictures Navigator screen as seen on your TV.

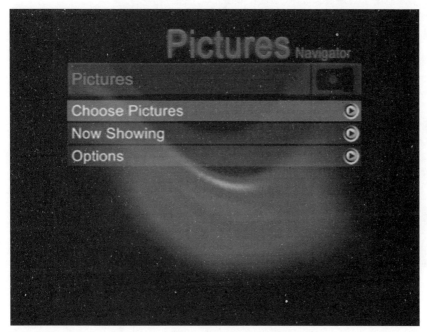

Figure 12-10: The main Pictures Navigator screen lets you select the pictures you want to see.

If you have your pictures organized into folders, the Pictures Navigator will let you select the folder you want to view. If your pictures are all lumped into one folder, you can use the Navigator to scroll through a thumbnail display of your images until you find the one you want to see. Figure 12-11 shows the thumbnail display.

As you can see in the example in Figure 12-11, the currently selected picture (on the lower left) is highlighted with a light gray frame. Pressing the Select button will show a full-screen image of the picture; pressing the Play button begins a slide show of all the pictures in the current folder, beginning with the selected picture

It may be difficult to tell from the small figures in this book, but the Media Adapter has no way of knowing which pictures are framed horizontally and which are vertical. For example, the picture at the bottom right of Figure 12-11 is a vertical picture, and it will display sideways on the screen. To correct this, you need to open the image in an image editor and then rotate and resave the image—or just turn your head sideways to view the vertical images.

Figure 12-11: The Pictures Navigator's thumbnail display lets you see six pictures at a time.

TiVo

I'm not a big TV watcher—or at least I wasn't one before I bought a TiVo. TiVo defined a new class of products collectively known as digital video recorders, or DVRs. With a TiVo in the house, you never have to worry about missing a TV show because the TiVo DVR records your favorite shows automatically. You can also pause live TV for up to 30 minutes, so you won't miss half of your pay-per-view movie just because Aunt Mabel decided to call.

TiVo not only changes the way you watch TV; it changes the way you think about TV. Instead of watching TV in real time, you tell TiVo what you want to see, and it takes care of the details—like the time, channel, and length of the program. When you have some free time, you can browse through your archive of recorded programs and pick one to watch. TiVo is easier and simpler to use than a conventional VCR. There's no tape to buy, no rewinding, and no programming.

TiVo is amazingly simple to use. TiVo uses a series of simple, easy-to-understand on-screen menus and one of the best remote controls I've ever used. Figure 12-12 shows the main TiVo menu screen and the TiVo remote control.

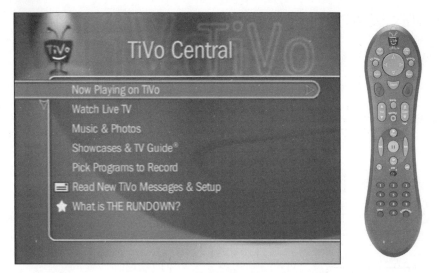

Figure 12-12: The TiVo Central screen (left) is the gateway to TiVo's features. You get there by pressing the TiVo button at the top center of the TiVo remote (right). © 2002 TiVo Inc. All Rights Reserved.

HOW TIVO WORKS

The TiVo system consists of a TiVo DVR and the TiVo service, a continually updated list of what's playing on each channel in your area. The TiVo DVR works with conventional over-the-air TV, as well as with cable and most satellite systems. You can purchase TiVo as a standalone device that you add to your existing home entertainment system, and several manufacturers offer satellite receivers and DVD players with TiVo built in.

The standalone TiVo DVR is a VCR-sized box containing a CPU and a large, fast hard drive. The DVR connects to your TV or home entertainment system in much the same way as a conventional VCR. Figure 12-13 shows a diagram of the TiVo system.

The TiVo DVR contains a standard TV tuner so that you can watch a live program on your TV while the TiVo records a different channel at the same time. You can also connect a satellite receiver or cable TV box to record programming from those sources.

TiVo records programs on the system's hard drive rather than on tape. When you play back a recording, the DVR converts the digital data stored on the hard drive back into standard audio and video signals that you can watch on any TV. Because disk storage allows random access to any part of the program, the TiVo playback experience is very much like watching a DVD rather than a tape. You can skip ahead or back, pause the playback, or fast-forward at high speed using the buttons on the TiVo remote control.

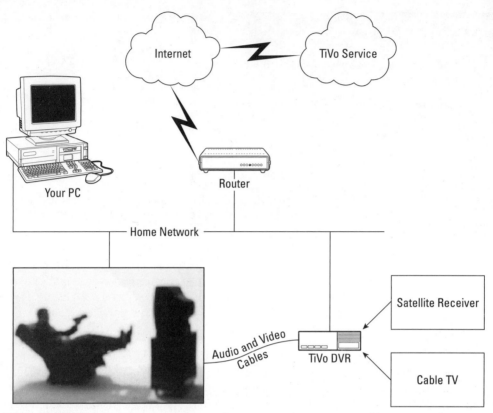

Figure 12-13: The TiVo DVR connects to your home entertainment system and home network.

NETWORKING YOUR TIVO

So what does any of this have to do with home networking? As you can see from Figure 12-13, the TiVo DVR can connect (using a wired or wireless connection) to your home network. The network connection is optional (and you'll need to hook your TiVo to a phone line if you don't have a LAN), but it adds several important features to the TiVo system.

Note

The networking features described in this section are available only on TiVo Series2 DVR systems.

Every TiVo DVR needs to connect to the TiVo service every day or two in order to download information on upcoming programs. If you subscribe to cable or satellite TV service, that's a lot of information. The TiVo DVR can make the connection using a dial-up telephone connection, but the daily call can take 20 minutes or more. If you connect the TiVo to a home network with a broadband Internet connection, the TiVo DVR will use the Internet connection instead of the phone line.

Networked TiVo DVR users can also take advantage of several features designed specifically for TiVos on a LAN:

- You can use your TiVo and home entertainment system to view photos and listen to MP3 audio files stored on your computer.

- If you have two TiVo DVRs in your home, you can view programs recorded on one DVR from another DVR. The TiVo DVRs use the home network to transfer the digitized recording from one DVR to the other.

- You can transfer recordings from any TiVo in your home to any PC equipped with TiVo's (free) software. This feature lets you use your PC or laptop as an additional TV set.

- LAN TiVo users also gain access to TiVo Central Online. This unique feature lets you add programs to your TiVo's to-do list over the Internet from any browser-equipped PC.

Figure 12-14 shows the TiVo Central search results screen. In this example, I went to TiVo Central and searched for all upcoming movies with "Brando." (The list shows some duplicate entries because some channels are duplicated on my cable and satellite services.) To add a recording to the TiVo's to-do list, click the title of the program and then acknowledge that you want to record this program. The next time your TiVo DVR connects to TiVo, the new recording is added to the to-do list.

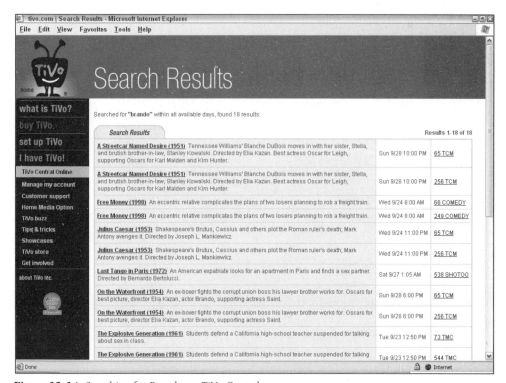

Figure 12-14: Searching for Brando on TiVo Central.

Tip

When I first heard of this feature, I didn't think I'd ever use it—but it is the one TiVo feature that I use the most. If I'm out of town, or if someone tells me about a must-see movie or TV show while I'm at the office, I can add it to TiVo's to-do list right away.

CONNECTING YOUR TIVO TO THE LAN

To connect a TiVo DVR to your network, you'll need a USB network adapter. The TiVo DVR has two USB ports on the rear panel, and the network adapter can connect to either port. You can use an Ethernet or WiFi wireless adapter; I've used a wireless adapter for this example.

Note

You'll need to purchase a network adapter that is on TiVo's list of approved network adapters. You can find a current list of adapters on the TiVo Web site.

The installation process is simple and usually takes only a few minutes, using the remote control, your TV set, and a series of onscreen menus. I won't go into all of the details here, but the screen in Figure 12-15 shows the main network setup screen as shown on your TV.

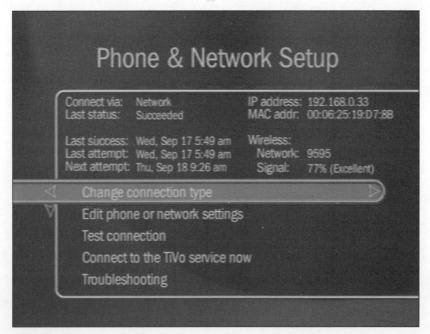

Figure 12-15: TiVo's network setup screen is about as easy as it gets.

The Phone & Network Setup screen shows your current network settings, and it also shows the TiVo DVR's current IP address and wireless signal status. When you think you have everything configured correctly, you can make a test connection to the TiVo service, as shown in Figure 12-16.

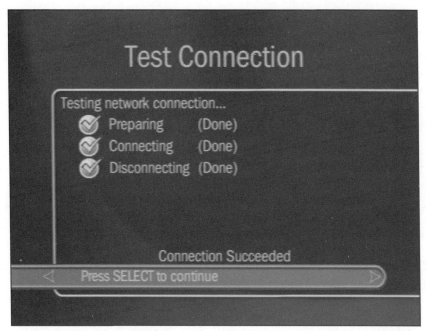

Figure 12-16: The Test Connection screen confirms that your connection is working correctly. If it isn't, the onscreen display will offer some useful troubleshooting tips.

Tip

After you've successfully connected your TiVo DVR to your network, you can disconnect the phone line from your TiVo DVR. This is a big plus for those of us who live in lightning-prone areas of the country because it eliminates a major source of lightning damage.

USING TIVO'S NETWORK FEATURES

To take advantage of many of TiVo's networking features, you'll need to install the TiVo Desktop software, a free download available on the TiVo site.

The TiVo's Desktop software consists of two separate programs that run on your PC. The TiVo Server program loads when you start your PC and runs as an icon on the system task tray. Double-clicking the TiVo Server icon starts the TiVo Desktop program, shown in Figure 12-17.

Figure 12-17: The TiVo Desktop lets you choose the files available for playback on the TiVo DVR.

The TiVo Desktop allows you to choose the files that will be available for playback and display on the TiVo DVR. After you've selected the files to publish, you can close the TiVo Desktop program, and the TiVo Server program will remain active.

You can view pictures or play back MP3 files from your home entertainment system by pressing the TiVo button and selecting Music & Photos from the TiVo Central menu, as shown in Figure 12-18.

Listening to Music

To listen to your MP3 files, select Music & Photos from the TiVo Central screen and then choose the appropriate shared folder from the onscreen menu shown in Figure 12-19.

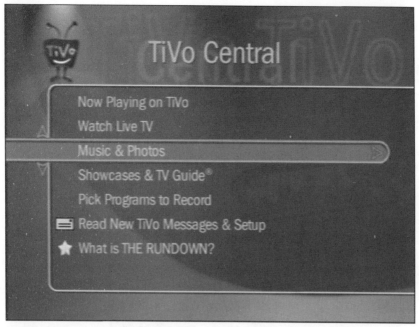

Figure 12-18: The TiVo Central screen.

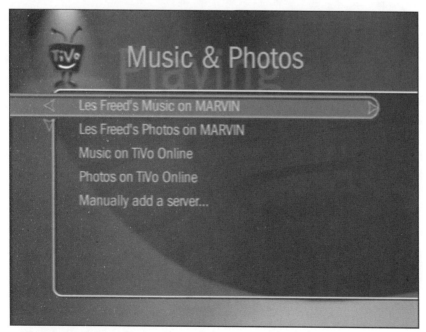

Figure 12-19: Your shared music and photo folders will appear on this screen.

In this example, I've chosen the folder called Les Freed's Music on Marvin. Pressing the Select button on the remote control shows the individual folders on my server, as shown in Figure 12-20.

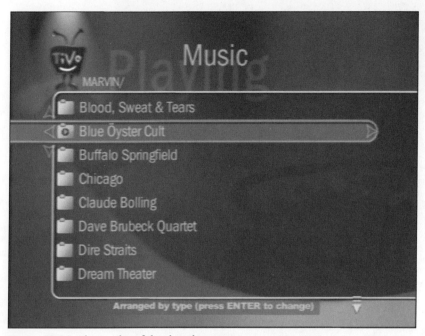

Figure 12-20: This is a list of the shared music on my computer.

To choose an individual artist, press the Select button again, and you'll see a display of all the album titles by that artist, followed by a display of the individual songs. After you've selected an artist to play, the TiVo DVR plays your music. The screen display shows the artist, title, and album name of each song, as you can see in Figure 12-21.

Viewing Your Digital Photos

To view your digital photos on the TiVo, you start at the Music & Photos screen and select a folder. As with the digital music playback, you can use the TiVo remote to navigate through your shared folders until you see the folder you want to view. After you've selected an individual image, you'll see a thumbnail display of the image, along with the date and time the photo was taken. A menu at the bottom of the screen lets you view the photo, rotate the photo (handy for those of us who take lots of vertical pictures), or begin a slide show of all the images in the folder. Figure 12-22 shows the individual photo display.

Figure 12-21: TiVo displays information about each track as it plays.

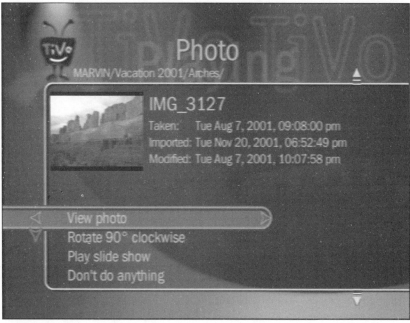

Figure 12-22: After selecting a photo folder, you can view details about each image.

WATCHING RECORDED PROGRAMS ON YOUR PC

If you see someone watching Leno or Letterman on their laptop during your morning commute, don't be surprised. A new TiVo feature called TiVoToGo lets you copy programs recorded on your TiVo to any PC and then watch the program at your convenience.

Note

As we went to press, the TiVoToGo feature was not available in the Mac version of TiVo Desktop.

TiVoToGo is part of the TiVo Desktop program (see Figure 12-17). When you click the Now Playing icon in TiVo Desktop, you'll see a list of available programs like the one in Figure 12-23.

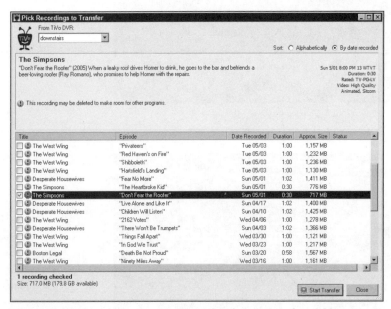

Figure 12-23: TiVo Desktop's Now Playing list shows a list of available recordings on your TiVo DVR.

To transfer a program to your PC, click the checkbox next to the program name(s) and then click the Start Transfer button. After the programs have been transferred to your PC, you can watch the programs using Windows Media Player.

Note

If you're in a hurry to catch your morning train, you'd better skip last night's Letterman show. It takes about 20 minutes to download a 30 minute program, even on a very fast LAN.

PURCHASING TIVO

TiVo makes its own DVRs, and it also licenses its technology to other equipment manufacturers. TiVo is available as a standalone DVR device, but you can also purchase TiVo as part of a DVD player or satellite receiver system.

All TiVo users must subscribe to the TiVo service to receive programming information and software updates. TiVo charges a monthly fee for the service, or you can purchase a lifetime subscription to the TiVo service. Keep in mind that *lifetime* means the lifetime of the TiVo DVR, and not the owner. If you upgrade to a newer TiVo device a few years down the road, you'll need to purchase a new subscription.

The TiVo system is much more powerful and much easier to use than a conventional VCR. If you're a dedicated TV watcher who can't stand to miss an episode of your favorite shows, TiVo is a must-have. And even if you're not a TV junkie, TiVo lets you watch your shows and movies on your terms at a time—and even a place—of your choosing.

Media Center PCs

So far, I've discussed the Linksys Media Adapter, which moves your still picture and MP3 audio files into the living room. I've also introduced you to the TiVo DVR, which lets you time shift TV and gives you the option to move recorded program files from the living room back to your PC. The Media Center PC combines elements of each of these devices, but in a completely different way.

A Quick Tour of Media Center

A Media Center PC is just the name says: It is a PC designed to be the center of your electronic media universe. Under the hood, a Media Center PC is a mid- to high-powered PC with a high end graphics card, a large, fast, hard drive, a network connection, at least one DVD drive, a wireless remote control with standardized buttons, audio and video input and output connectors, an (optional) TV tuner card, and a quiet design.

Microsoft originally required that Media Center PCs come equipped with a TV tuner, but they recently dropped this requirement. Media Center works with most USB and PCI TV tuner devices—including some HDTV tuners—so you can always add a tuner later.

The Well-Connected PC

The standard audio/video outputs make it simple to connect a Media Center PC to virtually any existing home entertainment system. For example, my own Media Center PC has four types of video outputs (standard composite video and S-Video, plus DVI digital and 15-pin VGA monitor video) connectors), plus analog stereo and digital 5.1 surround sound audio outputs.

Through a happy coincidence, my home entertainment center is just on the other side of the wall between my home office and my living room. I used the PC's DVI output to connect my LCD desktop monitor, and I ran an S-video cable and digital audio cable through the wall to connect my PC to my home entertainment system.

Microsoft has encouraged PC makers to get creative with the physical design of their Media Center PCs, and some PC makers offer Media Center PC boxes in all shapes and sizes. HP, for example, offers a small, cube-shaped Media Center PC that blends right in with most other home entertainment gear. A few PC makers have come up with super-quiet PCs that use liquid cooling (in place of noisy fans) and rubber-mounted hard drives to reduce noise.

Depending on your needs (and your home entertainment budget), you can use a Media Center PC as a standard desktop PC, or you can set it up to be a dedicated home entertainment center PC. Media Center PCs run a special version of Windows XP called Windows XP Media Center Edition, or MCE for short. You can switch between Media Center mode and standard PC operation with the push of a button or with the click of a mouse, so your PC can do double duty as a computer and as a Media Center. In fact, it can do both at once, as we'll see later in this section.

The Media Center menu screen (shown in Figure 12-24) covers the entire Windows desktop. It was designed to be operated at a distance, so it features large letters and icons that you can see from across the room. Although the Media Center menu uses the entire screen, it is actually a Windows application program like any other, so you can resize, minimize, or close the Media Center screen at any time.

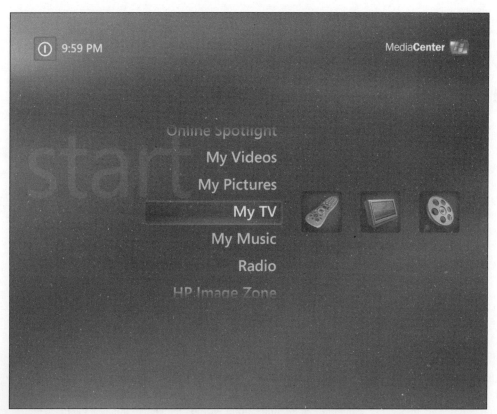

Figure 12-24: The main Media Center menu screen is readable from a distance and simple to navigate.

You operate the Media Center menu with your keyboard (if you're using your PC screen) or with the wireless remote control include with most Media Center PCs. As you can see from Figure 12-24, Media Center provides simple, point and click access to TV and radio (if your PC is equipped with an appropriate tuner card), music, and videos, including home movies created with Windows Movie Maker or virtually any other video editor program.

One of the strong points of Media Center is its excellent onscreen programming guide, shown in Figure 12-25.

Figure 12-25: Media Center's program guide shows you everything coming up on TV (talking horse not included).

If you're thinking that this looks and sounds a lot like TiVo, you're right. Media Center provides many of the same TV recording features as TiVo, including the capability to record all occurrences of your favorite programs. Figure 12-26 shows the Record Series option screen.

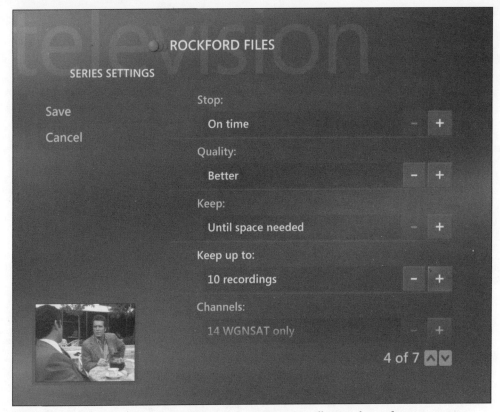

Figure 12-26: Media Center provides the capability to automatically record your favorite programs whenever they air.

Like TiVo, Media Center gets information on upcoming programming over the Internet. (Hey, you knew there had to be a network connection here someplace!) But unlike TiVo, which charges a monthly or lifetime subscription fee, Media Center's program guide is free.

Media Center Extenders

As I mentioned earlier, I am fortunate that my home entertainment system is located close to my PC, so my Media Center PC does double duty as my everyday PC and as my home entertainment PC.

If your home entertainment center is located some distance from your PC, it may not be possible to connect the PC directly to your entertainment system. Video signals can only travel relatively short distances before the picture quality degrades, even if you use high-quality (and expensive) cables. Even if you can overcome the distance issue, you'll need to run separate audio, video, and USB (for the remote control receiver) cables from your Media Center PC to the entertainment system. That's a lot of cables, and it can be difficult to hide them, especially in your living room.

That's where the Media Center Extender comes in. A Media Center Extender (Figure 12-27) connects to your wired or wireless LAN and to your home entertainment system.

A Little Media Math

A Media Center PC costs about $200 to $300 more than a similar PC without Media Center. At press time, a 40-hour TiVo DVR cost $200, plus $12.95 per month or $299 for a lifetime subscription to the TiVo service. So which one is the better buy?

If you're in the market for a new PC, you should consider a Media Center PC. Even if you don't plan to use Media Center's DVR features often, it is handy to be able to watch TV on your PC. If you're building a high-end home entertainment system, one of the made-for-the-living-room Media Center PCs makes an impressive addition to your system.

If you're looking for a dedicated DVR device to replace that old VHS machine, TiVo is probably the better choice.

Keep in mind that whichever you choose (Media Center PC or TiVo) you'll need to keep the machine powered up 24/7 to be able to record programs. A standalone TiVo uses substantially less electric power than a Media Center PC, an important factor given today's high energy costs.

Figure 12-27: A Media Center extender, such as this model from Linksys, connects your home entertainment center to your Media Center PC over your home LAN.

The Media Center Extender (about $300) is essentially a dedicated Media Center PC with no storage of its own. The Extender has standard audio and video connections on the back, including composite, S-Video, and component RGB video outputs as well as analog and TOSLink digital audio outputs. The Linksys Media Center Extender shown in Figure 12-27 includes 100 Mbps Ethernet and dual-band (802.11a and 802.11g) WiFi adapters.

A single Media Center PC can host up to three Extenders at the same time, so you can get double or triple duty out of one Media Center PC. The Extender's main menu is nearly identical to that of the Media Center PC, as you can see in Figure 12-28.

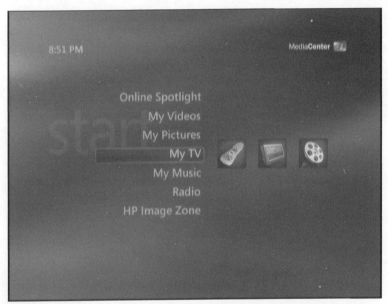

Figure 12-28: Media Center PC or Extender? It's hard to tell, but this is the Media Center Extender menu screen.

Tip

Media Center Extenders deliver a high-quality analog picture, but they do not work with digital TVs and can not play back high-definition digital content. If you have a high definition TV and want to use Media Center to record and play back HD content, you'll need to connect your Media Center PC directly to your TV.

My own experience with the Linksys Media Center extender has been very positive, but I've learned a few things the hard way, so I'll pass them on to you:

- If you'll be recording TV programs overnight, you'll need to leave the PC on 24/7. It is essential (and good computing practice in any case) to have a standby power supply or UPS for your Media Center PC.

- If you live in an area with frequent lightning hits, invest in good AC power surge protectors for your PC and your Extender, and make sure your cable TV or external antenna has adequate lightning protection. Most standby power supplies include built-in surge protectors, so you don't need both.

- Although the Extender works well over a wireless connection, it can be a bandwidth hog at times. You'll get better and more reliable performance using a wired Ethernet connection.

Network Gaming

Today's game consoles and high-end gaming PCs feature graphics, sound, and realistic animation that bring arcade-quality gaming into your living room. One of the hottest trends in gaming joins gaming and Internet technology to create a real-time, multiplayer gaming environment. Instead of competing against a programmed opponent built into the game's software, players can compete head-to-head against real, live opponents.

All three of the major game consoles—Sony's PlayStation2, Nintendo's GameCube, and Microsoft's Xbox—offer players the ability to connect their console to a local network or a dial-up Internet connection. Using the local network, gamers can connect two or more game consoles to play head-to-head games with their friends. Many games also include an Internet play feature that allows gamers to compete against players around the world.

Tip

If you hang around with online gamers very long, you'll almost certainly hear about *lag time*, *latency time*, or *ping time*. This is the amount of time it takes for one player's move to make its way over the Internet and over to the other player's computer. Lag time is a critical factor in multiplayer games because the person with the lowest lag time has a distinct advantage over the other players.

Dial-up modems typically have much longer lag times than cable or DSL connections. If you take your gaming seriously, broadband is the only way to go.

Of the three major gaming consoles, only the Xbox comes from the factory with an Ethernet connection as standard equipment. GameCube and PlayStation2 users can purchase inexpensive network adapters that add Ethernet and/or dial-up modem connectivity to their game consoles. Nintendo sells separate dial-up modem and Ethernet adapters; Sony offers a combination modem and Ethernet adapter.

All three game consoles use DHCP for automatic address assignment, so they require very little setup or configuration to connect to a home network.

Going Wireless

Online gaming is great fun, but most of us didn't have the foresight to run an Ethernet cable into the living room or den. Several manufacturers have addressed that problem with wireless adapters designed specifically for home gaming. In Chapter 11, I mentioned the D-Link Wireless Bridge as a great tool to connect a printer to a wireless network. That same product can also be used to connect any Ethernet-equipped game console to your wireless home network.

Linksys makes two wireless game adapters. The Wireless-B gaming adapter works on 802.11b networks, and the Wireless-G adapter works with 802.11b and 802.11g networks. The figure shows the two Linksys adapters.

The Linksys Wireless-B (left) and Wireless-G network gaming adapters add wireless connectivity to Ethernet-equipped game consoles.

These two products are exceptionally easy to install. The Wireless-B adapter requires little or no configuration at all; the Wireless-G adapter must be configured using an Ethernet connection to a PC. Both come with a short Ethernet cable to connect the adapter to your game console. The Linksys wireless adapters can be used with an existing access point, or you can use two or more of the adapters to create an ad hoc wireless network without an access point.

Although Linksys markets these products as game adapters, they will work with any Ethernet device. They are especially useful for connecting network-ready printers to a LAN, but they can also be used to connect desktop PCs, media hubs, and just about anything else with an Ethernet connection.

Video on Your LAN

LANs aren't just for data anymore. A new generation of TV products lets you use your LAN for video applications, too. The two products in this section leverage your Internet connection to provide closed-circuit TV monitoring and two-way videoconferencing on your LAN. D-Link's Wireless Internet Camera is exactly what the name says—and perhaps more than you'd expect.

The Internet Camera shown in Figure 12-29 combines a video camera and a Web server into one compact package.

Figure 12-29: The D-Link Wireless Internet camera has a built-in Web server, along with wired Ethernet and WiFi wireless connections.

The Internet Camera has wired and wireless network connections, so you can install the camera just about anyplace—as long as there is an electrical outlet nearby. The camera has a built-in microphone, so you even get sound along with the pictures. A mounting bracket included with the camera lets you mount the camera to a wall or ceiling.

There are several ways to view the images from the Internet Camera. The simplest way is to connect to the camera's IP address using a Web browser. Figure 12-30 shows how the camera works in this configuration.

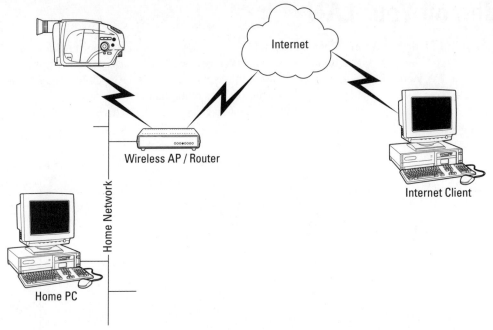

Figure 12-30: The camera's built-in Web server lets you see a live video stream from the camera using any Web browser.

Note

If you are using the Internet Camera behind a firewall router, you'll need to configure your router to allow Internet users to access the camera.

If you want, you can require viewers to enter a user ID and password before they can view images from the camera. Figure 12-31 shows how the camera's Web server appears over the Internet.

Streaming video over the Internet uses a lot of bandwidth, especially if several users are connected to the camera at the same time. To reduce bandwidth demand, you can reduce the image quality and the frame rate of the camera so that the camera traffic doesn't overload your Internet connection.

If you don't need a live video feed, you can configure the Internet Camera to take still images at a predefined interval, and the camera can upload the still images to an FTP server or send it to you by e-mail. A motion detector feature lets you set the camera to upload a new picture only when something in the image moves. The image quality from the Internet Camera is surprisingly good, and the camera automatically adjusts for changing lighting conditions. The camera includes relay contacts so you can control an external device (such as a light or siren) from the Internet.

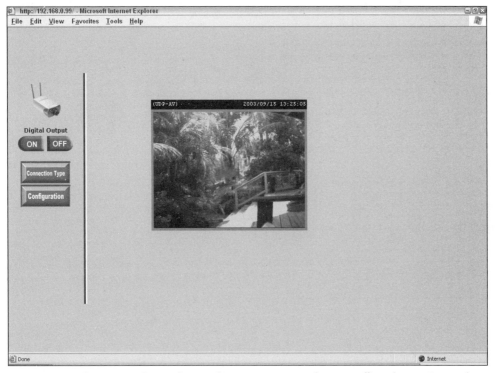

Figure 12-31: The Internet Camera lets you keep an eye on your home or office when you're not there.

D-Link provides surveillance software with the Internet Camera. You can use the IP Surveillance Software to view and optionally record the images from up to 16 Internet Cameras. This software lets you build a completely wireless video surveillance system for your home or office.

This is a great product for security-conscious home or business users who want to keep an eye on their property from a distance.

D-Link i2eye VideoPhone

I've been waiting for the video telephone to arrive ever since I attended the 1964 World's Fair in New York City. The one thing I remember from the fair (other than the giant Unisphere globe that still stands in Flushing Meadows) was the AT&T exhibit, where World's Fair visitors could enjoy a free video telephone call to the AT&T pavilion in Disneyland.

As you know, the video telephone never took off. A too-high price, technical problems, the Bell System breakup, and consumer resistance put the concept on hold for nearly 40 years. The biggest technical hurdle for the video telephone is that full-motion video requires much more bandwidth than an analog telephone line can deliver.

With broadband connections becoming more common, the bandwidth issue isn't a problem any more. Several companies have marketed add-on videoconferencing systems for PCs. These systems—called Web cams—provide decent-quality video, but they require a PC to handle the data connection.

D-Link's $200 i2eye VideoPhone combines the best aspects of AT&T's original video telephone with the data compression and transmission techniques of the Web cam. The resulting product is a standalone videoconferencing system that is very simple to install and use. Figure 12-32 shows how the i2eye system connects to your TV and LAN.

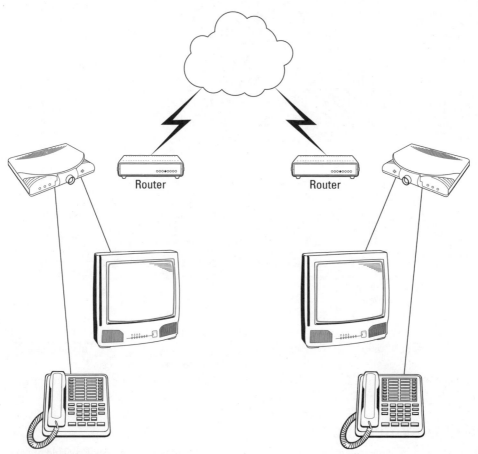

Figure 12-32: No computer required: The i2eye connects to your TV, not your PC. The telephones can be used in place of a microphone and speaker to provide a clear, feedback-free, audio connection.

As you can see in Figure 12-32, the i2eye connects to your TV and LAN, but not to your PC. Installation is very simple and is nearly automatic if you have a DHCP server on your LAN. Figure 12-33 shows a close-up of the i2eye system.

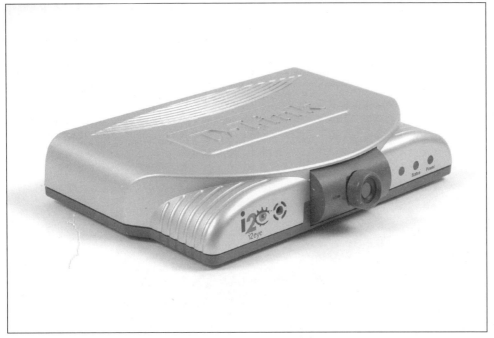

Figure 12-33: The D-Link i2eye sits on top of your TV set. The lens (center) swivels up and down to adjust for the height of your TV screen.

Videoconferencing, the Hard Way

When I first started writing for *PC Magazine* in the early 1990s, I spent a lot of time at our LAN testing lab in California. Our main offices are in New York City, and our Senior Networking Editor lived in Florida. To overcome the twin demons of time and distance, we used videoconferencing over digital ISDN telephone lines.

Despite having dozens of technically proficient people at both ends of the connection, we could never quite get the videoconferencing system to work. And even when we did, we would dial up a separate telephone call using speakerphones at both ends because the conferencing system's audio was awful.

After a few years of struggling with several videoconferencing systems, we realized that even when it worked well, we all saw pretty much the same blurry picture of the same people sitting at the same spot at the conference table every week. We eventually gave up on it and went back to the phones.

Installing the i2eye is a simple matter of connecting the cables and running through the onscreen configuration menu using the provided remote control. As part of the setup process, you enter your area code and telephone number, which is used to identify your i2eye system to other i2eye users on the Internet.

The i2eye can work using an external microphone and the speaker in your TV, but you'll get better results if you connect a standard telephone to the back of the i2eye. The telephone can't be used to place phone calls, since it is not connected to a telephone line.

Placing a video call to another i2eye system is also simple. You can "dial" other i2eye users by entering their telephone number or public IP address. Figure 12-34 shows the main i2eye menu screen.

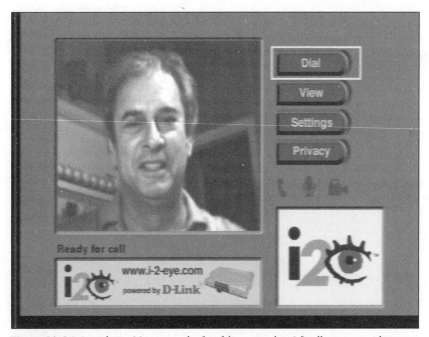

Figure 12-34: It took me 39 years and a few false starts, but I finally got my video telephone!

Given my exposure to videoconferencing systems, I was prepared not to like the i2eye, but I was pleasantly surprised by both the simplicity and the image quality. The only—and major—drawback to the i2eye system is that it only operates with a broadband Internet connection. This means that you can't buy one and send it to the grandparents—unless they have a broadband connection. On the plus side, i2eye calls are essentially free because they travel over the Internet and not over the public telephone network.

Summary

My goal in this chapter was to have a little fun and to introduce you to some new and interesting products that are outside the computing mainstream. The products and services in this chapter were all pie-in-the-sky ideas just a few years ago. Today, you can walk into any major electronics store and buy any of them off the shelf.

The key points in this chapter are as follows:

- Media convergence is finally here!

- Equipment makers are finding new and innovative ways to join computing and home entertainment technologies.

- New technologies make it easier than ever to monitor your home or office over the Internet.

- Easy, affordable videoconferencing has finally arrived.

Coming up next, I'll show you why you need to protect your LAN from the bad guys. They really are out there, and they're trying to break into your computer right now!

Chapter 13

Security

Who needs security? You do. Unless you've been hiding in a cave for the past few years, you've no doubt read or heard about one or more of the Internet attacks, virus outbreaks, or security breaches that have made the headlines. When Internet hacking first became a competitive sport in the mid-1990s, the majority of attacks were directed toward large corporate and government Web sites. But many crackers, snoops, and identity thieves have turned their attention away from the big Web sites toward the huge number of smaller—and often less protected—home computers.

What are the bad guys looking for? Some crackers do it just for fun, as a sort of competitive sport to see who can break into the most computers in an hour, a day, or a week. Some do it for profit, trolling thousands of home PCs looking for personal data, especially for credit card numbers that can be used to purchase merchandise, often over the Internet. Others do it for pay, intentionally breaking into specific computers, looking for information that can be used to blackmail, discredit, or otherwise humiliate the computer's owner.

In this chapter, I'll explain each of the types of security threats, including:

- Viruses

- Spyware

- Hoaxes and scams

- Intrusion and denial of service attacks

After explaining each type of threat, I discuss the tools that you can use to combat them, focusing on firewalls as the first line of defense. I also discuss security measures for wireless networks, and the software you can use to protect each PC from viruses and spyware.

Although most security threats have been targeted at Windows PCs, a large number of what I call equal opportunity threats apply to both Macs and PCs.

Note

The security precautions described in this chapter are appropriate to protect a typical home LAN. Business LANs, especially those containing sensitive or proprietary information, require much more stringent security measures.

Protecting Your LAN

To secure your network and computers from the bad guys, it's important to know and understand the different types of security threats. Table 13-1 summarizes the most-common security threats.

Table 13-1   Common Security Threats

Threat Type	How It Works	Protection
Denial of service (DoS) attack	Hackers bombard your IP address with traffic in an attempt to shut down your Internet connection.	Firewall
Port scan	Intruders probe your IP address, looking for vulnerabilities to exploit.	Firewall
Backdoor/Trojan horse programs	Hackers trick you into installing a program that appears to be beneficial (such as a screen saver) but is actually a "backdoor" program that allows them complete control over your computer.	Firewall, antivirus software
Virus	A malicious program arrives, most often disguised as an e-mail attachment. Many viruses replicate themselves by sending a copy of itself to everyone in your e-mail address book.	Antivirus software
Spyware/adware	Similar to a virus, spyware and adware are often "silently" installed as part of a free download such as a game or browser helper. Spyware programs track your Web site visits to gather marketing information. Adware programs replace content in your browser with paid advertising, often obscuring the content you are trying to see.	Spyware removal tools
Browser hijack	Malicious code on a Web site changes your browser's start and search pages to point to another site, often with pornographic content.	Antivirus software, special browser repair tools

Note

The bad news is that new security threats (and patches to fix them) appear almost daily. The good news, however, is that there are a number of online resources you can turn to for help in dealing with those threats. See Appendix C for a list of online security resources.

As you learned in Chapter 4, a firewall is a device or a piece of software that protects your network from intruders. Software firewalls, like the ones included in Windows XP and OS X, are typically used to protect a single computer that is directly connected to the Internet; hardware firewalls, whether independent or part of a combination router, are used to protect two or more computers connected to a LAN.

Tip

Broadband-connected PCs are much easier targets for hackers than computers using a dial-up connection.

Dial-up connections are slow, and dial-up users come and go. The always-on nature of broadband connections, coupled with broadband's higher connection speeds, makes broadband-connected PCs faster and easier to hack.

As you can see from the table, a hardware firewall is the first line of defense for your LAN. Microsoft also includes a software firewall with Windows XP, and I encourage you to keep it turned on because it provides an additional (and unobtrusive) layer of protection.

But a firewall alone isn't enough. You'll need to invest in (and use!) a good antivirus program and a spyware monitor program. You'll also need to educate yourself on current and new threats. This last point is important because many viruses use clever and persuasive tactics to convince people to open e-mail attachments that they know they shouldn't open.

Think of your firewall as the fence around your property. Even with a secure fence, you'll probably want to have good, secure locks on your doors. You may even want to have some locks on selected rooms in your house. In the following sections, I discuss the most common security threats and describe the tools you can use to avert those threats.

DoS Attacks

Denial of service (DoS) attacks are a major headache for corporations and ISPs, but they are not a major issue for home users. A DoS attack happens when someone (or a group of people acting together) on the Internet bombards your public IP address with traffic. When this happens, your Internet connection slows down because your router is overwhelmed with traffic.

A few years ago, DoS attacks were commonly used to take down a specific Web site or mail server. DoS attacks can't be prevented, but a properly configured firewall can minimize your chances of being the target of a DoS attack. Virtually all firewalls—including the inexpensive products sold for home use—simply ignore unsolicited incoming traffic. This simple tactic is very effective against DoS attacks, so DoS attacks aren't as effective as they once were.

Port Scans

The second category of attack is the port scan. Although a port scan isn't an attack in and of itself, it is often a prelude to a subsequent attack at some point in the future.

Each packet of data traveling on the Internet has a port number (also called a protocol number) assigned to it. The port number identifies the type of traffic contained in the data packet. For example, Web browser traffic uses port 80, outbound e-mail uses port 25, and FTP connections use port 21.

Computers on the Internet communicate with one another using well-defined procedures called *protocols*. Each protocol—and there are hundreds—defines the methodology that two devices will use to communicate. In most protocols, the first step is called a *connection request*. This happens, for example, when you open your Web browser and request a page from a specific site. Your computer attempts to open a communications session on port 80. The Web server responds by accepting the connection request.

Crackers use a software tool called a *port scanner* to scour the Internet, looking for IP addresses that respond to connection requests on the most commonly used ports. For example, if a specific IP address accepts connection requests on ports 21, 25, and 80, there's a good chance that the computer is running FTP, SMTP, and Web servers.

Port scanner programs can scan thousands of IP addresses at a time, and they keep track of the addresses that responded to connection attempts. This allows the cracker to build a list of potentially vulnerable IP addresses. Some ports, such as port 139 that is used for Windows file sharing, are especially vulnerable to this type of attack. Virtually all firewalls use a technique called *port filtering* that lets you decide which ports are (or aren't) visible on the Internet. Most home firewalls keep incoming ports invisible to the Internet, so crackers don't get a response to port scans.

Note

Most firewalls allow you to open specific ports to allow certain types of incoming connections. I discuss this topic in detail in Chapter 14.

Backdoor Protection

So far, I've discussed attacks that originate outside the firewall. But some attacks actually begin *inside* the firewall.

Such is the case with backdoor and Trojan horse programs. These programs find their way onto your computer in a variety of ways. They are often disguised as screen savers or games. When installed, they send a message back to the program's creator. This message acts as a homing beacon, allowing the hacker to easily and positively identify your (now infected) computer. Backdoor programs are so named because they create a back door that allows a hacker nearly complete access to your computer and its files.

Trojan horse programs are similar, but instead of taking over your computer, they run silently in the background, performing some dedicated (and usually undesirable) task. The most recent wave of Trojan horse programs are designed to send out huge quantities of e-mail spam, often advertising porn sites or get-rich-quick schemes.

Most antivirus software (described in the next section of this chapter) can catch these programs before they do any harm. But if a Trojan horse or backdoor program slips past your virus protection, a firewall can minimize the damage by preventing the program from making outbound connections.

Wireless LAN Security

Wireless LANs pose a special problem for security-conscious users. As wireless networks become more popular, so does the number of people seeking unauthorized access to wireless LANs.

Internet hackers need to get past your firewall to break into your network, but wireless hackers can get into your LAN—completely undetected—from hundreds of feet away. To make matters worse, a firewall is no protection against wireless hacking. Virtually all home wireless APs are installed inside of the firewall. If someone can connect to your wireless LAN, their computer is a peer on your LAN, just like all the other computers in your home.

Fortunately, there are a few simple steps you can take to protect your wireless network:

1. Change the default administrator name and password on your wireless access point and/or router. Hackers know all of the default names used by the manufacturers. Use a strong password of at least eight characters, preferably with a mix of letters, symbols, and numbers. "7xG%23OP" is a pain to type, but it offers a great deal more protection than "mypassword."

2. Enable the WEP or WPA security features on your access point. Although WEP has received a great deal of bad press, it still provides decent security. Most intruders will simply seek out an unprotected access point, rather than trying to defeat WEP. WPA is much more secure than WEP but may not be available on some older access points.

3. Some access points allow the administrator to restrict access based on the MAC address of each client. This provides an extra—but sill not unbreakable—level of security. Unfortunately, it is tedious to implement, since it requires you to manually enter the MAC address of any new wireless clients into the access point as your network grows.

4. Set your network workgroup name to something unusual, and refrain from using your name, company name, or address as part of the workgroup name.

5. Audit your network periodically and remove any unnecessary shared drives and folders.

Does Your Favorite Hotspot Have an Evil Twin?

When I first heard of this security exploit, I was sure it had to be a hoax...and I still haven't heard a first-hand report of this actually happening. It sounds a bit far-fetched to me, but it certainly could happen. Here's the scam:

You go to your favorite coffee shop, hotel, or other place with a public WiFi hotspot. While you're sipping your triple-shot latte, you fire up your laptop to check your e-mail, bank account, or just to browse the Web. Your computer connects to the hotspot as usual, and you're good to go—or so you think.

Continued

Does Your Favorite Hotspot Have an Evil Twin? *(Continued)*

What you don't know is that a hacker—maybe the guy with the laptop at the next table—has set up a phony hotspot. Instead of connecting to the real hotspot, your laptop is connected to the fake hotspot, called an Evil Twin. While you're surfing the Web, the Evil Twin is monitoring everything you do online, possibly even capturing user IDs and passwords for your e-mail, electronic banking, or online shopping sessions. Some Evil Twins reportedly even mimic popular e-commerce and banking sites so that identity thieves can capture your credit card and online banking information.

As I said earlier, I'm still not sure if this is a real threat or an urban legend. What is far more likely to happen is that someone with a laptop and a commonly available "sniffer" program could hang out in your favorite coffee shop, watching the traffic on the wireless LAN. It would be possible for an observer to obtain confidential information, such as account names, passwords, and credit card information, just by watching the traffic between your laptop and the shop's AP.

Fortunately, there are several simple steps you can take to protect yourself against these and similar security exploits:

- When connecting to an unfamiliar access point, check the list of available wireless networks in the area. If you see two APs with the same name, be suspicious.

- Use WEP or WPA security if at all possible. Most commercial hotspot operators offer this option, and many of them are starting to require it. WPA is always the better choice and gradually replacing WEP in most public hotspots.

- Use common sense. Don't use public hotspots to conduct business online unless you absolutely need to.

Protecting Your PCs

Even if you've secured your network with a firewall and the appropriate wireless security measures, you're still not completely protected until you secure each of the computers on your LAN.

To do this, you'll need a good antivirus software package and a spyware checker program. While commercial antivirus software has been available for many years, spyware checkers are a new, specialized breed of program designed to sniff out and remove spyware and adware programs. In the following sections, I'll explain what each one does, and you'll understand why you need both.

Antivirus Software

Computer viruses have been around almost since the beginning of the PC era. I don't know why people create computer viruses, but I do know that more than 50,000 viruses have been detected over the years. Some, like the Michaelangelo virus (first reported in 1991), do irreparable harm to your computer by deleting files or even formatting your hard drive. Many, like the Klez virus, spread by remailing copies of themselves to everyone in the infected computer's address book. Some viruses don't do anything at all, possibly as the result of a programming error. (After all, who is going to volunteer to beta-test a virus?)

Tip

Many viruses arrive as e-mail attachments, and they often appear to come from someone you know. Never open an e-mail attachment from an unknown sender, and be very, very wary when you receive an unexpected e-mail from someone you do know!

Virus writers and the antivirus software companies play a continual game of cat and mouse, 24 hours a day, 365 days a year. The virus protection on your computer is only as good as the most recent virus update, so it is possible for a new virus to slip past your antivirus software and onto your computer. Many viruses attempt to bypass, disable, or even uninstall popular antivirus software, making them difficult to remove.

Some recent viruses are network-aware, meaning that they know how to spread themselves to all of the computers on a LAN. If a single computer becomes infected, it is only a matter of time before the virus spreads to the rest of your computers.

I Can't Have a Virus—I Have a Firewall!

A router with a built-in firewall (or a separately installed firewall) is your first line of defense against Internet hackers. But many computer users think that because they have a firewall, they no longer need to worry about viruses, worms, Trojan horse programs, spyware, or other security issues. This is not at all the case.

A good firewall offers a great deal of protection at a relatively low cost, but it is not a magic bullet. The firewall's primary job is to create a private IP network that is connected to the public Internet. The firewall allows traffic in from the Internet, but only at the request of one of the client PCs on the LAN. Unfortunately, the firewall has no way to know what that traffic contains.

For example, when you open your e-mail program, the firewall sees that your PC is establishing a connection to an e-mail server on the Internet using the POP3 and SMTP protocols. The firewall knows the address of your PC, it knows the address of the mail server, and it knows that your mail program opened two connections (one using each protocol) to the mail server. Because your PC is expecting a response from the mail server, the firewall temporarily allows incoming traffic—but only SMTP and POP3 traffic—from the mail server. When your mail program closes the session, the firewall closes the inbound connections.

So far, so good. The firewall did its job, allowing you to connect to the mail server and collect your e-mail. The only problem is that one of the e-mail messages you just downloaded contains a nasty virus. Ten minutes from now, that virus will infect all the PCs on your LAN. Worse still, the virus will e-mail a copy of itself to everyone on your PC's address book—and everyone in the address books of the other PCs on your LAN. Thirty minutes later, your LAN—and the PCs connected to it—are sending out copies of the virus . . . and you won't even know it.

Tip

If you don't have an antivirus software program installed, you aren't completely out of luck. Most of the major antivirus software vendors offer a free online virus check. See Appendix C for a list of antivirus software vendors. If you don't want to spend the money for antivirus software, there are several free alternatives. See http://www.freebyte.com/antivirus/ for details.

All of the major antivirus software vendors offer on-demand updates for their software. In many cases, your initial purchase of the software gives you access to updates for a period of time, usually for a year. It is important to keep your antivirus software updated, and I strongly urge you to purchase a good antivirus software package and keep it updated.

Most antivirus programs offer several levels of protection, including file, e-mail, and Web browser protection. It is important to understand how each type of protection works.

File-level protection is the most important. The antivirus software intercepts all operating system file requests so that it can examine every file as files are created, opened, and modified. File protection makes sure that you will not be able to open an infected file.

E-mail protection works in a similar way. When you send or receive e-mail, the antivirus software scans the contents of any message attachments to scout for viruses.

Browser protection is a relatively new and increasingly important feature. Because many people know not to open e-mail attachments, some virus writers have taken to the Web instead. It is possible for a hacker to introduce a virus into your system through a script embedded in a Web page. Although Internet Explorer contains some safeguards to deal with this problem, antivirus software is more effective and provides better protection.

Painless Updates by Broadband

One of the real benefits of having a broadband-connected LAN is that it makes it easy to keep your software up to date. If you already have an antivirus package, make sure that it is set to update itself automatically.

Virus signature files—used by antivirus software to identify viruses—can be quite large. If you've been using a dial-up connection as your primary Internet connection, you may have disabled your software's auto-update feature to avoid the lengthy downloads. When you make the switch to broadband, don't forget to enable the auto-update feature on your software.

All versions of Windows since Windows 98 have a feature called Windows Update that allows your computer to automatically download and install Microsoft-issued updates to the Windows operating system. Many of the Windows updates are related to security, so it is important to check for updates on a regular basis.

To make sure your system is configured for automatic updates, open the System icon from the Control Panel. (If your Control Panel is set to Category View, select the Performance and Maintenance icon, and then select the System icon at the bottom of the screen.) Select the tab marked Automatic Updates.

Figure 13-1 shows the main configuration screen for Symantec's Norton AntiVirus, one of the most popular antivirus programs.

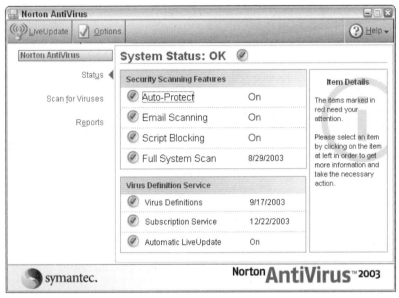

Figure 13-1: Norton AntiVirus protects your computer's file system and also monitors incoming e-mail and Web content.

As you can see from Figure 13-1, Norton AntiVirus provides all three levels of protection. Like most antivirus software, Norton AntiVirus offer an automatic update feature that automatically downloads and installs new virus update files. This feature is essential; an out-of-date virus signature file provides no protection against new viruses.

There are dozens of antivirus products available for Windows, and we regularly review antivirus programs at *PC Magazine*. If you need help choosing an antivirus program, check www.pcmag.com for our most recent antivirus roundup, or check the appropriate Web sites listed in Appendix C.

Spyware Protection

Spyware is a generic term that includes two subcategories of programs called spyware and adware. The two are similar in concept, but they have different goals. Both are usually installed on your computer without your knowledge. Both monitor some or all aspects of your online activity, and both can slow your computer to a crawl.

Spyware programs do just what their name implies; they spy on your online activity. These programs are typically used to track Web browsing habits, but some spyware programs log every keystroke and mouse click you make!

Adware programs are similar, but they watch your online activity and occasionally display ads on your computer's screen. Some adware programs substitute sponsored content in place of the content that would normally appear on your screen. For example, if you were visiting an airline's reservation page, an adware program might pop up an ad for a competing airline or an online reservation service.

Privacy issues aside, the bigger problem with spyware and adware programs is that they are often poorly written and unreliable. They use memory, disk space, and CPU cycles that you paid for in order to provide ads that you don't want to see. They can cause system lockups and slowdowns.

Spyware and adware programs are often installed "on the sly" as part of a free download like a screen saver, browser helper, or utility program. Some are installed using a technique called "drive-by download," which installs the software when you visit a Web page. The majority of adware programs are bundled in (and invisibly installed by) peer file sharing programs. Because these programs technically aren't viruses, most antivirus programs don't recognize them as such. Although adware and spyware programs aren't malicious in and of themselves, they are an annoyance at best.

The best way to deal with these programs is to simply not install them in the first place. Because they often install without your knowledge, it can be difficult to tell if a spyware or adware program is running on your computer. Fortunately, two free tools—Spybot Search & Destroy and Ad-aware—can do the job for you. Both programs can locate and uninstall common spyware programs. As with antivirus software, it is important to keep these programs updated, since new spyware programs appear almost daily. See Appendix C for more information on these products.

A Spyware Saga

How bad can spyware get? My sister is a very bright person and a long-time PC user. When I went to visit her a few months before I started work on this book, I used her computer to check my e-mail.

I couldn't help but notice that her reasonably fast and newer PC took almost 10 minutes just to start up. After the computer finally started, it took another minute or so just to launch the Web browser. When I asked my sister if it was always this slow, she replied that the computer had been getting slower and slower over the past few months but because it happened gradually, she really hadn't noticed anything unusual.

A quick check with Ad-aware uncovered no fewer than seven separate spyware programs running on her PC. The spyware programs were using so much memory and CPU time that the computer hardly had time left over to do anything else! It took over an hour to restore her computer back to a normal state.

Ironically, one of the programs doing the most damage was a trial version of a program that supposedly improved PC performance. It did, in a strange way—the computer ran about twice as fast after I removed that program!

Vigilance Is Good Protection Too!

Antivirus and spyware removal programs are a big help, but sometimes you simply have to watch out for yourself. Most computer users know that they shouldn't open attachments from unknown senders. But what do you do when you receive a message appearing to come from a well-known company?

Most computer users—me included—consider unsolicited e-mail, or spam, to be a nuisance. It's often annoying, but other than the occasional offensive picture or subject title, it is mostly harmless. But two ugly new types of spam are much more dangerous.

A few days before I began working on this chapter, I received two e-mails that appeared to be completely legitimate. The first was a security update message from Microsoft, urging me to install a security update file. The second was from PayPal, urging me to update my account information.

Fortunately for me, I already knew that these messages were both phony—but far from harmless. I'm sharing them with you because they show how spam can become much more than a nuisance. If they gave out Emmy Awards for spam, these two would certainly be finalists.

YOU WANT A VIRUS WITH THAT UPDATE?

It's no secret that Microsoft has had some serious security issues with all versions of Windows. The majority of the Windows updates issued since the release of Windows XP have been patches to improve security or to close some known, exploitable security hole. There have been so many patches and updates that even those of us who work with computers for a living have had a hard time keeping track of them all.

I receive quite a bit of e-mail from Microsoft and many other companies, so I didn't pay too much attention to the message shown in Figure 13-2 when it first arrived.

On closer inspection, I realized that something was very wrong. Although it has the Microsoft logo at the top of the page and looks like a Microsoft security bulletin, it contains several grammatical errors. More important (and less noticeable), Microsoft never refers to itself as "MS," which this e-mail does in several places. Finally, the message contains a large attachment named pack.exe. Microsoft never issues updates by e-mail; all official updates are handled through the Microsoft Windows Update Web site.

Because I was one of the first people to receive this "update" (lucky me!), my antivirus software did not recognize the attachment as a virus—not that I would have opened it anyway. But thousands of people did. The enclosed virus—technically a "worm" because it can spread by itself—spread very quickly over the next few weeks.

The moral of this story: *Don't believe anything you receive by e-mail.*

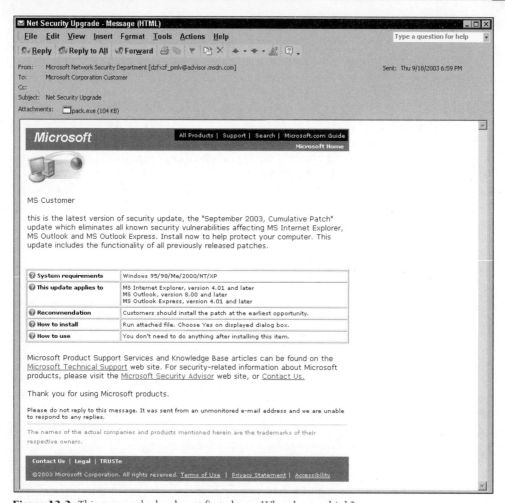

Figure 13-2: This message looks okay at first glance. What do you think?

ANATOMY OF AN E-MAIL SPAM SCAM

Con artists have always intrigued me. While I deplore their motives, I have to admire the cleverness and ingenuity of their methods. Thanks to the Internet, the world has a new breed of con artist to deal with: the spammer-scammer.

I sold some items on eBay a few months ago, so I set up a PayPal account to collect the proceeds from the sales. I hadn't used the account for several months when I received the official-looking e-mail shown in Figure 13-3.

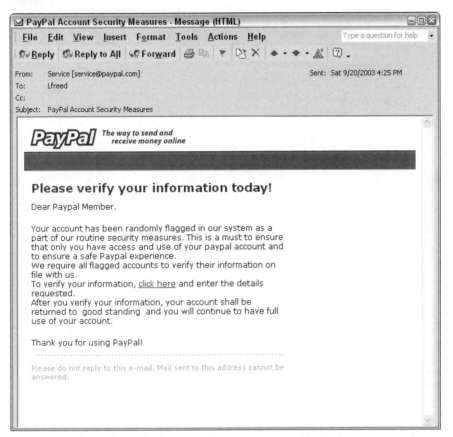

Figure 13-3: This authentic-looking PayPal message is not at all what it seems.

As you can see, the message looks authentic. It uses PayPal's logo, color scheme, and typeface, and the return address, `service@paypal.com`, sounds reasonable. But this message was sent to an ISP account that I rarely use, and my PayPal account is registered to a different e-mail address. Smelling a scam, I decided to play along to see where this scam was headed. Clicking the link in the e-mail took me to the Web page shown in Figure 13-4.

As with the e-mail, this looks just like an authentic PayPal site. But this page is asking for an awful lot of information—enough information to clean out my checking account, run up my credit card, and steal my online identity.

Even if this was a legitimate site, wouldn't PayPal use a secure connection to collect such sensitive information? And wouldn't PayPal already have much of this information?

As you've probably guessed, this isn't a PayPal site at all but a very skillfully forged page designed to collect information from unsuspecting Internet users. A close look at the site page properties (visible by right-clicking the page and selecting Properties from the menu) proved my suspicions, as you can see in Figure 13-5.

Your Billing Information - Enter your information as it appears on your credit card and bank account.

Card Type: Credit

Card Holder Full Name:

Card Issuing Bank

Credit Card Number:

Expiry Date: 01 / 2003

Card Verification
Number:

Card Pin Number: (your 4-digit credit/debit card pin number)

Your Verification Details - Your Details are required to verify your account.

Social Security Number:

Mother's maiden name:

Driver License:

Issued State for License:

Date of Birth: (mm/dd/yyyy)

Your Email Address and Password - Enter the email address which you used at the time of registration for PayPal.
Remember - Your password is at least **8 characters** and is case sensitive.

Email Address:

Figure 13-4: The PayPal scam letter takes you to this Web site.

Properties

General

PayPal - Verify Your Information

Protocol: HyperText Transfer Protocol

Type: Not Available

Connection: Not Encrypted

Address: http://www.paypal.com/@211.113.186.42/pp/updat
(URL) e.htm

Size: Not Available

Created: Not Available

Modified: Not Available

Certificates

OK   Cancel   Apply

Figure 13-5: The page properties for the fake PayPal
site shows the true source of the Web page—Korea.

The first part of the address, www.paypal.com, looks right. But the real address is in the 211.113.x.x address space and points to a server in Korea. This technique has become so common that scammers have coined a term—*phishing*—to describe the scam.

Scammers send out thousands of these messages every day. If even a tiny fraction of recipients respond with their account information, it can still mean big profits for the scammer. By the time most people realize that they've been scammed, it is far too late to do anything about it. The same scam has been used to collect user IDs and passwords from eBay, other auction sites, and banks.

There are three morals to this story:

1. Never trust anything you receive by e-mail.

2. Never give out personal information, either by phone or over the Internet. If PayPal really wanted me to verify the information it had on file, it would have asked me to log in using my PayPal ID and password—this scam site didn't.

3. Be careful—the bad guys really are out there!

THIS MUST BE TRUE—I READ IT ON THE INTERNET!

Every week, I receive at least two or three e-mail chain letters passed on by well-meaning friends and family. Almost without fail, these messages are part of a hoax.

One famous e-mail hoax from a few years back promised a free pair of Gap jeans if you forwarded the message to 10 friends. Other variants on the same hoax promised free food, plane tickets, and even cars. The motive behind these messages is unclear, but many of them claim to reward users for participating on a test of a new e-mail tracking system. The only problem is that there is no such system.

Most of the time, these hoaxes are harmless time-wasters. But hoaxes can be harmful too. A recent hoax claimed that a horrific new virus was on the loose. According to the chain letter, the virus remained dormant for 14 days before activating itself and wasn't detectable by traditional antivirus software. The message told users to search for and delete a file named jdbgmgr.exe.

The file in question is actually a legitimate part of Windows. Although most people don't need the file (it is a Java debugger program), thousands of people did indeed delete the file from their systems. A few weeks after the original hoax, a new variant of the message appeared, offering a recovery program that would restore the missing file for those who had deleted it. The recovery program was itself a virus.

Like the phony Microsoft security bulletin discussed earlier, these hoax e-mails claim to originate from Microsoft, AOL, and even the federal government.

If you receive one of these messages, ignore it. If you aren't sure whether the messages is a hoax or the real thing, check one of the major antivirus or hoax sites listed in Appendix C.

Summary

Computer users are faced with very real and serious security threats nearly every day. If you have a home network with multiple computers and an always-on broadband connection, you absolutely must have firewall, antivirus, and spyware protections.

The key points in this chapter are as follows:

- The bad guys really are out there.
- A firewall (or firewall software) is your first line of defense against crackers.
- Antivirus software is only effective if you keep it updated.
- Don't believe anything you read on the Internet—be especially wary of unsolicited e-mails of all types.

Coming up, I'll introduce you to some topics and concepts that take your home LAN beyond the basics.

Chapter 14

Advanced Networking Topics

The networking products and techniques in the preceding chapters of this book cover 99 percent of what most home users will need to know about networking. For that other 1 percent, I've included three important topics in this final chapter:

■ Customizing your firewall

■ Using a dedicated server

■ Using a Network Attached Storage (NAS) server

Customizing Your Firewall Configuration

Most home firewalls come from the factory with default settings designed to provide maximum protection with minimal end-user configuration. As a rule, these settings allow every user on the local network to have unrestricted access to the Internet connection. Conversely, the default settings typically block all incoming connection attempts.

In most cases, you'll want to leave your firewall's settings just as they came from the factory. But there are several situations where you may want to adjust your firewall settings to allow or deny specific types of traffic through the firewall. By adjusting your firewall's settings, you can:

1. Route specific types of incoming traffic to a specific computer on your LAN. This feature is typically used to set up a Web or e-mail server on your local network and is also used for online gaming.

2. Route all incoming traffic to a specific computer on the LAN. This is essentially the same as item 1, but it passes all incoming traffic to a specific computer. This is useful when you have multiple services (Web, e-mail, FTP, and so on) running on the same computer.

3. Restrict Internet access from a single computer or group of computers.

4. Restrict Internet access to certain times of the day.

It is important to keep in mind that not all routers provide all of these features. Most routers can perform the first three items on the list, but relatively few offer scheduled operation.

Note

If you plan to set up a Web, mail, or other publicly accessible server on the Internet, check your ISP's Terms of Service to make sure you aren't breaking any rules. Most cable and DSL service providers specifically prohibit running a server on your home connection.

If you think they're not watching, think again. Many ISPs routinely use automated port scanner programs (just like the hackers do!) to track down illicit servers on their network. If you really want to run a Web or mail server, you should consider using one of the many companies that specialize in Web and e-mail hosting.

Setting Up a Public Server

The private IP addresses used on your local network aren't normally reachable from computers and other devices on the public Internet. If you want Internet users to be able to connect to a server on your network, you'll need to configure your firewall to allow limited access to that one PC.

Firewalls use a technique called *port forwarding* to route specific incoming traffic to specific computers on your network. You can use this feature to make a Web, mail, or other server available to the public Internet. When a user on the Internet connects to your public IP address, the firewall automatically routes the incoming traffic to a specific computer using one of the private addresses on the LAN. Figure 14-1 shows the port forwarding screen from a Linksys router.

Tip

If you make use of port forwarding, you should make sure that the target computer on your local LAN has a static (permanently-assigned) IP address, not a dynamic address assigned by your DHCP server.

The screen in Figure 14-1 allows you to specify a port number or a range of port numbers, a protocol type, and a destination address. The port number tells the router which ports to forward, and the destination address tells the router where to send the traffic. The protocol type (UDP or TCP) will vary depending on the ports being forwarded; in most cases, you can leave this setting on Both to forward all traffic.

Tip

If you want to be able to connect to your LAN from a remote location such as your workplace, while traveling, or from a friend's house, you may want to consider using a virtual private network instead. A VPN provides secure, encrypted remote access to your network. See Appendix A for information on setting up a VPN.

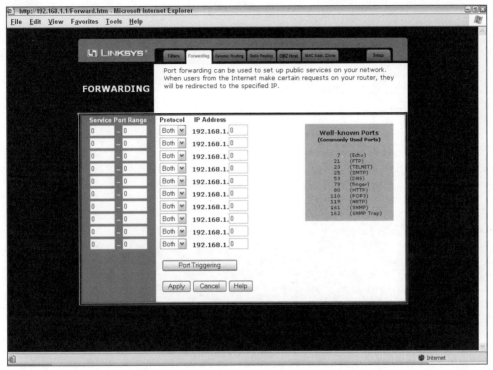

Figure 14-1: The Forwarding screen on this Linksys router lets you forward incoming traffic to specific computers on your LAN.

Some routers include a DMZ (demilitarized zone) feature that routes all incoming traffic to a single IP address (see Figure 14-2). The DMZ essentially opens all incoming ports to traffic, and it hands all of the traffic off to the DMZ computer. This is handy when you have a single computer on your LAN that provides more than one type of service.

Caution

I strongly recommend that you not use the DMZ feature unless you have a software firewall installed on the destination computer. When you put a computer into the DMZ, it is not protected by your hardware firewall and is wide open to Internet attacks.

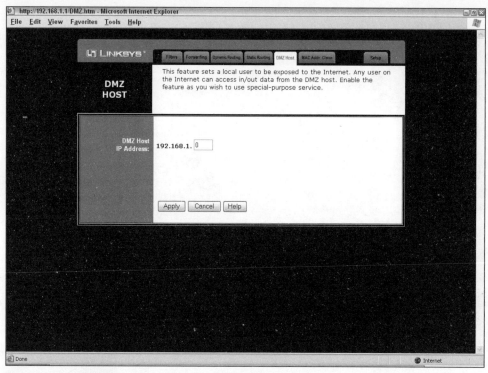

Figure 14-2: The DMZ Host feature routes all incoming Internet traffic to a single IP address.

Tip

Keep in mind that, in most cases, your public IP address may change at any time. If you want to be able to reach your home LAN even if your IP address changes, you may want to use a dynamic DNS service provider. These providers assign a host name to your IP address, and they keep track of changes to your IP address so that your host name is always reachable, even if your IP address changes. Many dynamic DNS providers offer free services for home users. Do an Internet search for "dynamic DNS service providers" to learn more. Also, see the entry for DYNDNS.COM in Appendix C.

Restricting Internet Access

In an always-connected, multi-PC home, any computer can access the Internet at any time—but that may not be a good thing. If you have children in your home, you may not want them to have Internet access at all times of the day—or at all.

Many routers include a feature called *port filtering* that lets you control the extent (and even the time of day) of each computer's Internet access. You can use this feature to selectively allow or deny access to one or more Internet protocols for each PC on your network.

For example, you could create a filter that allows Web access while blocking other protocols such as e-mail, instant messaging, and peer file sharing. Figure 14-3 shows a typical Filters screen from a Linksys router.

This particular router allows users to create up to five filters, each containing a range of addresses and ports. To create a filter, you enter the address or range of addresses for the filter in the top half of the screen and the port or range of ports to be blocked in the lower half.

Keep in mind that port filters aren't foolproof. Even if, for example, you block the ports for instant messaging or Internet Chat, dozens of Web sites provide access to IM and IRC Chat via a Web browser.

Some routers, like the D-Link unit shown in the next figure, let you specify the days of the week and the hours of the day that the filter is effective. Figure 14-4 shows the Advanced Filters screen from a D-Link wireless router.

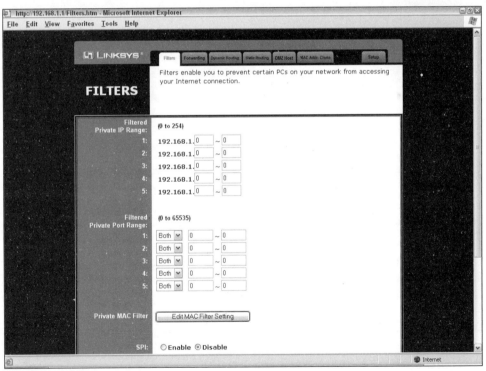

Figure 14-3: This router uses filters to selectively block Internet access to certain protocols.

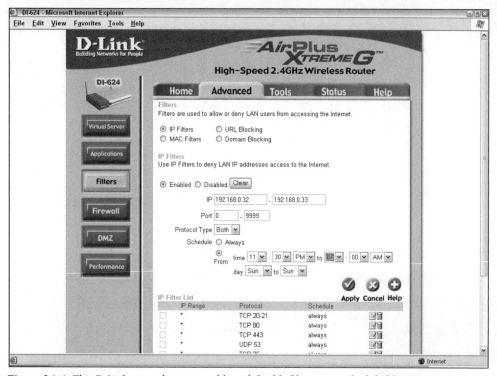

Figure 14-4: This D-Link router lets you enable and disable filters on a scheduled basis.

This screen is similar in concept to the one in Figure 14-3, but each filter has a scheduled time of operation. By default, all protocols are allowed to all IP addresses at all times. You can create any number of custom filters that override the default filters.

Port Number Roulette

To create an effective filter, you need to know the port number of the protocol you want to filter. Thousands of port numbers are in use on the Internet, so it can be difficult to locate the port assignments for a particular program.

You can find a complete list of port assignments at `www.iana.org/assignments/port-numbers`.

Using a Dedicated File Server

One of the main benefits of a home network is file and resource sharing between LAN clients. In the typical home, the types of files a networked PC stores tends to depend on who has access to it and who uses it the most. For example, the family gaming PC might also store all of your digital images, the home office PC may be the central point for financial files and family documents, and the family's vast collection of MP3 music files is usually scattered among all networked computers.

Because the systems are all attached to your home network, you easily can access or transfer files across systems. But to do that, you have to remember which LAN client has the files you want, and you also have to make sure that the other client is up and running. You also have to be diligent about backing up each LAN client's data. Pretty soon you'll be asking yourself, "Isn't there a better way to do this?" As you saw back in Chapter 3, the answer is yes, and it's easy to do in a peer-to-peer networking environment with a dedicated file server.

Advantages of a Dedicated File Server

In the home network, a file server is a computer dedicated to storing files and making them available to network users. Setting up a dedicated file server may sound like something you'd see only in a business environment, but it's actually a very sensible and affordable part of any network, even a relatively small home network.

Business-class file servers can be very expensive and require significant know-how to set up and administer, but home network file servers are easily configured and maintained. In fact, almost any PC you already have (maybe even that old Pentium II you stuck in the closet when you upgraded) is likely to be a good candidate for file serving duties at home.

You can also purchase an inexpensive device called a Network Attached Storage (NAS) server to handle network file sharing duties. I discuss NAS servers later in this chapter.

Your own home network file server gives you many advantages, including:

- **Centralized file storage.** Having all your shared files—digital pictures, music files, and work or family documents—in one place makes them easier to find, organize, and maintain.

- **Easier file backup.** With all your files in one place, backing them up is simplified. And by using recordable CD or recordable DVD technology, you can back up a lot of data in one step. Even better, you can purchase an inexpensive USB 2.0 external hard drive with enough capacity to back up several PCs worth of data on one drive.

- **Large storage capacity.** Rather than putting larger hard drives in each of your client PCs, you can use one or more large hard drives on the server. Drives as big as 400GB are commonly available and cost less than $300.

- **Printer sharing.** Although not directly related to file sharing, a dedicated file server can also provide print server functions for your LAN, automatically handling document queuing for the entire network. One or more printers attached to the server can be made available to all LAN clients and is ideal for sharing more-expensive or special-purpose printers.

Setting Up a File Server

Setting up a file server is no more difficult than setting up any of the other systems on your network. In fact, a file server can be any machine you want to define as the central storage point for shared files.

As you saw in Chapter 3, the network you're setting up operates in peer-to-peer fashion. This means that the dedicated file server is really just another peer, but one you've dedicated to file storage, resource sharing, and data backup. In other words, the file server computer is generally not a computer you'll use for applications (like word processing, e-mail, and so on), but in terms of general hardware setup and configuration, the file server need not be very different from one of your other networked computers.

Where you physically locate the file server is up to you, and it can really be placed just about anywhere. If you're going to use it strictly for file sharing, you could keep it in a seldom-used room, or tucked away in the basement. If the server is also going to serve printers, you'll probably want to make it a bit more easily accessible. Wherever you place it, remember that you'll need to get to it easily to do data backups.

Server Backup Options

Frequent backups are a critical part of computing. Computers aren't fail-safe, and your computer system will eventually fail for one reason or another—taking your data with it. If you plan to install a central server, you're putting all of your faith—and your data—onto a single computer.

Without a central file server, you have to be especially diligent about backing up each LAN client's data files, and this means you have to go to each computer to do the backup. Yes, you could back up files across the network, but this is very inefficient, especially for large data files. It could take hours to do a simple backup.

After you've moved your data files to the server, backing them up is a matter of transferring them to your storage media of choice. In general, this is going to be one of two formats: optical storage media or an external hard drive attached to a networked PC or to a NAS server.

OPTICAL STORAGE

A CD or DVD recorder (often called a *burner*) might be the most convenient way to back up your server files. Recordable optical media is fairly inexpensive, and it's a good and convenient choice for quick and frequent backups. The drives themselves are also reasonably economical and increasingly standard issue on newer computers.

With respect to storage capacity, recordable CD-ROMs offer roughly 700MB of storage and are good for backups of smaller batches of data, or project- and event-based backups. For example, you might back up each vacation's digital photos onto one CD per trip (or in my case, one CD per day.) Recordable DVDs, on the other hand, offer storage of just under 9 GB of data, about 15 times the capacity of a recordable CD-ROM. Recordable DVDs, then, could back up quite a bit more of your photos and other files onto fewer discs.

Keep in mind that there's a potential issue with the longevity of backups stored to optical media such as CDs and DVDs. Be sure to use high-quality discs to ensure the best long-term archival reliability.

POWER PROTECTION

To protect your file server system during power failures and fluctuations, you should add a good-quality uninterruptible power supply (UPS). A UPS is essentially a continuously charged battery with electronics to monitor power line conditions and provide an automatic switchover to battery power when standard line power is interrupted.

UPS devices are available in a range of sizes that correspond to the amount of output power they can supply. The larger the UPS in terms of output power capacity, the longer the file server can operate on battery power when the power fails. You'll want a UPS with sufficient capacity to keep the system running while you safely shut down your file server.

Although the least expensive UPS models provide adequate power backup, slightly better models provide a communication cable from the UPS to the computer that allows the computer to know when the power has failed. Most UPS units that have this feature supply software to handle messages from the UPS and initiate appropriate actions. For example, if the power goes out and remains out, the UPS software can instruct the computer to perform an orderly shutdown before the UPS battery is completely discharged.

Network Attached Storage Servers

Many home network users don't know about Network Attached Storage (NAS) servers. That's unfortunate because a NAS is one of the most useful and least expensive items you can add to your home LAN. A NAS is essentially a small, dedicated file server device with one or more attached hard drives.

When I wrote the first edition of this book just two years ago, I didn't even mention Network Attached Storage (NAS) servers because the then-current NAS servers were designed for the corporate marketplace. They were far too expensive and complex for most home users to consider. Today, home users can choose from a variety of inexpensive NAS servers starting as low as $100.

Regardless of size, all NAS servers share some common characteristics. They provide shared storage space for all of the users on a LAN. You can use a NAS server as a central repository for commonly-shared files (including digital photos and MP3 files), or as a convenient place to back up files from several network-connected computers.

NAS servers, and particularly the products designed for home use, consume far less electric power and generate less heat and noise than a dedicated server PC. The majority of NAS servers run some variant of Linux, and most offer a user-friendly, browser based configuration and management interface. Linux uses the SMB protocol for file sharing, so they work equally well with Windows, Mac OS X, and Linux client computers.

In the following section, I'll show you how to configure and use a typical NAS server.

Linksys NSLU2

One of my favorite home NAS devices is the Linksys NSLU2. I like it because it is cheap (less than $100), silent, small (about the size of a paperback book), expandable, and incredibly easy to use. Figure 14-5 shows a front view of the NSLU2.

Figure 14-5: The Linksys NSLU2 NAS
server packs a lot of power into a 5 1/2" box.

The rear panel of the NSLU2 has the usual power and Ethernet connectors, plus two USB connectors. As you might have guessed from its diminutive size, the NSLU2 does not have an internal disk drive.

You can connect the NSLU2 to virtually any external USB hard drive. I personally use a 160 GB drive I bought on sale for less than $100, mounted in a universal USB 2.0 case that cost less than $40. Sure, the drive and case cost more than the NSLU2, but for less than $300, I have a 160 GB file server that is fast, reliable, and nearly silent (the drive makes a barely perceptible sound when running.) Best of all, it takes up very little space and uses so little power that I don't even think about leaving it on all the time.

More than a NAS?

The NSLU2 is built using an open-source version of Linux, and Linksys has taken the unusual step of including the source code for the NSLU2's firmware and operating system on the CD-ROM packed with the unit. Not surprisingly, this has created a swarm of activity in the computer hobbyist community. Do a Google search on NSLU2 and you'll see that some clever folks have modified the NSLU2 to operate as a Web server, an FTP server, and even as an iTunes server!

If you're interested in seeing what people are doing with their NSLU2s, see www.nslu2-linux.org.

The NSLU2 isn't a speed demon, but it is more than fast enough to use for music and photo file sharing, and it is especially useful as a backup device. But my favorite thing about the NSLU2 is that it is exceptionally easy to install and operate.

Installing the NSLU2

You begin the installation by connecting the provided Ethernet cable to your LAN switch and connecting the power cord. You can configure the NSLU2 with or without a disk drive attached. After you connect the cables and power on the unit, you run a configuration wizard from the CD-ROM packed with the NSLU2. (Sorry, Mac users, but Linksys doesn't provide a Mac version of the configuration wizard. You can still use the browser-based interface, shown in the next step.)

The configuration wizard consists of four simple steps. In the first step, the wizard searches your local network looking for NSLU2 units. When it finds one, you'll see a screen like the one in Figure 14-6.

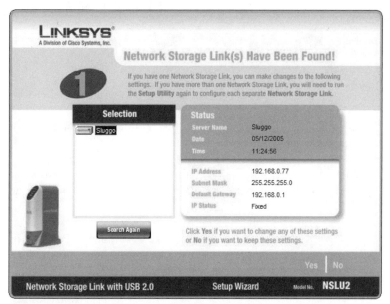

Figure 14-6: In Step 1, you identify the NSLU2 you want to configure.

If you have more than one NSLU2 on your LAN, you'll need to click the one you want to configure. When you've identified the correct unit, click the Yes button to continue. You'll see the IP Settings screen, shown in Figure 14-7.

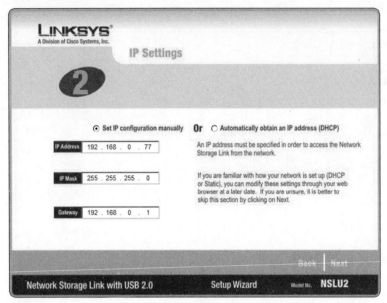

Figure 14-7: In Step 2, you can change the unit's IP address or choose to use an automatic address provided by your network's DCHP server.

By default, the NSLU2 comes configured to use a fixed address, although the preconfigured address may not be in the proper address range for your LAN. I recommend that you use a fixed address for your NSLU2, although you can use an automatic (dynamic) address if you prefer.

If you're not sure what IP address to use, check your router's IP address settings to learn the address of your router and the range of the router's DHCP addresses. You'll need to choose an address that doesn't conflict with another device on your LAN.

For example, my home LAN router is at 192.168.0.1, and the router is set up to provide automatic (DHCP) addresses in the range of 192.168.0.100 to 192.168.0.200. All of the addresses between 192.168.0.1 (the router) and 192.168.0.99 are available for manual assignment. I chose 192.168.0.77 as the address for the NSLU2, and this address will probably work on the majority of home LANs.

After you've entered the IP address, click the Next button to move on to the Date and Time settings screen, shown in Figure 14-8.

Unlike many NAS servers and routers, the NSLU2 does not obtain the current date and time from the Internet, so you'll need to set it manually. The unit does have a real-time clock chip and a backup battery, so you should only need to set the clock this one time. Enter the correct date, time, and time zone, and click Next to move to the Confirmation screen, shown in Figure 14-9.

This final screen lets you confirm your changes. Make sure the IP address is correct, or you may not be able to connect to the NSLU2's Web interface in the next step! You may want to write down the IP address so you can refer to it in the future.

At this point, your NSLU2 is configured and almost ready to use. You'll still need to attach a disk drive (if you haven't already), and you'll need to format the drive for use with the NSLU2. If you are using a single disk drive, connect the drive to the USB port labeled DISK 1 on the back of the NSLU2.

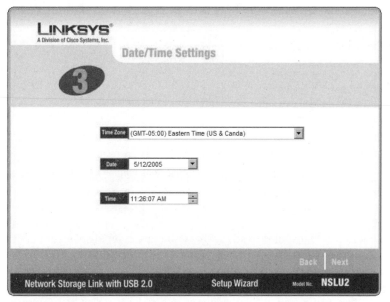

Figure 14-8: Make sure you set the correct date, time, and time zone so your files will be correctly time-stamped.

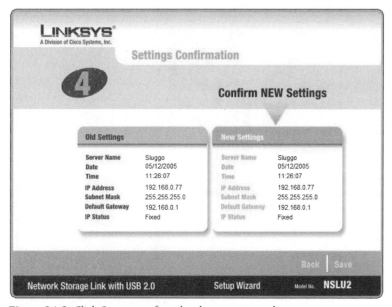

Figure 14-9: Click Save to confirm the changes you made.

Caution

Although the NSLU2 will work with virtually any USB disk drive (including USB "keychain" flash drives), there are two important things you need to know before you proceed.

1. Unlike Windows and Mac PCs, the NSLU2 does not allow for "hot swapping" of drives. You must power down the unit before you attach or disconnect a USB hard drive. You can swap out flash drives at any time.

2. The NSLU2 runs Linux and uses a different file structure than Windows or Mac systems. You will need to format the drive using the NSLU2's format utility (described in the next section) before you can use the drive with the NSLU2. If you plan to use a USB drive that contains important files, you should copy the files to another system before you connect the drive to the NSLU2.

After you've connected the drive, you're almost ready to go. From any computer on your LAN, open your Web browser and point your browser to the IP address assigned to the NSLU2. (Now you know why I told you to write it down!) You should see the NSLU2's Home screen, shown in Figure 14-10. In most cases, you can also reach the NSLU2 using the name you gave the server when you ran the setup wizard. As you can see in the following example, I can reach my server at `http://sluggo`.

Figure 14-10: The NSLU2's Home screen provides quick access to all of the NSLU2's features.

Figure 14-11: The disk status screen shows the operational status of the disk drives attached to the server. Note that in this example, I have already formatted Disk 1.

If you are sure that you are ready to format the drive, click the appropriate button for Disk 1 or Disk 2. (See Figure 14-11.) A window will pop up to confirm that you really do want to format the drive. Click OK if you are sure you want to proceed. The format procedure takes anywhere from a few minutes to nearly an hour, depending on the size of the drive.

After the drive is formatted, you're almost finished. In the next step, you'll create user accounts for each user who will have access to the shared drive. To add new user accounts, click Users from the Administration menu. You'll see the users screen, shown in Figure 14-12.

To add a new user, enter the user's name and password in the lower half of the screen. If you want to create a private directory that is accessible only by that specific user, check the box next to Create Private Folder. If you like, you can create a quota for that user, which limits the amount of storage for that user. When you are finished entering the information, click the Save as New User button to save the changes.

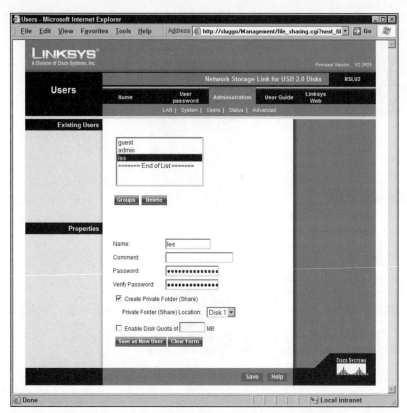

Figure 14-12: Use the Users screen to add and delete authorized users for the server.

Observant readers may have noticed the "guest" account in Figure 14-12. This is a default account automatically created by the NSLU2. Files placed in the guest directory are accessible by everyone on the LAN, and there is normally no password on the guest account.

The last step is to set the server's network name and workgroup name. Back in Chapter 8, I showed you how to set the workgroup name for your Windows LAN. You'll need to use the same workgroup name for your NSLU2, and you'll also need to give the NAS server a unique network name. To change these settings, click System from the Administration menu. Fill in the workgroup name, the server name, and an optional description of the server, using the example in Figure 14-13.

At this point, your NAS server is fully configured and ready for use. In the next section, I'll show you how to use your server.

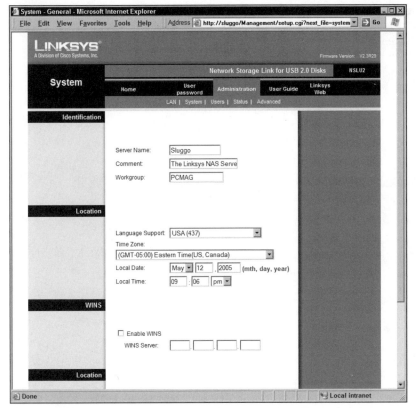

Figure 14-13: Use the System screen to set the server and workgroup names.
(To find out why my NSLU2 is named Sluggo, Google "NSLU2 Slug".)

Using the NSLU2

The NSLU2 uses the industry-standard SMB protocol for network communications, so it works equally well with Windows, Linux, and Mac OS X (10.3 and later) client computers. In most cases, the NSLU2 will appear like any other server in your computer's network browser.

On Windows client PCs, the NSLU2 should show up as a server in the Network Neighborhood. To see a list of the available servers on your LAN, open the Network Neighborhood and then click View Workgroup Computers on the left side of the screen. You should see a list of servers like the one in Figure 14-14.

Note

It can take up to 15 minutes for a new server to appear in the Workgroup Computers list. This is the result of the complexities of Windows networks. For an explanation of why this happens, see http://support. microsoft.com/kb/102878/EN-US/ for the gory details.

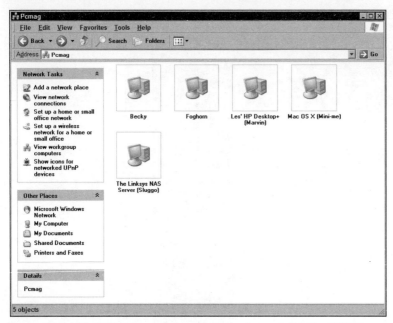

Figure 14-14: The Workgroup Computers display for my LAN. The NSLU2 (Sluggo) is at the bottom of the list of servers.

On Mac OS X systems, the NSLU2 will appear as a server in the Finder. To see a list of available servers, open the Finder and click the Network icon. If the server doesn't appear (probably due to the 15 minute delay I mentioned earlier), you can manually create a connection by selecting Connect to Server from the Finder's Go menu, as shown in Figure 14-15.

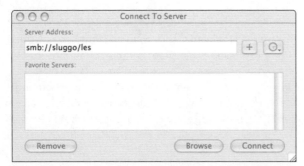

Figure 14-15: To manually connect to a server, you'll need to know the server and share names.

As you can see from the example, you'll need to enter `smb://` plus the server and share names to connect to the NAS server. If you plan to use the server connection frequently, you can click the plus icon next to the server address to add it to your list of favorite servers.

Summary

This chapter showed you several ways to extend the capabilities of your home network. The key points in this chapter are as follows:

- You can customize your firewall to give Internet users access to a server on your LAN.

- A file server is an affordable and very sensible (almost necessary) part of a home network.

- A file server provides centralized file storage and printer sharing for the entire home network.

- You can set up a Microsoft Windows system to share files or use a dedicated, inexpensive NAS server.

- A small NAS makes an excellent addition to most any home LAN.

Appendix A

Home Networking Cookbook

So you're enjoying the benefits of high-speed cable or DSL service: no more competition for the phone line, always-on convenience, and easy sharing of large image files of the kids with their grandparents, among many other things. The problem now is that now everyone in the house wants to use the one computer connected to the Internet, and usually at the same time.

Fortunately, setting up a home network to share the connection is relatively easy and inexpensive, and it also lets you share printers, files, and other resources among all the computers on the LAN. And the flexible nature of Ethernet and wireless LANs means you have many configuration options. In fact, there are so many options that planning your network can be a bit daunting.

To help narrow the field, this Home Networking Cookbook presents a series of arrangements to suit almost anything you're likely to need in home networking. Most of the layouts also work in a small-office environment, though there may be some differences in the service type and the type of equipment that supplies it. On the LAN side of things, the scenarios are essentially the same for home- and small-office settings. All use Ethernet (either wired or wireless) and the standard TCP/IP communications protocol.

The wired options presented are particularly suitable if you can run cables within your home. The ideal situation is to have your network cables run as the house is built (or as you have your basement finished) so that you can plan to put an Ethernet jack in every room, and you can even combine your Ethernet and telephone connections into a single wall plate for a compact and nicely finished appearance (see Chapter 6 for more on connector types).

If your house is already built or if you rent your home, you won't be able to install cabling quite as easily. But wired networks are still your best choice if most of the networked computers are in the same or adjacent rooms, or if your home has an unfinished basement or attic with easy access to the rooms above or below. In the latter cases, you can often route your CAT5 cables using existing telephone cable runs as a placement guide.

Note

It is also possible to use your home's existing AC power or telephone wiring to carry LAN traffic. See Chapter 4 for more details.

Wired LANs offer the best speed performance and are the best option for networks (or network segments) that handle a lot of data (like large image or file transfers, video, and so on). The wireless LAN configurations presented here are a very good alternative if your speed requirements are not as great, if you want more flexibility, or if you need to extend network access to parts of the house in which cabling is not an option. Also presented are a number of combined wired/wireless network configurations useful if you can run cable in some parts of the house but not others.

Wired, wireless, or a combination of the two, one thing's for sure: After you have your home network set up, you'll wonder how you ever got by without it.

The scenarios presented here assume you already have working DSL or cable modem service, and that it is delivered to your home via an external (standalone) modem. If you don't have a broadband connection, you can use Windows' Internet Connection Sharing feature to share a dial-up connection. But even if you don't have an Internet connection, the routers, switches, and wiring that create the LAN for you still let you share folders, printers, and other resources. That's because the LAN is independent of the Internet connection and doesn't require the Internet connection to operate.

A Quick Reference to the Sections

Here's a quick guide to the sections in this appendix. The first five network configurations cover the foundations of wired, wireless, and mixed wired/wireless home networks; the balance of the sections build on these basic layouts.

- **Individual Internet Access with Router/Firewall.**   Even if there's just one computer connected to your high-speed cable or DSL service, you can still benefit from using a router to manage and protect your connection. Plus, the router gives you a ready expansion point for when you're ready to add more computers or need to connect a laptop you've brought home from the office.

- **Ethernet LAN with Router/Gateway.**   The standard router-based wired Ethernet home network. The router handles Internet connection sharing, network management, and firewall functions. This all-wired configuration offers the best networking performance for all your LAN clients.

- **Ethernet LAN with Internet Connection Sharing (ICS).**   A home network arrangement that puts one of your existing PCs to work as the Internet connection and network management point.

- **Ethernet LAN with Separately Located Router and Modem.**   Just because the cable or DSL modem and the router have to be interconnected doesn't mean they have to be in the same room, or even on the same floor. This section tells you how to set up the router and modem where it's most convenient for you.

- **All-Wireless LAN with Router/Gateway.**   An all-wireless LAN offers you the greatest LAN client-placement flexibility. It also means you can move about with your laptop, from room to room, while staying connected to your home LAN—and to the Internet.

■ **Mixed Wired/Wireless LAN.**　Adding a wireless segment to a wired network gives you the best of both worlds: the high speed and performance of the wired section and the mobility and ease of installation of wireless.

■ **Expanded LAN with Two Ethernet Switches.**　A wired network is easily expanded with additional Ethernet switches. This section builds on the preceding configuration Ethernet LAN with Router/Gateway, and describes where the additional switches fit into the LAN and how to interconnect them.

■ **Expanded Wireless LAN with Two Access Points.**　A basic, single-access-point wireless LAN configuration doesn't always cover every area you need to reach within your home. This section explains how to use a second access point to expand the range of your LAN.

■ **Ethernet LAN with HomePlug Extension.**　One of the newer alternatives to running cabling for home networking, the HomePlug standard uses power line adapters to route Ethernet traffic over your home's electric cables. It's especially useful for connecting a LAN client in a difficult location.

■ **Secure Remote Access to Your Ethernet LAN.**　You can easily set up private and secure access into your own home network. Here you'll see how to interconnect your remote client PC (desktop or laptop) to your home LAN through a specially equipped router.

■ **Ethernet LAN with User-Installable DSL.**　You can easily extend user-installable DSL service into a full home network with shared Internet access. This section explains how this type of DSL is set up within your home and outlines what you need to network it.

Happy home networking!

Individual Internet Access with Router/Gateway

Even if you have only one computer today, you can still benefit from using a router between your system and the broadband modem. The router removes your computer from direct exposure to the Internet and gives you an easy way to set up a LAN for future (or occasional) expansion. Perhaps you have a home desktop machine that the kids also use, and you plan eventually to get them their own computer and reclaim yours. Or maybe you occasionally bring home your office laptop, and you'd like to be able to connect directly, with easy access to your home printer and Internet connection.

What You'll Need
For this project, you'll need the following:

■ A cable or DSL router, with or without a built-in Ethernet switch

■ An Ethernet switch (if using a router without a switch), when you're ready to expand

- One CAT5 interconnect cable for connecting your broadband modem, plus one cable for each computer (length will vary)

- One Ethernet adapter for each computer (desktops and laptops)

- One Ethernet printer server for each printer to be directly networked (optional)

Configuration Overview

You can use a router with or without a switch for a single-user configuration, but remember that to create a LAN and share the Internet connection, you'll need a switch somewhere, either in the router or as an external switch connected to the router. Either way, the router and switch combination provide both the Ethernet LAN and Internet connection sharing functions. The router also includes a number of important network management functions that will be especially useful as other devices are added. In addition, most routers include extended security and firewall features to protect systems within the LAN. A simple, single-user scenario is depicted in Figure A-1.

All routers have two types of ports, usually labeled WAN and LAN. Home routers usually have just one WAN port, and it connects directly to the cable or DSL modem that delivers your high-speed service. One or more LAN ports connect to the rest of your network. For routers without an internal switch, a single LAN jack connects to an external switch.

You can connect any Ethernet-capable desktop or portable computer to your router or switch. On desktop machines, an internal Ethernet card usually provides this function. Laptop computers either have Ethernet built in or can easily accommodate it with the installation of an Ethernet adapter. It doesn't matter whether you're running Windows, Apple, or Linux systems (or any combination), but the systems themselves have to be properly configured to use Ethernet. Printers, too, can connect to the LAN via Ethernet so that they're always available to your other LAN systems.

Note

For more Ethernet LAN installation information, including details on how to run cables and install Ethernet cards, see Chapter 6.

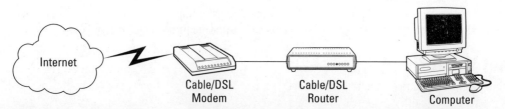

Figure A-1: Even a single-user configuration benefits from using a router's built-in security and network management functions. The configuration is then easily expanded when necessary to support more computers and/or wireless access.

Physical Layout and Connections

The basic setup for a single user is actually similar to that of the wired multiuser network configurations described in this appendix. The WAN side of the router connects directly to the DSL or cable modem with a standard RJ-45-terminated CAT5 cable. The cable/DSL modem and router can be in the same room, interconnected via a short CAT5 cable, or they can be located in two different parts of the house, as long as the distance between them doesn't exceed the 100-meter (about 300 feet) cable length limit.

LAN-side connections are made at the switch. On a router with a built-in switch, individual cables interconnect switch ports to each LAN client. With an external switch, there's one additional cable between the router and the switch, and then one cable between each LAN client and the switch. In the case of a single PC, you'll be running just one cable for the LAN side. Physical connections for the LAN are handled by the switch (internal or external), while the router itself handles traffic control, address translation, and IP addressing.

When you're ready to expand the network, note that the LAN generally supports as many Ethernet devices as there are connection jacks on the switch. For example, if your router has a built-in eight-port switch for LAN support, you can have any combination of eight Ethernet-capable computers and printers on the LAN. On the other hand, if you have a single-port router connected to an external eight-port hub or switch, you end up with only seven LAN-side connection points available on the hub; that's because one of the connections on the hub has to connect back to the router.

Each LAN client (a computer, Ethernet printer, and so on) connects via its own CAT5 Ethernet cable directly to a port on the Ethernet switch, also with a maximum cable length run of 100 meters (about 300 feet). Naturally, each computer and device to be connected to the LAN must have Ethernet capability. In the case of desktop computers, this usually means adding an internal Ethernet card. Many laptop computers are already equipped with an RJ-45 Ethernet jack. Those that don't have Ethernet built in can use a USB-to-Ethernet adapter (which would also work for any USB-equipped desktop) or a CardBus (or PC Card) Ethernet adapter.

A printer connected to a networked computer can be accessible to other computers on the network. However, note that sharing a printer this way requires that the computer to which it is connected be running. On the other hand, if a printer is directly connected to the LAN, it is always available to all your other systems. To be on the LAN, the printer must have its own Ethernet connection. Many newer printers have built-in Ethernet print servers. For printers that don't have it built in, a separate Ethernet printer server (basically, an Ethernet-to-printer port converter) supplies this function. Some printer servers can drive multiple printers, a handy feature if you have more than one printer to network.

Network Management, Software Configuration, and Security

After your computer is equipped with an Ethernet connection, you are ready to connect it to the Ethernet switch. Even if you're starting out with just one LAN client, it will need a unique identifier, which is assigned partly by the router and partly by you. Fortunately, routers have many built-in features to handle this part of network management and configuration for you.

Routers feature a DHCP server to automatically assign IP addresses and other network settings to clients as they connect to the LAN. The LAN client must run DHCP clients, but this is generally a one-time configuration that is very easy to set up (see Chapter 3 for a Windows example). Note that Ethernet-equipped peripherals like printers and print servers run DHCP clients by default and automatically receive network settings from the DHCP server upon connection to the LAN.

The router usually also functions as a DHCP client, in this case to negotiate settings between itself and your service provider's DHCP server. This is how the router receives its public IP address (the one that's visible to the outside world) and related service configuration settings.

That single public IP address obtained by the router is used only for external communication. All LAN traffic, on the other hand, uses a private network address, which the router does not pass to the outside world. The conversion between the two address types is done by Network Address Translation (NAT).

In doing this, NAT hides internal LAN addresses and provides a first line of defense. To the outside world, your networked systems are invisible; all traffic appears to originate from the router at the single, public IP address. Only the router knows how to direct traffic into and out of your network, and to the right LAN client internally. Your networked computers can access the outside world through the shared Internet connection, but people and other systems on the Internet can't initiate access to resources within the LAN. As a result, detection of the systems and capabilities within the LAN is very difficult.

Routers with built-in firewalls provide additional security for your LAN by filtering inbound and outbound data. All inbound traffic encounters the firewall first, and any data that does not meet specific security criteria is rejected. Data traffic is examined by means of a packet filter, a set of rules that determine what passes and what gets rejected. Outbound traffic is typically also checked, and some routers allow specific traffic types to be limited or completely disallowed, giving you a way to control the services (or times of day) during which certain functions (like gaming, for example) can take place.

Although the firewall is an important component of LAN security, note that a firewall alone won't protect you from everything and, in particular, cannot protect you against viruses spread through e-mail. For more-complete protection, you should consider running virus detection, software firewall, and spyware detection software on each computer.

For network and router management, most routers include a Web server that is accessible from any of the systems on the LAN. (Older routers are also remotely managed, but may not include a Web interface.) To access router controls, simply open a browser window at one of the systems and connect to the router at a specific network address or URL.

Ethernet LAN with Router/Gateway

Are there are multiple computers in your home, but only one that's connected to your high-speed cable or DSL Internet service? Do you sometimes bring your laptop home from work but have to steal the printer away from the family PC to print an important document? If any of this sounds familiar, you need to set up a LAN with the ability to share the Internet connection and other resources among all your computers' devices.

What You'll Need

For this LAN you'll need the following:

- A cable or DSL router, with or without a built-in Ethernet switch

- An Ethernet switch (if you are using a router without a switch)

- One CAT5 interconnect cable for each connection (length will vary)

- One Ethernet adapter for each computer (desktops and laptops), either internal or external

- One Ethernet printer server for each printer to be directly networked (optional)

Configuration Overview

The router provides the basis for both an Ethernet LAN and Internet connection sharing. You can think of your router as a one-to-many distribution center for your Internet connection that also supplies a number of important network management functions. Many routers also include extended security and firewall features to protect systems within the LAN. Typical router-based LANs with Internet connections are shown in Figures A-2 and A-3.

All routers have two types of ports, usually labeled WAN and LAN. A home router will usually have just one WAN port. It connects directly to the cable or DSL modem that delivers your high-speed service. One or more LAN ports connect to the rest of the network.

Note

Some manufacturers offer routers with Ethernet and serial (RS-232) WAN ports. These routers normally operate with a cable or DSL modem connected to the Ethernet WAN port as the primary connection, and a dial-up modem connected to the serial WAN port as a back-up connection. It is possible to use these routers with a dial-up modem as the only WAN connection.

The router in Figure A-2 includes a multiport Ethernet hub or switch that provides connection points for your Ethernet computers, printers, print servers, and other devices. For routers that don't have multiple LAN-side ports, an external hub or switch serves the same function, as in Figure A-3.

You can connect any Ethernet-capable desktop or portable computer to your network. On desktop machines, an internal Ethernet card usually provides this function. Laptop computers either have Ethernet built in or can easily accommodate it with the installation of an Ethernet adapter. It doesn't matter whether you're running Windows, Apple, or Linux systems (or any combination), but the systems themselves have to be properly configured to use Ethernet. Printers, too, can connect directly to the network via Ethernet so that they're always available to your networked systems.

Cross-Reference

For more Ethernet LAN installation information, including details on how to run cables and install Ethernet cards, see Chapter 6.

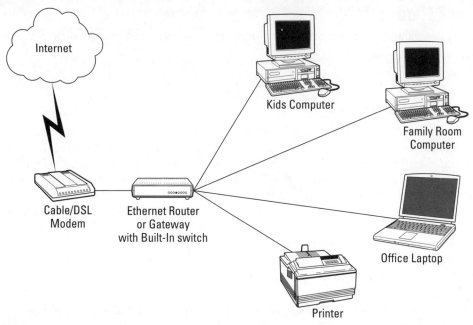

Figure A-2: A router-based Ethernet LAN in which the router itself provides multiple Ethernet jacks for direct connection to desktops, laptops, and other Ethernet-ready devices.

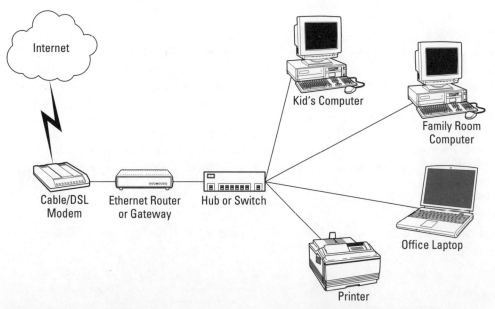

Figure A-3: If the router doesn't have a built-in hub or switch, a separate hub or switch can be used to create the LAN. Ethernet-equipped computers and other devices then connect to this device.

Physical Layout and Connections

The two scenarios shown here are functionally equivalent but differ in the location of the hub or switch. The router in Figure A-2 includes a multiport switch, and all LAN clients connect directly to the router. The single-port Ethernet router of Figure A-3, on the other hand, requires an external switch for connection to the LAN. Physical connections for the LAN are handled by the switch (internal or external), while the router itself handles traffic control, address translation, and IP addressing.

The WAN side of the router connects directly to the DSL or cable modem with a standard RJ-45-terminated CAT5 cable. The router and cable/DSL modem can be in the same room, interconnected via a short CAT5 cable, or they can be located in two different parts of the house, as long as the distance between them doesn't exceed Ethernet's 100-meter (about 300 feet) cable length limit. A router using an external switch (or hub) needs another CAT5 cable to connect its LAN connector to the switch.

In general, the LAN supports as many Ethernet devices as there are connection jacks on the switch or hub. For example, if your router has a built-in eight-port switch for LAN support, you can have any combination of eight Ethernet-capable computers and printers on the LAN. On the other hand, if you have a single-port router connected to an external eight-port hub or switch, you end up with only seven LAN-side connection points available on the hub; that's because one of the connections on the hub has to connect back to the router.

Each LAN client (a computer, Ethernet printer, and so on) connects via its own CAT5 Ethernet cable directly to a port on the Ethernet switch, also with a maximum cable length run of 100 meters (about 300 feet). Naturally, each computer and device to be connected to the LAN must have Ethernet capability. In the case of desktop computers, this usually means adding an internal Ethernet card. Many laptop computers are already equipped with an RJ-45 Ethernet jack. Those that don't have a built-in adapter can use a USB-to-Ethernet adapter (which would also work for any USB-equipped desktop), or a PC Card or CardBus Ethernet adapter.

A printer connected to one of your networked computers can be accessible to other computers on the network; however, note that sharing a printer this way requires that the computer to which it is connected be running. On the other hand, if a printer is directly connected to the LAN, it is always available to all your systems. To be on the LAN, the printer must have its own Ethernet connection. Many newer printers have built-in Ethernet print servers. For printers that don't have it built in, a separate Ethernet printer server (basically, an Ethernet-to-printer port converter) supplies this function. Some printer servers can drive multiple printers, a handy feature if you have more than one printer to network.

Network Management, Software Configuration, and Security

Once each device to be networked is equipped with Ethernet and connected to the network, you're ready to configure everything. Each device will require a unique identifier, which is assigned partly by the router and partly by you. Fortunately, routers have many built-in features to handle this part of network management and configuration for you.

Routers feature a DHCP server, which automatically assigns IP addresses and other network settings to clients as they connect to the LAN. Each of the networked devices must run DHCP clients, but this is generally a one-time setting that is very easy to configure (see Chapter 3 for a Windows example). Ethernet-equipped peripherals like printers and print servers run DHCP clients by default and are automatically configured for your network settings upon connection to the LAN.

The router usually also functions as a DHCP client, in this case to negotiate settings between itself and your service provider's DHCP server. This is how the router receives its public IP address (the one that's visible to the outside world) and related service configuration settings.

That single public IP address obtained by the router is shared by all of the LAN-side systems. The Internet connection is shared through Network Address Translation (NAT), a scheme to translate traffic between *private* LAN addresses and the one public address that represents your connection to the Internet.

By hiding private addresses, NAT provides a first line of defense for your LAN. To the outside world, your networked systems are invisible; all traffic appears to originate from the router at the single public IP address. Only the router knows how to direct traffic into and out of your network, and detection of the systems and capabilities within the LAN is very difficult as a result. The computers on your LAN can access the outside world through the shared Internet connection, but people and other systems on the Internet can't initiate access to the resources within the LAN.

Routers with built-in firewalls provide additional LAN security by filtering all data traffic that flows between your network and the outside world. Inbound traffic encounters the firewall first and is examined, and any data that does not meet specific security criteria is rejected. The traffic is examined by means of a packet filter, a set of rules that determine what passes and what gets rejected. Outbound traffic is typically also checked, and some routers allow specific traffic types to be limited or completely disallowed, giving you a way to control the services (or times of day) during which certain functions (like gaming, for example) can take place. Filtering criteria is typically determined through router configuration.

Although the firewall is an important component of LAN security, note that a firewall alone won't protect you from everything and, in particular, cannot protect you against viruses spread through e-mail. For more-complete protection, you should consider running virus detection and security software on each computer. (See Chapter 13 for more details on security features.)

For network and router management, most routers include a Web server that is accessible from any of the systems on the LAN. (Older routers are also remotely managed but may not include a Web interface.) To access router controls, you simply start a browser window at one of the systems and connect to the router at a specific network address or URL.

Ethernet LAN with Internet Connection Sharing (ICS)

If you have at least one computer running Microsoft Windows, you may be able use it to set up an Ethernet LAN and share your Internet connection, without installing a router. Microsoft Windows 98 Second Edition, Windows Me, Windows 2000, and Windows XP include Internet Connection Sharing, or ICS, a feature that allows you to use one computer to share an Internet connection among others within your LAN. The computer that runs ICS becomes your network gateway and essentially performs the same function as the router in other configurations.

What You'll Need

For this LAN, you'll need the following:

- One computer equipped with two Ethernet cards to function as the ICS system

- An Ethernet switch for interconnecting other computers and networked peripherals

- One CAT5 interconnect cable for each connection (length will vary)

- One Ethernet adapter for each networked computer (desktops and laptops)

- One Ethernet printer server for each printer to be directly networked (optional)

Configuration Overview

The ICS gateway machine is the point through which data passes between your LAN and the Internet. To do this, the gateway machine uses two Ethernet cards, one to connect to the cable or DSL modem, and the other to connect to either another Ethernet-enabled PC or to an Ethernet LAN.

A connection to a single PC, as shown in Figure A-4, is a simple scenario, but it's also the most limited because it doesn't allow for adding other computers or Ethernet-enabled peripherals. But if you have just two computers, this may be the least-expensive connection-sharing configuration (although you'll still need to get a second Ethernet card for one of the systems). If you start with this, you can always expand later by adding a hub or switch. Note that the second machine (the one labeled Desktop) need not be a desktop. It can be any Ethernet-equipped device, like a laptop system.

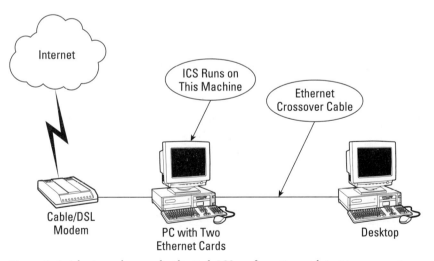

Figure A-4: A basic, and somewhat limited, ICS configuration with just two computers sharing the Internet connection.

The second configuration, shown in Figure A-5, is far more flexible. By connecting the ICS machine to a relatively inexpensive Ethernet switch, you have a LAN that can support as many Ethernet devices as you have connections on the switch. You could even add a wireless access point to the network to support laptops and other mobile devices. In either configuration, your networked computers will have full access to the Internet, and to each other, if you like, for sharing printers and other resources.

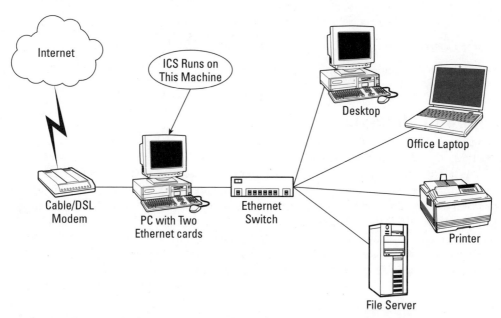

Figure A-5: This more flexible configuration adds an Ethernet switch to which many other computers and devices can be connected.

One particular advantage of ICS is that it can also share dial-up Internet connections over a standard modem. This is very useful if you can't get DSL or cable modem service where you live, or as an occasional backup for when your high-speed, always-on connection is down. Your Ethernet LAN configuration need not change in this case, but the system running ICS and some of the other systems' settings may need to be reconfigured when you switch between always-on and dial-up service.

By the way, the system running ICS need not be the latest-and-greatest PC. If the system is dedicated to this task, an older Windows machine you might not otherwise use (because it's slower, has a small hard disk, or has a limited memory capacity) can serve a very useful role as an Internet connection sharing gateway. However, it is vitally important to keep the gateway PC updated with the latest security patches. It's also a good idea to use the Windows XP firewall software (included in Windows XP Service Pack 2) on each of the client PCs.

Cross-Reference

For Ethernet LAN installation information, including details on how to run cables and install Ethernet adapters, refer to Chapter 6. For information on installing ICS, refer to Chapter 8.

Physical Layout and Connections

Whether you run the bare-bones setup shown in Figure A-4 or the more typical LAN configuration of Figure A-5, these two ICS configurations are pretty much equivalent with respect to the gateway machine.

The gateway is equipped with two Ethernet cards—one for the WAN connection and the other for the LAN. Windows categorizes the cards according to function in its list of network devices. The Ethernet card connected to the cable/DSL modem is called the TCP/IP(Shared) adapter, and the card connected to your Ethernet LAN is the TCP/IP(Home) adapter.

With respect to cabling, the simple ICS scenario depicted here requires a special CAT5 *crossover* Ethernet cable to interconnect the ICS system and the second PC. A crossover cable is needed when any combination of two PCs or other Ethernet devices are directly connected (though that's rarely the case). The more common and recommended method, even for a two-system LAN, uses an Ethernet hub or switch to interconnect all devices on the LAN. A standard CAT5 Ethernet cable then connects each device directly to the hub.

Network Management, Software Configuration, and Security

The service-side, or TCP/IP(Shared), Ethernet adapter is configured with the service connection information given by the cable or DSL service provider. This includes the IP address (unless the IP address is dynamically assigned) and other details specific to the service type. The LAN-side, or TCP/IP(Home), adapter is automatically configured by Windows as the gateway for all the devices connected to your Ethernet LAN.

On your LAN, Ethernet devices can use either fixed or dynamic IP addressing. If you have multiple devices on your LAN, it's best to use dynamic IP address assignment. Like routers, ICS includes a DHCP server for this purpose, and the server automatically assigns addresses to devices as they are added to the network. It also automatically releases the addresses when a device is turned off or disconnected.

Note, however, that even if you run ICS with DHCP, there is always one fixed address on the network. Because it functions as the gateway for all your LAN clients, the ICS system's LAN-side card must have a fixed IP address. The default address is 192.168.0.1. Other LAN-side systems are then assigned addresses within the 192.168.0.x range.

If your LAN computers were previously configured to use fixed IP addresses, you will need to configure each of your LAN clients to use DHCP automatic IP addressing. On Windows and most other operating systems, this is easy to do and is usually just a matter of selecting the appropriate option in a dialog (see Chapter 3 for a Windows example). Ethernet-equipped peripherals like printers and Ethernet print servers have built-in DHCP clients that automatically get network and configuration information from the DHCP server in the ICS system.

The core of ICS is Network Address Translation (NAT). NAT translates the *private* addresses of each LAN client into the single *public* address that represents the entire private network. To the outside world, private network elements are invisible and appear to be processes within the gateway machine. That is, all traffic appears to originate from the single service-provider-supplied IP address. Detection of the systems and capabilities on the LAN is very difficult as a result. Computers on the LAN can access the Internet, but people and other systems on the Internet can't directly access the computers within the LAN.

There's one important difference between ICS and the router-based configurations described in this appendix. Because the ICS system functions as your router, it means that this system is always directly exposed to the Internet. The Ethernet card connected to the cable or DSL modem has to use a public IP address, and this makes the ICS system especially vulnerable to attack. (The other Ethernet card, the one that's connected to your LAN, uses a private IP address.) But that's essentially the same situation as for any single PC connected to an always-on service. Just as in that case, it's essential to run firewall and antivirus software on the ICS PC to protect against tampering and unauthorized access. Windows XP includes a built-in firewall for this purpose, but you'll need to provide your own antivirus software.

Other Considerations

Note that for the Ethernet LAN to work and for devices to have access to the Internet connection, the gateway system has to be on and running ICS. Without ICS, there's no connection sharing, no way for the networked devices to get IP address assignments, and, basically, no LAN. Also, when the ICS machine is rebooting or otherwise not running Windows, ICS will not be available and the shared Internet connection will not work. If the ICS server goes down for a long period of time, the DHCP addresses originally assigned by the ICS server will expire, leaving the client PCs without a valid IP address.

The ICS software places only a minimal workload on the host computer, so the ICS host computer can still be used for other tasks, although I don't recommend it. Users should keep in mind that a very demanding application—like a graphics-intensive game program—running on the ICS host computer may temporarily slow Internet access for all the other computers on the LAN. Also, if an application program running on the ICS gateway crashes and requires a reboot, the shared Internet connection will not work until the ICS machine is rebooted.

Ethernet LAN with Separately Located Router and Modem

Most scenarios presented in this appendix assume that the cable or DSL modem and router are installed near each other, usually in the same room of your house. For example, the router and modem may be located in the mechanical room of your basement, your home "network operations center," from which the entire LAN is served. Or they may be both be in your family room or home office, wherever the service installer set up the connection for your cable or DSL service.

Sometimes the arrangement you have isn't desirable, especially since it requires running multiple cables, one from each LAN client back to the router (or router and switch combination, if your router doesn't have a built-in switch). If the router isn't centrally located, you may end up running a lot more cable and over greater distances. In other cases you may find that your cable or DSL modem connection is in an odd or difficult location that is inconvenient for you (and your router).

What You'll Need

For this LAN, you'll need the following:

- A cable or DSL router, with or without a built-in Ethernet switch
- An Ethernet switch (if using a router without a switch)

- One CAT5 interconnect cable for each connection (length will vary)

- One Ethernet adapter for each computer (desktops and laptops)

- One Ethernet printer server for each printer to be directly networked (optional)

Configuration Overview

There's no rule or requirement that says you have to keep your modem and router together. You could easily separate them by interconnecting them with long CAT5 cables. The maximum interconnecting cable length limit of 100 meters (about 300 feet) between Ethernet devices gives you a lot of placement flexibility for Ethernet devices.

Figure A-6 shows one possible setup in which the router is separated from the modem and moved closer to the systems on the LAN (on a separate floor from the modem, in this case). Because there can be about 300 feet of distance between the router and the modem, you could install the router one or two floors up from the modem location as necessary to accommodate the layout of the home and the location of the LAN clients.

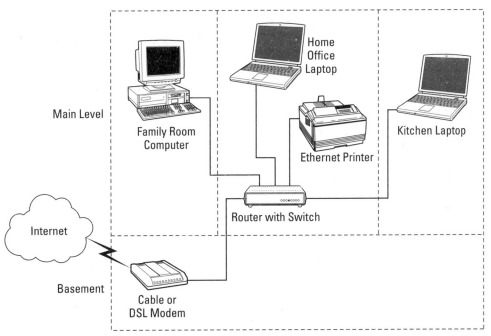

Figure A-6: The broadband modem and Ethernet router can be installed in separate parts of the house (in this example, the basement and main floor). You'll need a CAT5 cable between the floors, connecting the modem to the router. LAN clients connect to the router via its built-in switch.

Figure A-7 shows a similar approach but uses a separate Ethernet switch to serve the LAN on the main floor. This keeps the router in the basement, near the broadband modem, and may be a good approach if the router is already installed and you prefer not to move it.

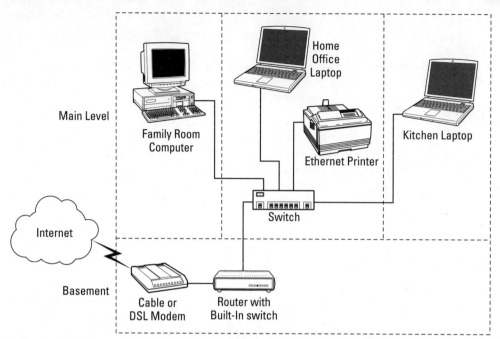

Figure A-7: Another option is to leave the router in the basement and use a separate switch to connect to the LAN.

If you're working with a two-story house and need to network systems on both floors, install the router on the main floor as in Figure A-6 to serve the main floor systems. Then, run another long CAT5 cable to a separate switch on the second floor to serve the systems there.

Any of these configurations are ideal if you need to serve separate LAN zones that are far apart, whether on different floors or in nonadjacent rooms on the same level.

Cross-Reference

For more Ethernet LAN installation information, including details on how to run cables and install Ethernet cards and network adapters, refer to Chapter 6.

Physical Layout and Connections

No matter which of these two scenarios you choose, there's going to be one fairly long connection after the cable or DSL modem. The router is either separately located (far from the modem but close to your networked devices), or the router is installed near the modem and an Ethernet switch is separately located.

Both are functionally equivalent; only the device to which the network devices connect varies. The router in Figure A-6 includes a multiport switch, and all LAN clients connect directly to the router's switch, via individual CAT5 cables. In Figure A-7, a long CAT5 cable interconnects the router to a separate switch. Physical connections for the LAN are handled by this switch, and each LAN client connects to it using an individual CAT5 cable. Either way, the router itself handles most of the traffic control, address translation, and IP addressing. (An external switch also does some network traffic control, but it's functionally no different from what happens within the built-on switch in a router.)

The WAN side of the router connects directly to the DSL or cable modem with a standard RJ-45-terminated CAT5 cable. This is the cable that can be up to about 300 feet long if you plan to use the router and modem in separate locations. If you're using an external switch, the long CAT5 cable is installed between the router and the switch.

With respect to how you run that long CAT5 cable, there are many choices. Of course, you want to have it end up in a location that's convenient for the router (or switch) with respect to your LAN clients. If most of the computers you use are in the same room (for example, a home office), you can probably just run the cable into that room. For the cleanest look, you should feed the cable through the floor below beneath a wall, up into the wall cavity, and into a wall box that's fitted with a CAT5, RJ-45 jack. During your quest to get the cable where you want it, you may be tempted to cut and splice the cable. Don't do it! A splice can ruin the electrical characteristics of the cable.

You could also consider running the cable right through the floor into the target room. In this case, it's best to carefully locate the corner of a closet in the target room, make a hole in the floor just big enough to fit the RJ-45 connector, and then carefully feed the cable through and connect it to your router or switch. (If any of this still seems like too much work or you're unsure about it, you can contact a local electrician, telephone, or cable TV installer for help. Or, you can consider going with one of the wireless configurations described in this appendix.)

Each LAN client (computer, Ethernet printer, and so on) connects directly to a port on the Ethernet switch via its own CAT5 Ethernet cable, also with a maximum cable length run of 100 meters (about 300 feet). Also, note that the LAN supports as many Ethernet devices as there are connection jacks on the switch or hub. For example, if your router has a built-in eight-port switch for LAN support, you can have any combination of eight Ethernet-capable computers and printers on the LAN. On the other hand, if you have a single-port router connected to an external eight-port hub or switch, you end up with only seven LAN-side connection points available on the hub; that's because one of the connections on the hub has to connect back to the router.

Each computer and device to be connected to the LAN must have Ethernet capability. In the case of desktop computers, this usually means adding an internal Ethernet card. Many laptop computers are already equipped with an RJ-45 Ethernet jack. Those that don't have it built in can probably use a USB-to-Ethernet adapter (which would also work for any USB-equipped desktop), or a PC Card or CardBus Ethernet adapter.

A printer connected to one of your networked computers can be accessible to other computers on the network; however, note that sharing a printer this way requires that the computer to which it is connected be running. On the other hand, if a printer is directly connected to the LAN, it is always available to all your other systems. To be on the LAN, the printer must have its own Ethernet connection. Many newer printers have built-in Ethernet print servers. For printers that don't have it built in, a separate Ethernet printer server (basically, an Ethernet-to-printer port converter) supplies this function. Some printer servers can drive multiple printers, a handy feature if you have more than one printer to network.

Network Management, Software Configuration, and Security

After each device on the LAN is equipped with its own Ethernet connection, you're ready to network. Each device will require a unique identifier, which is assigned partly by the router and partly by you. Fortunately, routers have many built-in features that automatically handle this part of network management and configuration for you.

Cross-Reference

Refer to Chapter 8 for more on setting up individual computers.

Routers feature a DHCP server to automatically assign IP addresses and other network settings to clients as they connect to the LAN. Each of the networked devices must run DHCP clients, but this is generally a one-time setting that is very easy to configure (see Chapter 3 for a Windows example). Most Ethernet-equipped peripherals like printers and print servers run DHCP clients by default, and the router automatically configures them for your network upon connection.

The router usually also functions as a DHCP client, in this case to negotiate settings between itself and your service provider's DHCP server. This is how the router receives its public IP address (the one that's visible to the outside world) and related service configuration settings.

That single public IP address obtained by the router is shared by all of the LAN-side systems. The Internet connection is shared through Network Address Translation (NAT), a scheme to translate traffic between *private* LAN client addresses and the one public address that represents your connection to the Internet.

By hiding private addresses, NAT provides a first line of defense for your LAN. To the outside world, the clients on your network are invisible and all traffic appears to originate from the router at the single public IP address. Private LAN-side addresses are never seen by the outside world. Only the router knows how to direct traffic into and out of your network, and detection of the systems and capabilities within the LAN is very difficult as a result. The result is that the computers on your LAN can access the outside world through the shared Internet connection, but people and other systems on the Internet can't initiate access resources within the LAN.

Routers with built-in firewalls provide additional security for your LAN by creating another level of separation between your network and the outside world. All inbound traffic encounters the firewall first, and any data that does not meet specific security criteria is rejected. Data traffic is examined by means of a packet filter, a set of rules that determine what passes and what gets rejected. Outbound traffic is typically also checked, and some routers allow specific traffic types to be limited or completely disallowed, giving you a way to control the services (or times of day) during which certain functions (like gaming, for example) can take place.

All-Wireless LAN with Router/Gateway

If you don't want to deal with running cables to each of your LAN clients, an all-wireless LAN is a great option. It gives you a lot of flexibility for computer placement and is quick and easy to install. If you have a laptop, it also means you can easily move from place to place while you use it. Want to look through recipe Web sites while you're in the kitchen? No problem. Want to read news online while enjoying your morning coffee in the family room? Just take the laptop with you. In many cases, you can even go out to the garden or sit on the porch while staying connected.

What You'll Need

For this LAN, you'll need the following:

- A cable or DSL router with a built-in 802.11 wireless access point (WAP)

- One 802.11 wireless adapter for each computer (desktops and laptops)

- One 802.11 wireless printer server for each printer to be directly networked (optional)

Configuration Overview

Wired networks have few specific requirements for where you place the router, switches, or even the broadband modem that delivers Internet service. A wireless network, on the other hand, can require a bit more planning. That's because the system operates best in a line-of-sight configuration between the access point and each of the LAN clients. In general, there needs to be a clear, unobstructed path between the transmitting and receiving antennas. Think of it as the antennas needing to "see" each other; if you can stand at the location of one antenna and see the other, then you're usually in good shape. The wireless signal can pass through walls and floors, but too many of either one will scatter the signal, resulting in a slow or unreliable connection.

Any desktop or notebook computer equipped with a wireless Ethernet adapter can be part of your wireless LAN and share the Internet connection through the router. Most desktop systems easily accommodate a wireless Ethernet card. Analogous to the cabled Ethernet card used for wired networks, wireless card installation is similar except that you'll likely end up with a small "whip" antenna protruding from the back of the chassis.

Laptop computers are even more easily set up for wireless, with a PC Card or CardBus adapter or a USB-to-wireless adapter (the latter also works for a USB-equipped desktop, by the way). Newer laptops may have wireless capability built in, so getting on the wireless LAN may be a matter of configuring for your particular wireless setting. An added benefit is that a laptop set up with wireless Ethernet will also work with the wireless "hotspots" springing up in public places like coffee shops, libraries, airports, and hotels.

Printers, personal digital assistants (PDAs), and other wireless-enabled devices can also connect to your wireless LAN. Printers that are not already wireless-ready are easily adapted with a wireless printer server. A printer may also be physically attached to and shared through a wirelessly networked laptop or desktop computer. Figure A-8 illustrates a wireless configuration.

Cross-Reference

For more on wireless LAN installation, including details on setting up the wireless network cards, see Chapter 7.

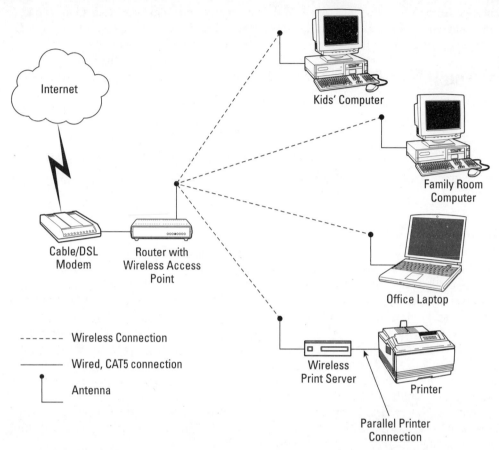

Figure A-8: This all-wireless LAN features a router with a built-in wireless access point. Each LAN client is wireless-enabled, including the printer (through an external, wireless print server).

Physical Layout and Connections

A wireless access point can be configured in multiple ways. These include setting it up as (1) the only AP on the network, (2) as a secondary access point on a multi-AP network, and (3) as one of two ends of a bridge to interconnect two wired network segments. This section covers the first configuration—a single wireless access point serving multiple wireless-enabled LAN clients: desktop and notebook computers, printers, and so forth.

Note

The type of wireless Ethernet network described here is called an *infrastructure* mode network because it uses an access point to connect wired and wireless clients into a single network. Another wireless network mode called *ad hoc* applies only to wireless Ethernet devices that communicate on a peer-to-peer level, without an access point in the network.

The ideal location for your wireless access point is at the center of the network, both vertically and horizontally. For best performance and good link quality, a clear line of sight to each of the clients is best. If one or more walls or floors stand between your LAN client and the WAP, you're likely to find link quality—and connection speed—substantially reduced, depending on just what sort of obstruction exists. This reduction in speed may not be a problem for casual use, but it's something to keep in mind for applications that need more bandwidth, like large file transfers.

That's not to say that your wireless connections won't work at all without a clear line of sight, but you'll have to experiment a bit to see if you can live with the resulting performance. Reflective surfaces within your home (the walls and ceilings, for example) alter the signals' direction of travel, and sometimes you can get a connection where you wouldn't expect to (or, you might not get a good connection where you thought you would!).

Cross-Reference

Chapter 7 includes a list of things to consider in deciding where to place your access point.

The distance between your wireless LAN device and the access point is another important performance factor. For best results indoors, you'll want each wireless LAN client to be within about 150 feet of the access point for 802.11b, 802.11g, and 802.11n. (Indoors, the 802.11b standard supports a maximum theoretical distance of 100 meters (about 300 feet) between devices. In practice, the effective range for best performance varies according to environmental factors and is usually less than 300 feet.) For 802.11a devices, the range is less, often under 100 feet. The practical working range for your situation depends on the specific conditions within your home, and you may have to experiment a bit to determine it. (If you discover that you need more coverage than you can get with a single access point, you can extend the range with additional units, as described in the *Expanded Wireless LAN* section of this appendix.)

With wired networks you don't usually have to worry about electrical or radio frequency interference, but this can be a big issue in some wireless networks. Most home-based wireless networks operate in the 2.4 GHz range, the same band as many other devices. Microwave ovens and 2.4 GHz cordless telephones are two such common household items. They can negatively affect your wireless network performance, though you shouldn't see change unless the devices are in use, close to your wireless LAN, or defective.

Note

Devices that use 802.11b and 802.11g (and the upcoming 802.11n standard) operate at 2.4 GHz. Devices using 802.11a operate in the 5 GHz band, where there are fewer competing wireless devices. Whether you choose a, b, or g, make sure everything on your network uses the same standard. Some newer access points and wireless Ethernet adapters support multiple standards and allow you to mix 802.11 device types; check your LAN hardware specifications for details.

To help assess your wireless network performance, wireless Ethernet adapters include a helpful software-based signal strength and link quality meter. It will tell you how well each LAN client is communicating with the WAP, and you can use it to experiment with wireless client (and WAP) placement. Moving the device just a few feet in one direction or another often makes a big difference toward resolving interference and signal strength problems.

The only wired connection you'll need to set up for your wireless network is between the router/WAP and your cable/DSL modem. A standard CAT5 Ethernet cable connects the router's WAN port to the modem. As for any wired Ethernet connection, you can use any cable length up to 100 meters (about 300 feet) between the router and the modem. This gives you a lot of flexibility in placing the WAP for optimum wireless network performance.

Network Management, Software Configuration, and Security

Each device to be networked requires a unique identifier. This is assigned partly by the router and partly by you. Fortunately, routers have many built-in features to handle this part of network management and configuration for you. The router's DHCP server automatically assigns IP addresses and other network settings to clients as they connect to the LAN. Each of the networked devices must run DHCP clients, but this is generally a one-time setting that is very easy to configure (Chapter 7 has wireless-specific setup details). Wireless Ethernet-equipped peripherals like printers and print servers run DHCP clients by default and in most cases are automatically configured for your network settings upon connection to the LAN.

Note

The extent of network autoconfiguration for any device will vary according to the specific WEP or WPA settings of your wireless LAN.

Note that the router usually also functions as a DHCP client, in this case to negotiate settings between itself and your service provider's DHCP server. This is how the router receives its public IP address (the one that's visible to the outside world) and related cable or DSL service configuration settings.

The public IP address is shared by all of the LAN-side systems through the router's implementation of Network Address Translation (NAT). This is the key standard for Internet connection sharing. It converts traffic between multiple *private* LAN-side IP addresses and the single public address that represents your connection to the Internet.

Network, router, and security management is done through the router's own Web server. This server is accessible from any Web browser window running on a LAN client. (Note that older router/wireless access point units are also remotely manageable but may not include a Web interface. Check the router's documentation for specific management details.)

GENERAL SECURITY FUNCTIONS

Besides allowing you to share a single public IP address among many private LAN addresses, NAT provides a first line of intrusion defense for your LAN. To the outside world, your networked systems are invisible; all traffic appears to originate from the router at the single public IP address. Only the router knows how to direct traffic into and out of your network, and detection of the systems and capabilities within the LAN is very difficult as a result. The computers on your LAN can access the outside world through the shared Internet connection, but people and other systems from outside can't initiate access to the resources within the LAN.

A firewall can provide additional security for your LAN. Routers with built-in firewalls provide additional LAN protection by filtering all the data traffic that flows between your network and the outside world. Inbound traffic encounters the firewall first and is examined, and any data that does not meet specific security criteria is rejected. Traffic is examined by means of a packet filter, a set of rules that determine what passes and what gets rejected. Outbound traffic is typically also checked, and some routers allow specific traffic types to be limited or completely disallowed, giving you a way to control the services (or times of day) during which certain activities (like gaming) can take place. Filtering criteria are configured through the router's configuration interface.

Note that while the firewall is an important component of LAN security, a firewall alone won't protect you from everything and, in particular, cannot protect you against viruses spread through e-mail. For more complete protection, you should consider running virus detection and security software on each computer.

WIRELESS SECURITY FUNCTIONS

The nature of wireless networks means they're very easy to find and are susceptible to unauthorized access attempts. For example, the WAP periodically sends "beacon" messages to announce itself to your potential network clients (your wireless Ethernet devices). If you leave your wireless network unprotected, it's open to unauthorized users who can easily detect the network and attempt to access and monopolize your Internet connection, or even tamper with your internal network resources. To prevent unauthorized access, WAPs include a number of security functions specifically for limiting access to your wireless network. These include the following:

- **Media Access Control (MAC) address filtering/authentication.**   A MAC address is a unique hardware-level identifier for each Ethernet device. By filtering out all other MAC addresses but those of your wireless network clients, only the Ethernet devices on your network are able to access its resources. The method isn't foolproof, as it's possible for a MAC address to be detected and hijacked, but address filtering is nonetheless a basic and important component of any security plan.

- **Wired Equivalent Privacy (WEP) data encryption.**   Designed to provide security similar to that of wired networks, WEP encrypts wireless data. Encryption comes in several strengths; 128-bit encryption is considered the most secure.

- **WiFi Protected Access (WPA).**   An enhanced security feature that uses a combination of user authentication (via a user name and password), as well as strong data encryption. WPA is found on many newer APs and was designed to address some security shortcomings in WEP.

There are several additional steps you can take to minimize unauthorized access, and all are configurable via the AP's Web interface. At a minimum, you should:

- **Frequently change the AP's administrator password.**   Because the administrator's password allows access to all wireless access point settings, its security is very important. Change it often and keep it in a safe place.

▦ **Change the default Service Set Identifier (SSID).** Your wireless access point is probably configured with a factory-set SSID. Change this to something unique as soon as possible after setting up the access point. And like the administrator password, you should change it often to maintain its security.

▦ **Disable SSID broadcasts.** By default, wireless access points broadcast the SSID setting for other wireless devices to pick up. This means, of course, that it's also likely to be picked up and used by unauthorized wireless users. Because you'll be setting up each wireless client with the SSID that you set up, there's no need to broadcast it.

▦ **Use WPA if your AP supports it.** WPA requires each wireless LAN user to have a unique user name and password and is the strongest security method available for wireless LANs.

▦ **Use your AP's logging feature.** Most APs can keep a log of wireless connections. You should enable the logging feature and check the log periodically to see if anyone has been trying to break into your wireless network,

▦ **Use multiple WEP keys, and change them periodically.** WEP (described in the previous list) uses a key to encrypt/decrypt your wireless data. To further increase your wireless security, most access points and wireless Ethernet cards allow you to specify multiple encryption keys. Note that there can be a performance trade-off when using multiple keys.

You can also increase wireless network security by making the network unavailable when you're not using it. Simply turn off or unplug the access point when it's not being used, such as when you're sleeping, at work, or on vacation. To make this easier, some newer APs include scheduling features in their Web interfaces. Older routers may need to be cycled the old-fashioned way[md]with the on/off switch or power cord.

Mixed Wired/Wireless LAN

Wired and wireless approaches to networking serve the needs of home users very well. But each has distinct advantages and disadvantages in performance, range, and ease of configuration. What if you could mix wired and wireless Ethernet networks for the best of both worlds? Fortunately, this is easy to do and offers the best coverage, performance, and flexibility.

What You'll Need

For this LAN, you'll need the following:

▦ A wireless Ethernet router with a built-in Ethernet switch

▦ One Ethernet adapter for each computer (desktop or laptop) to be wired to the LAN

▦ One CAT5 interconnect cable for each wired connection (length will vary)

▦ One wireless Ethernet adapter for each computer (desktop or laptop) to be wirelessly networked

- One wireless Ethernet print server for each printer to be wirelessly networked (optional)

- One Ethernet print server for each printer wired to the LAN (optional)

Configuration Overview

A combined wired/wireless network may seem much more complex in terms of arrangement and configuration, but it's really not. It's a good idea, however, to give some thought to how you'll arrange the systems on the LAN; some will perform better on the wired Ethernet side, and others will be more useful to you on the wireless side.

One important consideration is the potential difference in connection speed between the wired and wireless segments of your combined network. The wired segment is usually significantly faster than the wireless side, so you'll want to use the wired segment for LAN clients that need higher network performance, like a file server. Any other system that either shares or uses large files, like photos, MP3s, or MPG video, across the network will also perform better while connected to the wired part of your LAN. On the other hand, connection speed isn't everything. Placement flexibility and cable-free connection are big advantages for desktop computers in awkward locations and roaming laptops.

For both segments of your LAN, the router provides both the basis for the Ethernet LAN and Internet connection center. The router also supplies a number of important network management functions, and many include extended security and firewall features to protect LAN-side systems against intrusion. Figure A-9 shows a typical combined wired plus wireless LAN configuration that supports a file server, a shared Ethernet printer, multiple laptops, and desktop systems.

Any Ethernet-equipped desktop or portable computer can connect to your network. On desktop machines, an internal Ethernet card (either wired or wireless) usually provides this function. Laptop computers either have Ethernet built in or can easily accommodate it with the installation of an Ethernet adapter. It doesn't matter whether you're running Windows, Apple, or Linux systems (or any combination), but the systems themselves have to be properly configured to use Ethernet. Printers, too, can connect directly to the network via Ethernet so that they're always available to the network.

For best support of wireless LAN clients, a bit of experimentation with your wireless router may be in order. The system operates best using a line-of-sight configuration and a clear, unobstructed path between the router and your wireless LAN clients. Think of it as the antennas needing to "see" each other; if you can stand at the location of the wireless router and see the antenna of each of your wireless clients, you're probably in good shape.

Any desktop or notebook computer equipped with a wireless Ethernet adapter can be part of your wireless LAN. Most desktop systems easily accommodate a wireless Ethernet card. Laptops are even more easily set up for wireless, usually with a PC Card or CardBus adapter or a USB-to-wireless adapter (the latter also works for a USB-equipped desktop, by the way). Newer laptops may have wireless capability built in, so getting on the wireless LAN may be an even simpler matter of changing a few configuration settings.

Printers, PDAs, and other wireless-enabled devices can also connect to your wireless LAN. Printers that are not already wireless-ready are easily adapted with a wireless printer server. A printer may also be physically attached to and shared through a wirelessly networked laptop or desktop computer.

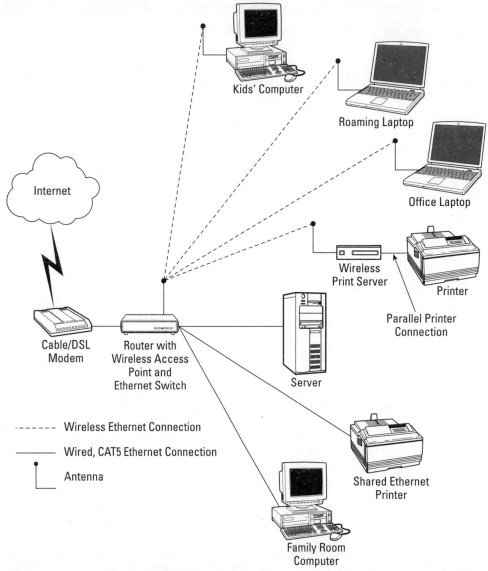

Figure A-9: A mixed wired/wireless LAN provides the best of both worlds: high-speed access for file servers and other devices that work best wired to the LAN, and wireless access for portables and other clients that are hard to reach with a cabled connection.

Cross-Reference

Chapter 6 contains more-detailed information on installing the wired portion of a network. For wireless LAN installation details, including how to set up wireless network cards, see Chapter 7.

Wired Segment—Physical Layout and Connections

The WAN side of the router connects directly to your DSL or cable modem with a standard CAT5 cable. The router and cable/DSL modem can be in the same room, interconnected via a short CAT5 cable, or they can be located in two different parts of the house, as long as the distance between them doesn't exceed the 100-meter (about 300 feet) cable length limit. A router using an external switch (or hub) needs another CAT5 cable to connect its LAN connector to the switch.

Most "wireless" routers, like the one depicted in Figure A-9, actually support both wired and wireless connections. The wired side is supported with a multiport Ethernet switch through which wired LAN clients connect. In general, the switch connects to as many Ethernet devices as it has jacks. For example, if your router has a built-in eight-port switch for LAN support, you can have any combination of eight Ethernet-capable computers and printers on the wired LAN segment. (If your wireless router doesn't include a switch but has a single Ethernet jack, you can connect this jack to an external Ethernet switch to provide the same function.)

Each LAN client (a computer, Ethernet printer, and so on) connects via its own CAT5 Ethernet cable directly to a port on the Ethernet switch, also with a maximum cable length run of 100 meters (about 300 feet). Naturally, each computer and device to be connected to the LAN must have Ethernet capability. In the case of desktop computers, this usually means adding an internal Ethernet card. Many laptop computers are already equipped with an RJ-45 Ethernet jack. Those that don't have Ethernet capability built in can use a USB-to-Ethernet adapter (which would also work for any USB-equipped desktop), or a PC Card or CardBus Ethernet adapter.

A printer connected to one of your networked computers can be shared and made available to other computers on the network; however, note that sharing a printer this way requires that the computer to which it is connected be running. On the other hand, if a printer is directly connected to the LAN, it is always available to all your other systems. To be directly attached to the LAN, the printer must have its own Ethernet connection. Many newer printers have built-in Ethernet print servers. For printers that don't have it built in, a separate Ethernet printer server (basically, an Ethernet-to-printer port converter) supplies this function. Some printer servers can drive multiple printers, a handy feature if you have more than one printer to network.

Wireless Segment—Physical Layout and Connections

The wireless access point (WAP) or your wireless router serves all your wireless-enabled LAN clients: desktop and notebook computers, printers, and so on. As described and configured here, you'll be running your wireless LAN in *infrastructure* mode. (Another wireless network mode called *ad hoc* applies only to wireless Ethernet devices that communicate on a peer-to-peer level, without an access point in the network, and is not covered in this appendix.)

You can use a long CAT5 cable to connect the router to your cable or DSL modem, so you have a good bit of flexibility in terms of wireless router placement. As for any wired Ethernet connection, you can use any cable length up to 100 meters (about 300 feet) between the router and the modem.

For the best wireless LAN performance, the ideal location for the wireless router is at the center of the network, with clear line of sight to each of the wireless clients, if possible. In the case of one or more walls between your LAN client and the router, you're likely to find signal strength—and link quality—substantially reduced, depending on the construction materials used and related factors. Reduced link quality may not be a problem for casual use, but it's something to keep in mind for applications that need higher throughput, like large file transfers.

You may have to experiment to find the best location for your wireless router. Keep in mind that reflective surfaces within your home (the walls and ceilings, for example) can alter the signals' direction of travel, and you can sometimes get a connection where you wouldn't expect to (or, you might not get a good connection where you thought you would!).

The distance between each wireless LAN device and the access point is another important performance factor. For best results indoors, you'll want each wireless client to be within about 150 feet of the access point for 802.11b and 802.11g. (Indoors, the 802.11b standard supports a maximum theoretical distance of 100 meters, or about 300 feet, between devices. In practice, the effective range for best performance varies and is usually less than 300 feet.) For 802.11a devices, the range is less, often under 100 feet. The practical working range for your situation depends on the specific conditions within your home, and you may have to find it by trial and error. (If you discover that you need more coverage than you can get with a single access point, you can extend the range with additional units, as described in the *Expanded Wireless LAN* section of this appendix.)

With wired networks you don't usually have to worry about electrical or radio frequency interference, but this can be a big issue in some wireless networks because most wireless networks operate in the 2.4 GHz range. This is the same band used by many other devices, including microwave ovens and 2.4 GHz cordless telephones. Interference can impact your wireless network performance, but you probably won't see degradation unless the devices are in use, close to your wireless LAN, or defective.

Note

Devices that use 802.11b, 802.11g, and 802.11n operate at 2.4 GHz. Devices using 802.11a operate in the 5 GHz band, where there are fewer competing wireless devices. Whether you choose a, b, or g, make sure everything on your network uses the same standard. (Some newer access points and wireless Ethernet adapters support multiple standards and allow you to mix 802.11 device types; check your LAN hardware specifications for details.)

To help assess the wireless network's performance, the wireless Ethernet adapters you install in your laptops and desktops include a helpful software-based signal strength and link quality meter. It tells you how well each LAN client is communicating with the WAP, and you can use it to experiment with wireless client (and WAP) placement. Sometimes, moving the device a few feet (perhaps just inches) in one direction or another makes a big difference.

Network Management, Software Configuration, and Security

Each device to be networked requires a unique identifier. This is assigned partly by the router and partly by you. Fortunately, routers handle much of this part of network management and configuration for you. The router's DHCP server automatically assigns IP addresses and other network settings as clients connect to the LAN. Each of the networked devices must run DHCP clients, but this is generally a one-time setting that is very easy to configure (Chapter 7 has wireless-specific setup details). Wireless Ethernet-equipped peripherals like printers and print servers run DHCP clients by default and in most cases are automatically configured for your network settings upon connection to the LAN. (The extent of network autoconfiguration for any device will vary according to the specific security settings of your wireless LAN.)

Note that the router usually also functions as a DHCP client, in this case to negotiate settings between itself and your service provider's DHCP server. This is how the router receives its public IP address (the one that's visible to the outside world) and other Internet service configuration settings.

The public IP address is shared by all of the LAN-side systems through the router's implementation of Network Address Translation (NAT). This is the key standard for Internet connection sharing, and it's the same address sharing technique used in many business routers. NAT converts network traffic between multiple *private* LAN-side IP addresses and the single public address that represents your connection to the Internet.

Network, router, and security management is done through the router's own Web server. This server is accessible from any Web browser window running on a LAN client, though many settings are best modified through a wired network client. (Note that older router/wireless access point units are also remotely manageable but may not include a Web interface. Check the router's documentation for specific management details.)

GENERAL SECURITY FUNCTIONS

Besides allowing you to share a single public IP address among many private LAN addresses, NAT provides a first line of intrusion defense for your LAN. To the outside world, LAN-side systems are invisible, and all traffic appears to originate from the router at its public IP address. Only the router knows how to direct traffic into and out of your network, and detection of the systems and capabilities within the LAN is very difficult as a result. The computers on your LAN can access the outside world through the shared Internet connection, but people and other systems from outside can't initiate access to the resources within the LAN.

Most wireless routers provide additional LAN security with a firewall, which is special software that filters data traffic flow between your network and the outside world. Inbound traffic encounters the firewall first and is examined, and any data that does not meet specific security criteria is rejected. Traffic is examined by means of a packet filter, a set of rules that determine what passes and what gets rejected. Outbound traffic is typically also checked, and some routers allow specific traffic types to be limited or completely disallowed, giving you a way to control the services (or times of day) during which certain activities (like gaming) can take place. Filtering criteria are configured through the router's configuration interface.

Note that while the firewall is an important component of LAN security, a firewall alone won't protect you from everything and, in particular, cannot protect you against viruses spread through e-mail. For better protection, you should consider running virus detection and security software on each computer.

WIRELESS SECURITY FUNCTIONS

The nature of wireless networks means they're easy to find and highly susceptible to tampering. If you leave the wireless section of your network unprotected, it's wide open to unauthorized users who can easily detect the network and attempt to access (or monopolize) your Internet connection, or even tamper with your internal network resources. To prevent unauthorized access, WAPs have a number of security functions specifically aimed at protecting your network. These can include the following:

▪ **Media Access Control (MAC) address filtering.**   A MAC address is a unique hardware-level identifier for each Ethernet device. By filtering out all other MAC addresses but those of your wireless network clients, only the Ethernet devices on your network are able to access its resources. The method isn't foolproof, as it's possible for a MAC address to be detected and hijacked, but address filtering is nonetheless a basic and important component of any security plan.

▪ **Wired Equivalent Privacy (WEP) data encryption.**   Designed to provide security similar to that of wired networks, WEP encrypts wireless data. Encryption comes in several strengths; 128-bit encryption is considered the most secure. Use the highest encryption level possible, but keep in mind that encryption slows network performance; the higher the encryption, the greater the impact on performance.

There are also several things you can do to minimize unauthorized access, and all are configurable via the WAP's Web interface. At a minimum, you should:

▪ **Frequently change the WAP administrator password.**   The administrator's password allows access to all wireless access point settings, and keeping it secure is highly important. Change it often and keep it in a safe place.

▪ **Change the default Service Set Identifier (SSID).**   Your wireless access point is probably configured with a factory-set SSID. Change this to something unique as soon as possible after setting up the access point. As for the administrator password, you should change it often to keep it secure.

▪ **Disable SSID broadcasts.**   By default, wireless access points broadcast the SSID setting for other wireless LAN devices to pick up. This means, of course, that it's also likely to be picked up and used by unauthorized users. Because you'll be setting up each wireless client with the SSID that you set up, there's no need to broadcast it.

▪ **Use WPA if your AP supports it.**   WPA requires each wireless LAN user to have a unique user name and password and is the strongest security method available for wireless LANs.

▪ **Use your AP's logging feature.**   Most APs can keep a log of wireless connections. You should enable the logging feature and check the log periodically to see if anyone has been trying to break into your wireless network,

▪ **Use multiple WEP keys, and change them periodically.**   WEP (described in the previous list) uses a key to encrypt/decrypt your wireless data. To further increase your wireless security, most access points and wireless Ethernet cards allow you to specify multiple encryption keys. (Note that there can be a performance trade-off when using multiple keys.)

Note that you can increase security by turning off the wireless access point when you're not using it: when you're sleeping, at work, out fishing, or on vacation. To make this easier, newer access points include scheduling features that are accessible through the Web configuration interface. Older routers may need to be cycled the old-fashioned way: with the on/off switch.

Expanded LAN with Two (or More) Ethernet Switches

If you have a wired Ethernet LAN, you probably have at least one Ethernet switch, either built into the router or serving as a standalone unit. And if you have just one switch, you're probably also either out of connections or getting close to using them all. Adding switches to your network is the easiest way to support additional LAN clients and to segment it into "zones" for better performance.

What You'll Need

To expand an existing wired network, you'll need the following:

- One or more Ethernet switches, depending on your expansion needs
- One CAT5 interconnect cable for each new connection (length will vary)
- One Ethernet adapter for each new computer to be networked (desktops and laptops)
- One Ethernet print server for each new printer to be directly networked (optional)

If you're just getting started with your wired home network, refer to the first section of this appendix for basic cabling and configuration information.

Configuration Overview

The arrangement of a switch-expanded network is fundamentally the same as that of any basic wired home Ethernet network. The cable/DSL router remains the central control point for Internet connection sharing, network configuration, security, and management for the entire network.

The problem with a single-switch LAN, whether part of the router or standalone, is that you very quickly run out of connections. If fact, any but the smallest of home networks quickly exhausts the connection capacity on a small switch, especially because most routers' built-in switches have only four Ethernet ports. A switch-expanded LAN enables you to segment the network into convenient or logical sections with more flexible connection options as shown in Figure A-10.

Physical Layout and Connections

If there are no more available connections at your main Ethernet switch, adding another switch at the same location is the easiest way to expand network connection capacity. In this case, one of the ports on the new switch connects to the main switch through its uplink port (on some switches you have to select the uplink function by pressing a switch), which allows you to user a straight-through Ethernet cable for the connection. The remaining switch ports are then available for connection to devices that await connection to the LAN.

Note that, as for any wired Ethernet connection, you can have up to 100 meters (about 300 feet) between Ethernet devices. This means that the switch you add to your network need not be near (or in the same room with) your router. If it's more convenient, you can place the new switch in another area of the house, like on another floor.

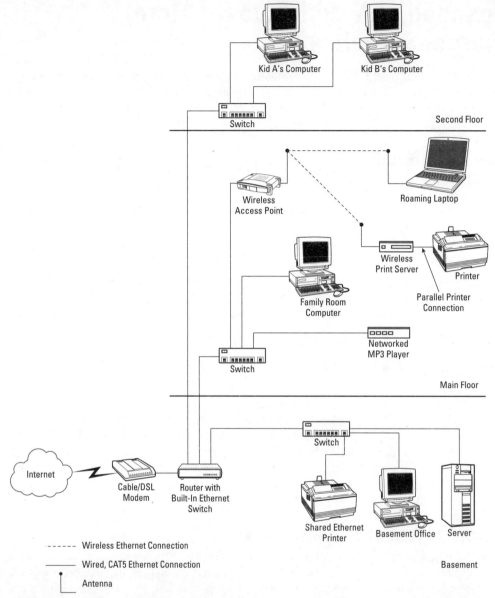

Figure A-10: A LAN expanded with one or more Ethernet switches offers a lot of connection capacity. This example uses one switch per floor. A wireless access point connected to the main floor switch serves wireless clients there.

Ethernet switches provide a good way to segment network traffic according to function or coverage area. For example, say you live in a two-story house with a basement and need LAN access on each floor. You could place your cable/DSL router with built-in four-port switch in the basement and then connect the router's switch to another switch on the main floor and a second switch on the second floor. This example uses two of the routers' four ports for switch connections on the other floors, and two left over for connection to LAN clients (or even other switches) in the basement (see Figure A-10).

Note that you can connect any type of Ethernet LAN client to any of the switches: desktop and notebook computers, Ethernet-equipped printers, print servers, and so on. If you want to set up wireless access in your home, you can connect a wireless access point (WAP) to any of the switches. Note, for example, that Figure A-10 also shows a WAP connected to the switch serving the main floor.

Switches are available in a variety of sizes, from small four- and five-port switches to models that support 24 or more connections. As a rule of thumb, always choose a switch with more connection capacity than you think you might need. That is, don't cut your connection needs too close; if you think you'll need to serve four LAN clients in a particular area of the house, use an eight-port switch to serve it. The larger switch may cost a bit more, but having the extra capacity more than pays for itself later on.

Network Management, Software Configuration, and Security

Switches are available in a variety of sizes and configurations. You may also encounter the terms *managed* or *unmanaged* when shopping for a switch. Managed switches are for much larger and complex commercial networks. A residential-grade switch, on the other hand, is unmanaged, meaning it requires no configuration. From the point of view of the other elements in your network, like your cable/DSL router and LAN clients, the Ethernet switches are essentially "transparent," self-configuring traffic directors.

The basic network management, software configuration, and security functions for your switch-expanded network continue to be handled by the cable/DSL router that enables Internet connection sharing. To summarize, the router's LAN management and security features include the following:

- **A DHCP server.**   For automatic network configuration of LAN clients, including IP address assignment.

- **Network Address Translation (NAT).**   The standard for sharing a single Internet connection among all the computers on your LAN.

- **Firewall functionality.**   For protecting the LAN against intrusion from the outside. The firewall may also include traffic control capability in which some traffic types can be completely disallowed.

- **A built-in Web server.**   For checking or modifying router configuration settings (like NAT, DHCP, and firewall,) from any client on the LAN.

For full details on router management features, refer to the *Ethernet LAN with Router/Gateway* section at the beginning of this appendix and to Chapter 3.

Expanded Wireless LAN

A wireless LAN has many advantages: You don't have to run cables, it's easy to configure, and you can roam about the house with while staying online through your laptop. But there are limits to the range of a basic, single wireless access point LAN. Physical obstructions, distance, and even the characteristics of the spaces between a client and the access point can directly affect the quality of a wireless connection. You may find, for example, that the main floor of a two-story house gets good coverage, while access from upstairs is spotty or completely unavailable. Fortunately, extending coverage is easy and relatively inexpensive with the addition of a second wireless access point in the underserved area.

What You'll Need

If you have a basic wireless network already installed, you need only add:

- A wireless access point (*not* another router/WAP device combination, just an access point) with wireless *repeater* capability. The repeater feature does exactly what its name implies; it receives and retransmits signals received from the main access point, thereby increasing the effective range of the main access point.

    or

- A wireless access point connected to your existing network with an Ethernet cable.

You may also need:

- One wireless Ethernet adapter for each new computer (desktops and laptops) to be supported, if any

- One wireless Ethernet printer server for each additional printer to be directly networked (optional), if any

If you're just getting started with your wireless network installation, refer to the *All-Wireless LAN with Router/Gateway* or *Mixed Wired/Wireless LAN* section of this appendix for information on setting up a basic wireless network, and then return here when you're ready to expand.

Configuration Overview

A second WAP extends your network over a much larger service area than is possible with just your router-based WAP. There are two ways to add a second AP to your existing wireless network.

The preferred method is to run an Ethernet cable from the main AP to the secondary AP. This approach offers the best performance, but it may be difficult (or impossible) to run the Ethernet cable to the second AP.

If you are using an AP with a *repeater* mode, the second AP can be located almost anywhere in your house as long as it's in a place where it gets a good signal from the main access point. The two APs work as a relay team, where LAN traffic is relayed from the main AP to the second one, and vice versa. To get this to work, you'll have to set up the secondary AP for repeater (sometimes called *relaying*) mode and you'll also need to tell the second AP how to find the main AP (usually through its MAC address or SSID, as explained later).

Note

In a repeater configuration, your second WAP gets its data connection wirelessly, so there's no need to run Ethernet cabling to it. Your router-based WAP sends wireless Ethernet data to the second access point, and the second WAP repeats (retransmits) the traffic to your more distant LAN clients. The whole thing works in reverse, too, of course; the second AP sends Ethernet traffic from your extended LAN clients back to the main AP, and to other parts of the network. This arrangement is very convenient and easy to install, but it decreases the available bandwidth on the entire wireless LAN.

An Ethernet-connected secondary AP works in much the same way, but it uses an Ethernet cable connection to provide communication between the two APs. In most cases, this is the better way to go because the secondary WAP communicates with the main WAP over the Ethernet cable, rather than over the wireless link. This conserves radio bandwidth, resulting in a faster connection while providing a broader wireless coverage area.

After set up, you'll have seamless roaming throughout the coverage area of the two access points. The additional wireless service range you'll get from a second AP depends on a variety of characteristics, but you can expect about a 50 percent increase in coverage area. Figure A-11 shows a LAN with two access points.

Physical Layout and Connections

If your secondary AP has a repeater mode, the physical installation of the second WAP is a simple matter of identifying the best location for it and plugging it into a power outlet. This is an advantage because it's easy to experiment with its location until you find a spot that extends the best performance to the more remote LAN clients it serves. The physical location and connection setup of your main, router-based WAP need not change to support the second wireless AP, though you could experiment with its placement, too, to see if you can further improve overall network performance.

Network Management, Software Configuration, and Security

Wireless access points can operate in a variety of modes. By default, the main access point for your wireless network, the one that's built into your cable or DSL router, operates in a plain *access point* mode. This role will not need to change in your expanded wireless network. An Ethernet-connected secondary AP works in exactly the same way.

Wireless secondary APs must be configured to operate in repeater (or *relaying*) mode. In most cases, this is done through the AP's Web interface. You'll need to know the MAC address or default SSID of the main access point (you can get this information through the main AP's Web interface) as well as the WEP or WPA password. When that's configured, the two access points should be able to communicate with each other and with the wireless clients within their respective ranges.

Note

Not all APs can operate in repeater mode. Check the product box or the manufacturer's Web site before you buy!

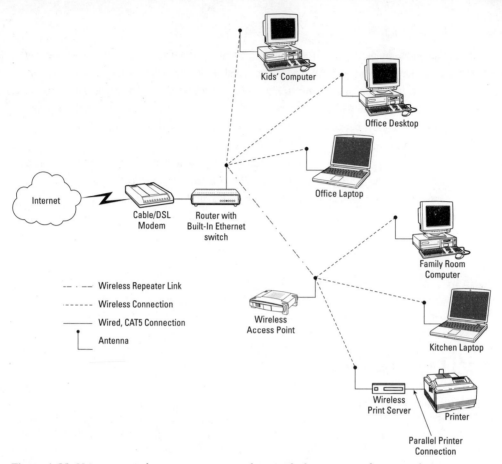

Figure A-11: Using two wireless access points greatly extends the coverage of your wireless LAN.

Note that your main WAP continues to provide network management and security functions to the entire network, including:

- **DHCP server service.** Automatic network configuration of LAN clients, including IP address assignment.

- **Network Address Translation (NAT).** For sharing a single Internet connection among all the computers within the LAN.

- **Firewall functionality.** For protecting the LAN against intrusion from the outside. The firewall may also include traffic control capability in which some traffic types can be completely disallowed.

- **A built-in browser interface.** For checking or modifying router configuration settings (like NAT, DHCP, and firewall,).

Cross-Reference

For more on the operation and configuration of these router features, refer to the section of this appendix that matches your existing network type (wired or wireless). See also Chapter 3.

ABOUT WIRELESS SECURITY SETTINGS

The security precautions taken for the first access point apply to the second. The same security features you've activated for the main AP should be implemented for the second AP. These include MAC address filtering—a scheme that lets only the wireless Ethernet hardware you designate connect to the wireless net—and Wired Equivalent Privacy (WEP) or WiFi Protected Access—two schemes for wireless data encryption/decryption.

You can further increase the security of your wireless network by adjusting several operational parameters within the router, including periodically changing the administrator's password and changing (or completely eliminating) the identifier broadcast by your router. These wireless security functions and recommendations are covered in detail in the *All-Wireless LAN with Router/Gateway* section of this appendix. You'll also find helpful information in Chapter 4's *Wireless Security* section.

Ethernet LAN with HomePlug Extension

HomePlug networking technology offers an interesting alternative to conventional wired and wireless networks. Like wired networks, HomePlug uses cabling to carry Ethernet traffic. But unlike wired networks, HomePlug doesn't require you to run cables to create the network. There are no new cables to run and no new holes to drill. How can that be? It's because HomePlug devices use the existing power wiring within your home as the networking infrastructure.

You can build a home network from scratch using HomePlug devices, or you can use HomePlug devices to extend an existing network. This section presents HomePlug devices as an option for extending the LAN to computers that can't be reached with cabling or by using a wireless LAN, either because of distance constraints or because getting cable to them is impractical (or just plain impossible). While HomePlug offers an additional tool for connecting PCs into a LAN, it is relatively slow, even when compared to an 802.11g wireless LAN.

What You'll Need

To extend an existing wired Ethernet network through HomePlug devices, you'll need the following:

- A HomePlug Ethernet bridge or USB adapter for each computer (zone) to be connected

- A HomePlug power line bridge for connection near the router

- One CAT5 interconnect cable between each power line adapter and computer

- An Ethernet adapter for each computer (desktops and laptops)

- One Ethernet printer server for each printer to be directly networked (optional)

Configuration Overview

All HomePlug devices have two connections[md]a standard wall plug and a computer connection (either USB or Ethernet). Some HomePlug devices look something like the kind of power "brick" used by laptops, printers, and other electronic equipment. The difference here is that the computer side of the connection carries data (instead of power) to your LAN client.

Because HomePlug works over power lines, and you're going to have a power connection anywhere you have a computer to be networked, you'll automatically also have a ready LAN connection at a nearby power outlet. In fact, any power outlet in your home is a potential LAN connection when outfitted with a HomePlug unit.

When expanding an existing Ethernet network, a HomePlug bridging device is used to interconnect standard low-voltage Ethernet cable-based signals and power-line-level Ethernet levels, as shown in Figure A-12.

Physical Layout and Connections

HomePlug devices have two types of connections: a power plug and a data connection, either Ethernet or USB (depending on the model). The power plug connects to any standard 110-volt AC outlet in your home; the data connection accepts a data cable (Ethernet or USB) for connection to a LAN client.

The physical layout and connection arrangement for the main section of your wired Ethernet LAN is essentially like that of the *Ethernet LAN with Router/Gateway* section at the beginning of this appendix. To interconnect, or bridge, the conventional LAN and the power line networks, you need only add a HomePlug Ethernet bridge device.

To connect the bridge to the router's built-in switch (or to an external switch), note the following cable requirements:

- Use a *crossover* CAT5 cable to connect from the bridge to any of the regular (nonuplink) switch ports.

- Use a *straight-through* CAT5 cable to connect from the bridge to the uplink port (check for an uplink/normal switch, and set it to the uplink position).

Some device brands may have different requirements; check the device documentation to determine specific cabling needs. The power plug cable connects the bridge's power connector to any available standard AC power outlet. Note that you can not plug a HomePlug device into a standby power supply or a surge protector, since those devices will block the HomePlug signal.

To connect LAN clients to your HomePlug extended network, you'll need to install one HomePlug power line adapter per client. You can choose either an Ethernet or USB power line adapter, depending on the connection type available on the client system. You do have to run some cabling with HomePlug devices, but it's needed only here, between the HomePlug device and the PC to be connected to your extended LAN. The cable will be either a standard CAT5 Ethernet cable or USB cable, depending on the type of HomePlug device you're using.

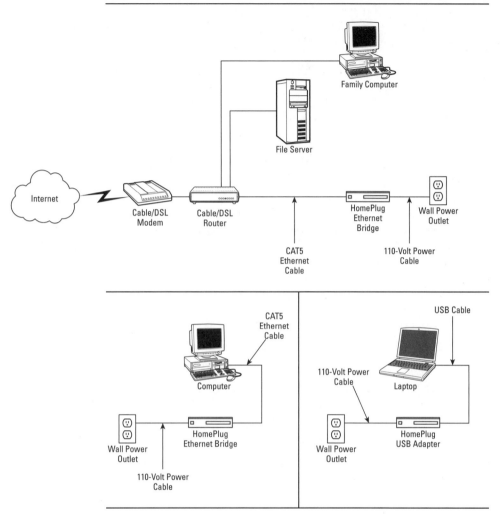

Figure A-12: A wired Ethernet LAN is easily extended with HomePlug devices that use your home's power lines to carry Ethernet traffic. The technology is especially useful for serving systems that are hard to reach with cabled (or even wireless) Ethernet.

Network Management, Software Configuration, and Security

A HomePlug network extension does not impact the administration of your existing wired Ethernet network. The cable/DSL router you're already using to share your Internet connection, manage the network, and provide a firewall continues to perform all management, configuration, and security functions.

Your HomePlug LAN extension devices, on the other hand, will need separate configuration. You'll have to individually configure each of the Ethernet and USB HomePlug devices on your power line network to select security options, an important step toward protecting the data on your power line network.

Your home is to some degree electrically interconnected with your neighbors' homes, so any data that travels over your power lines is conceivably accessible to other power customers on the same power distribution sub-grid. To address this, the HomePlug standard includes a 56-bit Data Encryption Standard (DES) that protects your data while it travels over your home's wiring with a unique key. This allows your HomePlug devices to encrypt data before putting it on the power line network and to decrypt it upon reception.

To enable password protection and data encryption, you'll have to select these features on each of the HomePlug devices you use. You should first change the password for each device, using the same password on all devices. You should also enable data encryption for each HomePlug device. To make this easier, the configuration software included with most HomePlug-compatible devices enables you to search for and configure all your power line adapters from one configuration utility. If this functionality isn't provided, you'll have to individually configure each LAN client supported by a HomePlug device for these and other applicable settings.

From the point of view of the wired part of your network (specifically, to your cable/DSL router), the HomePlug devices look like any other standard Ethernet network device; the fact that they're communicating over a power line is transparent to your router. HomePlug devices use the router's DHCP server to obtain their IP addresses, and each device is uniquely identifiable through a standard-format MAC address and is automatically configured upon power-up.

Ethernet LAN with User-Installable DSL

At one time, getting DSL service set up in your home was a fairly involved task. A technician had to make a site visit, run cables, and carry out other time-consuming tasks. This could also take up a good part of your day, waiting for the installer to arrive (often sometime within an eight-hour window) and then waiting for the installation process to be completed.

All that changed with the advent of user-installable DSL. The service provider still has to do some work to set up the connection, but it all happens behind the scenes and without an on-site visit. Instead, the provider sends you a self-installation kit that consists of a DSL modem and multiple telephone line filters. Installation is very easy and offers a lot of placement flexibility. You need only to add a few networking elements, such as a router and some cables, to set up a complete home network.

What You'll Need

For a wired Ethernet network, you'll need the following:

- DSL service with user-installable DSL modem and microfilters
- A cable or DSL router, with or without a built-in Ethernet switch
- An Ethernet switch (if using a router without a built-in switch)

- One CAT5 interconnect cable for each connection (length will vary)

- One Ethernet adapter for each computer (desktops and laptops)

- One Ethernet printer server for each printer to be directly networked (optional)

For a wireless Ethernet network, you'll need the following:

- DSL service with user-installable DSL modem and microfilters

- A cable or DSL wireless router (with or without a built-in Ethernet switch)

- One wireless Ethernet adapter for each computer (desktops and laptops)

- One wireless Ethernet printer server for each printer to be networked (optional)

Configuration Overview

DSL service comes into your home on the same telephone line that carries your standard telephone service. The two services can coexist because voice service and DSL do not interfere with one another. Still, to make doubly sure there's no interference, every user-installable DSL kit includes a set of *microfilters*, small plastic-cased devices that are easily installed.

One microfilter plugs into each wall jack that has a telephone, fax machine, or other telephone-enabled device, and the filter completely blocks DSL signals from getting through. The standard telephone jack you choose for your DSL modem doesn't need a filter. The beauty is that you can put your modem anywhere you have a phone jack. Just make sure the other jacks you use have filters, and you're done with the DSL setup. And if you ever want to rearrange things, moving things around is a matter of unplugging the DSL modem from one jack and connecting it to another. See Figure A-13 for an example.

Physical Layout and Connections

Conventional telephone service uses only a small portion of the frequency range that can be carried by the copper pair that delivers it. DSL capitalizes on this unused bandwidth capacity by communicating over a higher set of frequencies that do not overlap voice service. The microfilters included with your DSL kit are lowpass filters; they pass the lower voiceband frequencies used by your telephones, fax machines, and other telephone-enabled devices, like a TiVo digital video recorder. Connecting the DSL modem to an unfiltered jack enables it to pick up broadband data traffic, which operates at higher frequencies, and a highpass filter within the modem ensures that voiceband frequencies do not interfere with its data operation.

After you have DSL set up, extending your new high-speed connection is a matter of adding standard home networking components. Everything on the "home" side of the DSL modem, from the router on, is exactly the same as for other types of home networks. (The *What You'll Need* list for this section assumes a wired Ethernet network, but you could just as easily set up a wireless or mixed wired/wireless home network as described in detail in the early sections of this appendix.)

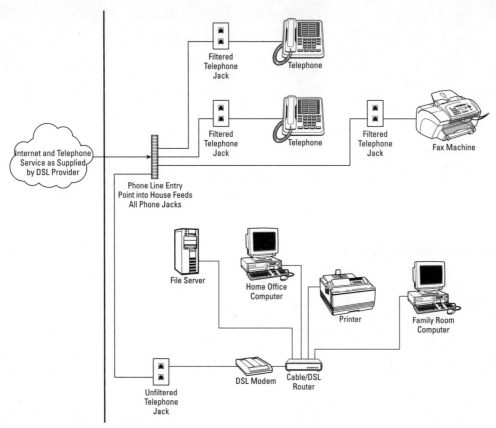

Figure A-13: User-installable DSL is easy to set up and lets you put the DSL modem where it's most convenient for you. The location then becomes the starting point for your home network, which can be wired, wireless, or a combination of the two.

For any Ethernet networking arrangement (wired or wireless), the DSL modem connects directly to your router. This is always a wired Ethernet connection using standard CAT5 cable, so you have up to about 300 feet of cable between the modem and the router. Keep in mind that the modem can be installed anywhere you have a (working) phone jack, so this means you have a lot of placement flexibility. Many installations have the DSL modem and the network router in the same place, but that need not be the case if a different arrangement is more convenient for you.

The rest of the network then connects to your router (by cable if you have a wired network), and the router is the central network management and security control point for the entire network. After the network is set up, you can connect any Ethernet-equipped computer or device to your network, including printers, print servers, dedicated file servers, and more.

Network Management, Software Configuration, and Security

With one exception, all network management, software configuration, and security functions are exactly the same for this network matching network type described earlier in this appendix. For example, if you're using an all-wired network, these functions are exactly the same as described in the *Ethernet LAN with Router/Gateway* section at the beginning of this appendix.

The one exception applies when only to DSL modems. Virtually all DSL service providers use an authentication method with the cumbersome name of Point to Point Protocol over Ethernet (PPPoE) to verify your DSL account name and password when you start a DSL connection. You will need to configure your router to use PPPoE, and you will need to enter your DSL account name and password in the appropriate configuration screen on your router.

To summarize, standard router-based network management and security features include the following:

- **A DHCP server.**   For automatic network configuration of LAN clients, including IP address assignment.

- **Network Address Translation (NAT).**   For sharing a single Internet connection among all the computers within the LAN.

- **Firewall functionality.**   For protecting the LAN against intrusion from the outside. The firewall may also include traffic control capability in which some traffic types can be completely disallowed.

- **A built-in Web server.**   For checking or modifying router configuration settings (like NAT, DHCP, firewall, and VPN) from any client on the LAN.

Cross-Reference

For more on the operation and configuration of these router features, refer to the section of this appendix that matches the network type you're setting up (wired, wireless, or combination). See also Chapter 3.

Appendix B

Troubleshooting Your LAN

Armed with the information presented in previous chapters plus a few bits of networking hardware, you should have your home network up and running pretty quickly. But what if something isn't working right off the bat? And what do you do if things are running smoothly for a while but one or more devices stop working sometime later?

Home networking equipment is pretty reliable and easy to set up, so you probably won't have to refer to this appendix very often. But when your network or a LAN client isn't working as expected, determining the source of the problem can be a bit tricky. If you are using equipment from multiple manufacturers, you need to at least be able to determine which component is causing the problem before you can call for tech support.

Fortunately, checking for and fixing problems on your home LAN isn't rocket science. You'll find that troubleshooting most of your LAN connection problems is easily accomplished by a simple process of elimination and a bit of investigative work, as described in this appendix.

The troubleshooting guidelines and checklists presented in this appendix necessarily make a few assumptions. These guidelines assume that:

- You're working with a router-based LAN configuration (wired, wireless, or combination) as described in earlier chapters and in most of the examples in Appendix A.

- You have the Ethernet adapters appropriate to the LAN type you're setting up; on a wired network, the adapter speed should be supported by the device to which it's connected (a 100 mbps Ethernet card, for example, can be connected to a 10/100 switch but not to a 10 mbps switch).

- For a wired network, all cables have been run and connected to their relative endpoints.

- For a wireless network, you know your wireless LAN SSID and WEP or WPA keys.

- You know the IP address of your LAN router and how to access router settings via a Web interface.

Checking the Hardware

The first step in checking any LAN problem is to eliminate the possibility of a simple hardware or physical connection fault.

Power Connections

As trivial as it sounds, checking for power to the device in question should be the first thing you do. Sometimes devices are accidentally turned off (or unplugged), and many problems are truly this simple to solve. If your router doesn't have power, for example, your LAN clients can't get IP addresses, and nothing on your LAN will work.

Check your outlet strips for power, make sure your devices aren't plugged into switched wall outlets (i.e., outlets controlled by a wall switch so that you can conveniently turn on a lamp when you walk in), and make sure the family's pet iguana hasn't chewed through the power cord. Check that all on/off switches are set to the on position.

Cabling

Make sure all Ethernet cables are fully inserted into their jacks at every connection point, including at the LAN client's Ethernet adapter, at the LAN router, and on any intermediate connection points, such as switches and hubs. (Even if you have a wireless network setup, you'll have at least one cable connection, between the wireless access point and the cable or DSL modem.)

When inserting an RJ-45 cable connector into an Ethernet jack, it should slide in smoothly and click into position, similar to the way an ordinary modular telephone cord plugs into a wall jack. To double-check that a cable is properly seated in its jack, disconnect it by pressing the tab on the RJ-45 connector, slide it out, and reinsert it. If the locking tab is broken on any of the connectors, replace the defective connector or replace the cable.

Visual Indicators

All Ethernet adapters include at least one hardware indicator to provide network connection status. On desktop PCs, for example, most Ethernet cards include one or more of the following:

- **Link.** Indicates a connection to another Ethernet device (but does not indicate proper network configuration)

- **10/100 LED.** On dual-speed cards, indicates the current operating speed

- **Activity.** Blinks to indicate network traffic activity

Wireless Ethernet adapters usually have only the Activity and Link indicators. They provide the same functions described in the preceding list for wired Ethernet cards.

Understand that the Link light indicates only that you have a good electrical connection to a corresponding Ethernet device, but it does not provide any guarantee that the device is properly configured. For a wired connection, the Link lights at each end of the cable indicate that the cable is properly connected and wired, and that it's connected to an Ethernet router, switch, or hub. In the case of a wireless connection, the Link light tells you that you're in the vicinity of a compatible wireless access point. The

Link light does *not* indicate proper software, TCP/IP, or router connection settings for the adapter. (I'll go into detail about checking settings in the *Software Tools for Network and Connection Testing* section later in this appendix.)

Plug-In Ethernet Adapters

If you're using a CardBus, PC Card, USB, or other type of plug-in Ethernet adapter, make sure it's fully inserted into its slot. On a laptop computer, CardBus/PC Card and USB adapters in particular can pull out just enough to break a connection but still appear to be plugged in. For a CardBus/PC Card device, make sure that Windows knows the device is connected by clicking on the Safely Remove Hardware icon on the system task tray. This will tell you what's plugged in (and will also let you "stop" the card when you want to take it out). Of course, you should also know if the adapter in question is not fully connected by looking at its visual indicators (described previously); they will be off if the adapter is not fully inserted.

Hardware Diagnostics

Many networking hardware components, such as Ethernet cards and routers, include some form of self-checking diagnostic software. If you suspect a problem with a specific device, running the diagnostic will help to isolate the problem. (Plus, in the event that you have to contact the manufacturer for support, you'll be able to provide a bit more information about the nature of the problem.)

Also, if you suspect a problem with hardware setup or configuration, consult the hardware documentation. Most manufacturers include a helpful troubleshooting guide; your LAN router's manual is probably the best place to start.

If you're unsure of the specific hardware model you have, or the software required to test it, check the manufacturer's Web site. Most manufacturers feature support sections that include helpful product identification guides, utilities for testing your networking devices, and downloadable manuals.

Software Tools for Network and Connection Testing

After you've assessed the state of the physical connections for your networking devices, it's time to test your network configurations and connections with a few software tools.

Windows offers a number of software-based approaches to setting and checking network configurations. The Network Connections dialog box (described in the section that follows) is one way to do it, and this will offer everything you need for LAN client diagnostics.

The additional tools described here are included with Windows XP and most prior versions of Windows. (In fact, these tools are usually available on any TCP/IP network-enabled machine, including Apple and Linux-based systems.) These command-line tools run from the Windows command prompt. They're not pretty, but they're all you need to determine what's happening with your LAN clients, your home network, and even whether or not (or even to some degree, how well) you're getting to the outside world via the Internet.

Windows XP Network Properties

You can see how your network connections are set up by selecting Network Connections from Windows' Control Panel or by right-clicking the My Network Places or My Neighborhood icon and choosing Properties from the resulting menu. Here you'll see a list of all your LAN devices and other networking connections, including a couple of wizards for setting up the network and new connections. There are several ways to display this information. The Tiles and Details views (selectable via the View menu) include useful device status information. Figure B-1 shows the Tiles view.

You can right-click an individual item, like Wireless Network Connection in the following example, and then select Status to review connection and activity details in the resulting dialog box's General tab. The Support tab shows the most-relevant TCP/IP configuration information, including the IP address, subnet mask, and default gateway (see Figure B-2). The full details of this adapter, like its MAC address, can be displayed by clicking the Details button; this shows a new window with a Physical Address value that is your Ethernet card's unique hardware identifier.

Figure B-1: The Tiles display of connections and wizards in Windows' Network Connections window.

Figure B-2: The TCP/IP status details provided
by Windows XP let you know if your PC has
a valid IP address.

This dialog box is one place where you can see your Ethernet or WiFi adapter's IP address (labeled IP Address), as well as the IP address of your router (the Default Gateway). If values appear here, your adapter should be properly configured for the network, and you should be able to access the router, your file server, and other network resources. On the other hand, if this information isn't there, or if the values are incorrect, your computer won't be able to access the local network or the Internet. If you're using DHCP for dynamic addressing, you can click the Repair button to let Windows attempt to get a new IP address from the router.

If you need to change the adapter configuration (for example, if you want to use a fixed IP address rather than have one assigned by your router's DHCP server), right-click the device icon and select Properties. For more on setting the device properties, refer to Chapter 8.

Windows XP includes a fairly complete networking help and support center. To access the center, click the Start button, choose the Help and Support command, and choose Networking and the Web from the Help and Support Center window. For additional Windows-related help topics, consult the Microsoft Knowledge Base at `support.microsoft.com`.

Your Utility Software Toolbox: IPCONFIG, PING, TRACERT

Each of the software tools described in this section is included with Windows XP (in fact, they're available in most versions of Windows and many other operating systems) and can be run from any client on your LAN. Each utility has particular advantages depending on what you need to know about your system or network.

GETTING TO THE WINDOWS COMMAND PROMPT

These very useful utilities don't use the Windows graphical user interface. Instead, they run in Windows' command prompt dialog box, a special command-line interface window that's similar to older text-only PC DOS system interfaces. To access Windows' command line, follow these simple steps:

1. Click on Windows' Start button.

2. Select the Run command.

3. Type **cmd** into the Open: text box.

4. Click OK.

The resulting window will look similar to the one in Figure B-3. You'll end up with a command prompt on drive C: and in the folder that contains your user configurations. Where you are in your folder system doesn't matter, however, because the utilities you'll be running should be accessible from anywhere in the system's file hierarchy.

Figure B-3: The Windows command prompt as it looks right after starting. (This is what computing looked like before Windows!)

To close the Command Prompt window when you're done with it, type **exit** and press Enter at the prompt, or click the close box in the top-right corner of the window.

Note for Mac Users

Two of the tools described in this section—PING and TRACERT—are also available in OS X. You'll need to open a Terminal window (similar to the DOS command prompt shown above) to use the tools. To do this, you use the Terminal program, found in the Applications->Utilities folder on your Mac. The Mac version of TRACERT is called traceroute. There is no direct Mac equivalent to IPCONFIG.

CHECKING LOCAL ETHERNET DEVICE SETTINGS: IPCONFIG

The IPCONFIG utility provides a status display of all IP devices installed on your system. As you'll see, IPCONFIG is sometimes a better alternative to checking network configuration information through Windows' Network Properties display. If you enter IPCONFIG and press Enter in the Command Prompt window, the program shows you results only for the device in use for the local area connection, as shown in Figure B-4.

```
C:\WINDOWS\System32\cmd.exe                                    _ □ ×
Microsoft Windows XP [Version 5.1.2600]
(C) Copyright 1985-2001 Microsoft Corp.

C:\Documents and Settings\Les>ipconfig

Windows IP Configuration

Ethernet adapter Wireless Network Connection:

        Connection-specific DNS Suffix  . : siestk01.fl.comcast.net
        IP Address. . . . . . . . . . . . : 192.168.0.37
        Subnet Mask . . . . . . . . . . . : 255.255.255.0
        Default Gateway . . . . . . . . . : 192.168.0.100

C:\Documents and Settings\Les>
```

Figure B-4: The results of an IPCONFIG command without arguments. In this case, only the connection information for the current adapter is returned.

When used without arguments, IPCONFIG tells you the currently assigned domain name (DNS suffix), the IP address of the Ethernet adapter, the subnet mask, and the default gateway (router) address. To be able to communicate locally (intra-LAN), the last three settings must contain valid addresses. The DNS suffix setting affects only your ability to access other systems by "name" (like the URL you'd type into a Web browser) and is almost always provided by your ISP.

Note

DNS stands for Domain Name Service. This is the service that translates the URLs and other network addresses you know as, for example, www.google.com, to the IP addresses used by the routers and other network devices. See Chapter 3 for more on DNS.

If the IP address and other settings are incorrect (or if the IP address field is blank), the client PC will be not be able to communicate on the LAN. If your router and LAN adapter are configured for DHCP, you'll be able to "refresh" your connection configurations by typing IPCONFIG /refresh at the command line, as described following.

You can list IPCONFIG options by specifying the **/?** argument on the command line. That is, in the Command Prompt window, enter **IPCONFIG** and press Enter. The result will look something like Figure B-5.

```
C:\WINDOWS\System32\cmd.exe                                    _ □ ×

C:\Documents and Settings\Les>ipconfig /?

USAGE:
    ipconfig [/? | /all | /renew [adapter] | /release [adapter] |
             /flushdns | /displaydns | /registerdns |
             /showclassid adapter |
             /setclassid adapter [classid] ]

where
    adapter         Connection name
                    (wildcard characters * and ? allowed, see examples)

    Options:
        /?          Display this help message
        /all        Display full configuration information.
        /release    Release the IP address for the specified adapter.
        /renew      Renew the IP address for the specified adapter.
        /flushdns   Purges the DNS Resolver cache.
        /registerdns Refreshes all DHCP leases and re-registers DNS names
        /displaydns  Display the contents of the DNS Resolver Cache.
        /showclassid Displays all the dhcp class IDs allowed for adapter.
        /setclassid  Modifies the dhcp class id.

The default is to display only the IP address, subnet mask and
default gateway for each adapter bound to TCP/IP.

For Release and Renew, if no adapter name is specified, then the IP address
leases for all adapters bound to TCP/IP will be released or renewed.

For Setclassid, if no ClassId is specified, then the ClassId is removed.

Examples:
    > ipconfig            ... Show information.
    > ipconfig /all       ... Show detailed information
    > ipconfig /renew     ... renew all adapters
    > ipconfig /renew EL* ... renew any connection that has its
                              name starting with EL

    > ipconfig /release *Con* ... release all matching connections,
                                  eg. "Local Area Connection 1" or
                                      "Local Area Connection 2"

C:\Documents and Settings\Les>_
```

Figure B-5: The IPCONFIG tool has many options. The list of options can be displayed with the ipconfig /? command in the command prompt window. Commonly used options include /release, /renew, and /all.

There are a lot of features in IPCONFIG, and the **/?** option provides some help with option use and gives some command examples. For most home networking troubleshooting, however, you're likely to need only three of these command-line options (sometimes called *switches*), shown in Table B-1.

Table B-1   IPCONFIG Command Line Switches

Command	*Purpose*
/all	Lists all networked devices on a given client, with detailed configuration information on each device. (See Figure B-6.)
/release [*adapter*]	Releases the IP address assigned to the networking device by the DHCP server (usually your LAN router). The [*adapter*] parameter specifies the networking adapter whose IP address you want to release. For example, IPCONFIG /release 1 will release the address used by adapter number 1.
/renew [*adapter*]	Attempts to renew (or obtain) an IP address lease for a given networking adapter. The [*adapter*] option specifies the networking adapter whose IP address you want to renew.

You can use the /release and /renew options anytime you want to refresh your LAN adapter's TCP/IP settings. If you're running DHCP at the router, the adapter's network settings should be renewed automatically. There are times, however, when this isn't the case. This may happen, for example, when devices are disconnected from the network and later reconnected, as might happen with a laptop computer.

If you list LAN device settings with IPCONFIG and see an unusual or missing IP address for your LAN connection device (like 254.x.x.x and/or no subnet mask or gateway address), you'll know that the connection settings need to be refreshed.

You can force the network settings to refresh with the IPCONFIG /release and IPCONFIG /renew commands. (Incidentally, this is essentially the same thing that happens when you use Windows XP's connection Repair feature described earlier in the *Windows XP Network Properties* section.)

CHECKING AN IP ADDRESS: PING

The PING utility is useful for checking the validity of a specific IP address. It can also tell you how long traffic takes to reach that address and be reflected to you. In fact, it's very much like the idea of submarine sonar and the ever-present "pinging" you hear in submarine movie soundtracks: You send a signal, wait to see if it reflects back to you, and then make some determinations about the reflection source based on trip time and other factors.

Within your home network, you should be able to ping every device you have connected to the LAN: your router, wireless access points, and LAN clients (other computers, laptops, network-enabled printers, and so on). Getting a positive response to a ping means that at least the device in question is on the network and that both your local and remote network configurations are properly set up. For example, the result of pinging a LAN router is shown in Figure B-7.

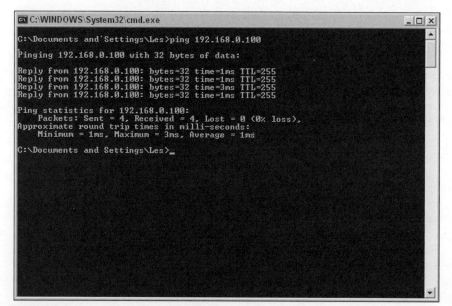

Figure B-6: The /all option returns information about the system ("tweety" in this example) and all of the installed network adapters.

Figure B-7: An example of PING being used to check for the presence of a device at 192.168.0.100 (which happens to be the LAN's router, in this case). Note the aggregate ping statistics provided at the end of the standard four-ping cycle.

In this case, PING sends a message (a network traffic packet) four times (the default number of pings), provides statistics related to each message, and then shows a summary of the completed process.

In the case of your LAN's router (or for any other device on the LAN), round-trip times should be very short (the example in Figure B-7 shows 192.168.0.100). If you know the IP address or network name of devices on your LAN, this is always a good way to verify that they're on and properly attached to the network. Figure B-8 shows a similar example, using the computer's network name rather than its IP address. This is helpful if you know the computer's name but not its IP address (which is often the case).

Note

Within your LAN, the network name option works only for accessing other Windows and OS X-based systems. Linux systems and many other devices may not be accessible by name, only by IP address.

```
C:\WINDOWS\System32\cmd.exe                                    _ |□| x|
Microsoft Windows XP [Version 5.1.2600]
(C) Copyright 1985-2001 Microsoft Corp.

C:\Documents and Settings\Les>ping elmer

Pinging elmer.siestk01.fl.comcast.net [192.168.0.38] with 32 bytes of data:

Reply from 192.168.0.38: bytes=32 time=2ms TTL=128
Reply from 192.168.0.38: bytes=32 time=1ms TTL=128
Reply from 192.168.0.38: bytes=32 time=1ms TTL=128
Reply from 192.168.0.38: bytes=32 time=1ms TTL=128

Ping statistics for 192.168.0.38:
    Packets: Sent = 4, Received = 4, Lost = 0 (0% loss),
Approximate round trip times in milli-seconds:
    Minimum = 1ms, Maximum = 2ms, Average = 1ms

C:\Documents and Settings\Les>
```

Figure B-8: You can ping LAN clients by name. In this case, PING is being used to ping a system named ELMER. Note that PING translates the name (ELMER) to an IP address (192.168.0.38).

You can generally also ping addresses outside your LAN, like the address of your employer's Web site, or the corporate network's VPN server. In this case, particularly if pinging a Web site, you can almost always use a domain name (the URL you'd type in a browser window) instead of an IP address to ping the system. PING gets the destination IP address from your DNS server. (Note, however, that some Internet destinations won't echo your ping request, even if they're working perfectly. This is done to protect the systems against malicious ping-related attacks.)

PING accepts one or more arguments followed by the destination you want to test. You can see all ping options by typing **PING** at the Windows Command Prompt. For home networking purposes, however, you'll very rarely need to use the options, and they're not described here.

Tip

The command PING –t will run PING continuously until you type control-c to stop it. This is useful for troubleshooting.

TRACING A CONNECTION PATH: TRACERT

An abbreviation of "trace route," the TRACERT utility checks connection paths. You probably won't need to use it within your home network, but TRACERT is most useful when you need to check how network traffic packets from your LAN client get to another system or service over the Internet.

For example, if a Web site you visit is responding slowly (if, for example, the home page takes a long time to come up), you can trace the connection path for getting there with TRACERT to see if there's a networking problem along the way.

Figure B-9 shows a TRACERT session to the Google site and all the hops your test packet takes to get to this destination from one particular Internet connection (your trace will vary according to your location and Internet service provider). Traffic begins at the LAN's router (in this case, the router is at the 192.168.10.100 address) and hops through a long series of Internet routers before getting to its destination.

```
C:\WINDOWS\System32\cmd.exe                                          _ □ X

C:\Documents and Settings\Les>tracert google.com

Tracing route to google.com [216.239.37.100]
over a maximum of 30 hops:

  1     1 ms     1 ms     1 ms  interjak.siestk01.fl.comcast.net [192.168.0.100]

  2    16 ms    25 ms    13 ms  10.51.176.1
  3    10 ms    11 ms    12 ms  172.30.84.145
  4    13 ms    10 ms    12 ms  172.30.84.186
  5    11 ms    17 ms    14 ms  172.30.84.252
  6    19 ms    11 ms    13 ms  68.56.0.50
  7    13 ms    12 ms    14 ms  12.119.95.53
  8    15 ms    15 ms    13 ms  gbr3-p100.ormfl.ip.att.net [12.123.218.34]
  9    19 ms    19 ms    27 ms  gbr4-p60.ormfl.ip.att.net [12.122.5.138]
 10    29 ms    27 ms    28 ms  tbr1-p012302.attga.ip.att.net [12.122.2.181]
 11    27 ms    27 ms    27 ms  ggr1-p360.attga.ip.att.net [12.123.20.249]
 12    27 ms    27 ms    27 ms  acr2-so-3-0-0.Atlanta.cw.net [208.172.65.121]
 13    28 ms    29 ms    27 ms  agr3-loopback.Atlanta.cw.net [208.172.66.103]
 14    28 ms    39 ms    27 ms  dcr1-so-0-2-0.Atlanta.cw.net [208.172.75.9]
 15    41 ms    41 ms    41 ms  dcr1-loopback.Washington.cw.net [206.24.226.99]

 16    46 ms    43 ms    43 ms  bhr1-pos-10-0.Sterling2dc3.cw.net [206.24.238.38
]
 17    44 ms    43 ms    47 ms  csr11-ve240.Sterling1dc2.cw.net [216.33.98.146]

 18    44 ms    43 ms    46 ms  209.225.34.218
 19    47 ms    50 ms    53 ms  216.239.48.94
 20    44 ms    43 ms    50 ms  www.google.com [216.239.37.100]

Trace complete.

C:\Documents and Settings\Les>_
```

Figure B-9: This sample TRACERT session shows the path taken by a trace from a home router (at 192.168.10.100) to www.google.com (at 216.239.37.100).

The trace shown here is good, and the response time is typical. If you see many *timeouts* in the path, you may be seeing a routing problem, such as a defective Internet service provider router, and this is probably what's causing a slow or broken connection. (Then again, it may be that the destination is not responding to traces, much like pings are sometimes not echoed. Note also that a working Web destination, like many popular news and search sites, may never respond to pings or to TRACERT sessions.)

If you look closely at the example in Figure B-9, you'll see that the TRACERT report is divided in to multiple columns. The first column is simply a count of the number of devices, or hops, in the path to that point. The second, third, and fourth columns show the average, maximum, and minimum response times for that device, and the last column shows the DNS name (if any) for the device. In the example, there is a 13 to 25 ms delay between my router and the ISP's gateway. This is a typical time for cable modems; DSL modems will show a similar but slightly longer delay, and dial-up connections will have a significantly longer delay.

Note that in many cases you won't see much of a hopping path change between one TRACERT session and another, but the nature of Internet connections means paths do change. In general, don't think too much about the specific addresses or number of hops between your LAN and a remote system; as long as you're able to reach the service by some path or another, that's the only thing that matters.

Note that if you're able to run a successful TRACERT session to a system or service outside your LAN, you can rest assured that at least your LAN router and the LAN client from which you're running TRACERT are properly configured to communicate with each other and with the outside world (at least in terms of TCP/IP settings anyway). E-mail, file transfer programs, and other applications will almost always require separate configuration for proper operation.

Wireless Considerations

A mismatch in one or more settings between your wireless access point (WAP) and network clients will keep your wireless connection from working. The following list provides a checklist of key settings to check for wireless connection problems:

- **Check the SSID setting.**   The SSID (Service Set Identifier) setting must be the same for all your devices, including the access point.

- **Check WEP settings for all devices.**   If you've enabled data encryption through Wired Equivalent Privacy (WEP), make sure all devices are using the same WEP key(s), and the same level of WEP encryption (e.g., 64-bit, 128-bit, and so on).

- **Verify that wireless operation is enabled.**   If your access point is built in to the router, make sure the wireless functionality is enabled.

- **Check the mode setting.**   When using an access point, all devices should be configured for *infrastructure* mode. If you're not using an access point and are instead connecting devices in a peer-to-peer configuration, use *ad hoc* mode.

- **Check the MAC address filtering table at the access point.**   If you've elected to use MAC address filtering, make sure each LAN client's MAC address is included in the access point's list of acceptable addresses.

- **Check connection signal strength and link quality.**   Most wireless card drivers install a signal-monitoring utility for this purpose and display a signal indicator in the system tray.

Also check the documentation provided with your wireless access point. It may point you to specific tests, software, and settings you can use to further investigate wireless anomalies.

Networked Printers

If your printer isn't printing when you send documents to it, you'll need to check several things:

- Is the correct printer software installed on the client PC?
- Does the printer work from any of the PCs on the LAN, or is the problem isolated to a single client PC?
- Is the printer driver configured correctly?
- Do you have the TCP/IP configuration for your print server or networked printer?

Note

These instructions assume you've checked the printer hardware to see that the power and cable connections are working.

All LAN clients must be configured for the networked printers they're going to use, even if the printer is not directly attached to the client. This includes both installing the printer's drivers and setting up the networked printer connection for each client. You can check all printer configurations and add printers by clicking Start → Control Panel → Printers to launch the Printer dialog box.

Most importantly, note that most Ethernet-connected printers, including network-ready printers and printers connected via an external print server, use a DHCP client for automatic configuration of network settings, including the IP address. If the printer's IP address changes after you have installed the printer driver on your client PCs, the clients will attempt to print to the old, and incorrect, IP address. You should use fixed IP addresses for your network printers whenever possible.

To check the printer's current IP address, many print servers (and printers with built-in servers) have a special button or menu selection for printing the configuration information. This is the easiest way to display the printer's settings.

If a printer is shared through a LAN client (a networked desktop or notebook computer), make sure the LAN client has a valid network connection and has printer sharing enabled.

For more information about sharing printers in your home network, see Chapter 11.

Internet Connection Performance and LAN Security Testing

One of the best ways to test the performance and security of your Internet connections is through Web-based services designed for this purpose. Following are several of the most popular and useful test sites. Check with your Internet service provider too; many offer their own network connection testing services. Appendix C offers a list of some other useful sites.

BROADBAND REPORTS

The Broadband Reports (formerly called DSL Reports) site (`www.broadbandreports.com`) has been around a long time by Internet standards and provides a number of DSL and cable modem connection speed tests for site visitors. The tests are available free of charge and are easy to run.

You can choose your test from the Tools section of the site (`www.broadbandreports.com/tools`). For plain speed testing, choose the Speed Tests option. These tests benchmark your broadband service speed and display it in the context of typical connection speeds for a variety of services. Most of these tests do *not* require you to install software on your system.

Read the site's Frequently Asked Questions (FAQ) page to learn more about it and what it provides. You'll find many other helpful tests here, including a port scanner (useful for checking your router firewall configuration) and IP address checker.

PC PITSTOP

Like DSL Reports, PC Pitstop (`www.pcpitstop.com`) offers a variety of speed and network security tests. The Internet Connection Test Center (`www.pcpitstop.com/internet/default.asp`) has separate upload and download tests, and ping and trace route tests. Note that many types of tests are offered on the site, ranging from a simple Internet speed test to a complete (and very thorough) computer checkup.

The site tends to steer you toward its automatic test sequence, but these require you to install a test component locally on the LAN client you're using to access the site. You can read more about how these work through the site's Our Technology link, and then decide if you want to run these tests. If you don't want to install the automatic software, seek out the site's manual tests.

GRC RESEARCH

Steve Gibson's interesting (and often controversial) Shields UP!! Web site (go to the main site at `www.grc.com` and then click on Shields UP!!) offers visitors a number of freeware utilities for checking the security of Internet connections, especially in terms of firewall vulnerabilities. Of particular value are the Common Ports and File Sharing tests, which check for potential vulnerabilities that result from improper configuration (or bad default settings). A list of all free utilities is available at `http://grc.com/freepopular.htm`.

There's a wealth of information at the Shields UP!! site. Run a few tests and read through some of the material to learn more about protecting your Internet-connected LAN and LAN clients.

Appendix C

Online Resources

T he Web is a great source of information; however, much of it is wrong.

The following is a directory of some of my favorite networking-related Web sites. I've included some equipment manufacturers, online testing and discussion resources, and a few watchdog sites that help keep the other sites honest.

Hardware Manufacturers

Dozens of companies are competing for your business in the home networking market. I chose the companies on this list because they all offer a complete line of home networking products, and they all have interesting and informative Web sites.

3Com Corporation

www.3com.com

About the company: 3Com Corporation was founded by Bob Metcalfe, the inventor of Ethernet, in 1979. Since then, the company has experienced a gut-wrenching series of ups and downs and shifts in corporate focus. Through all of this, 3Com has maintained a reputation for producing innovative, high-quality products for networks of all sizes.

The current 3Com product lineup includes a complete line of home and small-business networking equipment, including wired and wireless routers, access points, and network adapters. The company's NJ100 and NJ200 series of network jacks (see Chapter 6) are some of my favorite "sleeper" network products.

What's on the Web Site: In addition to the usual product information, 3Com provides several free online courses on the principles and practice of networking. You can view a complete listing of these free courses at www.3com.com/support/en_US/learning_center/catalog.html.

Cisco Systems, Inc.

www.cisco.com

About the company: Cisco Systems is the world's largest network equipment maker. The majority of Cisco's products are designed for medium and large businesses, and Cisco has never been a major player in the home networking market. That changed in 2003 with Cisco's acquisition of Linksys, one of the market leaders in home networks.

What's on the Web Site: Like the company's products, the Cisco Web site is designed for business network customers, so you won't find much product information specific to home networks. In fact, the home networking link on the Cisco Web page will take you directly to Linksys.com. What you will find is an excellent, if somewhat technical, series of background articles on virtually every networking technology. From the main page, click Products and Solutions, and select Networking Solutions to see a list of topics and technologies.

D-Link Systems, Inc.

www.dlink.com

About the company: Taiwan-based D-Link Systems is one of the two major players in the home networking market. D-Link has maintained a strong presence in the home- and small-office networking markets since the company's founding in 1986.

D-Link offers one of the most complete home networking product lines in the industry, including a full range of Ethernet adapters, Ethernet switches, wired and wireless Internet routers, and videoconferencing equipment.

What's on the Web Site: D-Link's site offers visitors a huge selection of downloadable drivers, firmware upgrades, and product manuals for just about every D-Link product ever produced. The searchable knowledge base is an excellent resource to turn to when you're having problems with a product.

If you haven't built your network yet, you might want to check out D-Link's Network Configurator. This online tool asks you a series of questions about your network needs and produces a list of the equipment you'll need (from D-Link, of course!) to build your network.

Linksys

www.linksys.com

About the company: Linksys Corporation is one of the world's largest producers of equipment for networks of all sizes. Linksys, founded in 1988, originally focused on the small office/home office markets. In recent years, the Linksys product line has expanded to include large Ethernet switches and associated equipment for larger, enterprise-class networks.

Linksys was acquired by Cisco Systems in the summer of 2003, but Linksys continues to operate as an independent company. Linksys produces a huge range of home networking equipment, including wired Ethernet, wireless, HomePlug power line, and HomeLink phone line networking products.

What's on the Web Site: The Linksys Web site contains drivers, documentation, and FAQs for all past and current Linksys products. An online configuration guide helps you determine what products you need to build a network. Each Linksys product has its own support page with links to the latest drivers and firmware updates.

Visitors can also take a series of short courses that provide an introduction and overview of networking technologies.

Microsoft

www.microsoft.com/hardware

About the company: The world's largest PC software company is also big in hardware. Microsoft's hardware division recently added home networking equipment to its existing product line. In addition to mice, keyboards, and game controllers, Microsoft now offers a small but focused line of routers and network adapters designed specifically for home networks.

What's on the Web Site: Microsoft's massive online knowledge base contains answers to nearly every PC technical problem ever recorded. You'll also find a wealth of product information, software updates, downloadable manuals, and a few nice tutorials on Windows networking.

NETGEAR

www.netgear.com

About the company: NETGEAR began life in 1996 as a subsidiary of Bay Networks. Bay was later acquired by Northern Telecom, and NETGEAR was spun off as a separate company in 2002. NETGEAR's focus on the small-business and home markets allowed the company to sidestep the tech downturn that hit many larger tech companies in 2001.

NETGEAR's networking product line is very complete and includes switches, routers, network adapters, and print servers. NETGEAR was one of the first companies to produce a range of Gigabit Ethernet products for the home- and small-office markets.

What's on the Web Site: In addition to the usual drivers, downloads, and product information, NETGEAR's site provides a nice overview of the benefits of home networking, with specific examples for home, travel gaming, and multimedia networks.

SMC Networks

www.smc.com

About the company: SMC Networks isn't as well known as some of the other major players in the home network market, but it offers a very full line of wired and wireless home networking products.

What's on the Web Site: SMC's Web site is heavy on product information but light on tutorials and how-to articles. Each major product category (routers, wireless adapters, and so on) features a thorough feature chart designed to help you locate the perfect product for your needs. After you've located the product with the features you need, you can click the product's link in the chart to go directly to that product's page.

Online Security and Performance Testing

The sites listed here offer online security/performance testing for your system.

Lavasoft

www.lavasoftusa.com

Lavasoft's Ad-aware software was one of the first spyware-removal programs, and it is still one of the best. Ad-aware is a simple, easy to use program that scans your computer for adware, spyware, and other malicious software.

Lavasoft provides several versions of Ad-Aware. Most home users will be perfectly happy with the basic version, which is free of charge The paid version is even better because it provides full-time protection against new spyware threats.

Broadband Reports

www.broadbandreports.com

Broadband Reports (formerly DSL Reports) was born out of necessity. Founder Justin Beech had so much trouble locating DSL service for his home that he decided to start a Web site where users could exchange information about DSL. The site now includes coverage of cable modem providers as well, so Justin changed the name of the site to reflect the site's broader audience.

There's so much to see at this site that your first visit can be overwhelming. Some of the must-see items are as follows:

- An active discussion forum where you can exchange messages with other broadband users around the world

- Reviews of routers, switches, broadband service providers, and networking equipment

- Some of the best and most informative networking FAQs on the Web

- An excellent set of tools to test the speed and reliability of your Internet connection

- Tips and tools to help you tweak your computer's IP settings for maximum performance

Gibson Research Corporation

www.grc.com

Former *InfoWorld* columnist and programmer extraordinaire Steve Gibson is on a one-man campaign to save the Internet—and I mean that in a good way. Gibson's site is full of great information, with a strong focus on security issues.

Don't miss the ShieldsUP!! page, where you can get a free online security checkup of your computer and router. I highly recommend that you visit this site to test your network's security settings. The test is very stringent, so don't be surprised if your system fails one or more of the tests—even if you are running a firewall.

McAfee

www.mcafee.com

As you might expect, antivirus vendor McAfee's site deals primarily with the detection and removal of viruses. If you look hard enough, you'll find some interesting free tools to scan your computer for viruses (even if you don't have McAfee's antivirus software!) From the McAfee home page, click Home and Home Office and then select one of the free tools at the bottom of the page.

Other free features include a real-time world virus map that shows the world's current virus hotspots, and a free program that assesses your computer's security vulnerabilities.

PC Pitstop

www.pcpitstop.com

PC Pitstop is one of my favorite online test sites. This free site performs a complete performance test on your PC and includes tests of CPU speed, disk drive speed and health, Internet security settings, and Internet connection speed.

The full suite of tests takes about five minutes to run, and you can compare your system's test results to results from similar systems. You can also perform separate antivirus and spyware checks to ensure that your system is free of uninvited guests. The site features tips and programs that can help you tweak every bit of performance out of your PC.

Spybot Search & Destroy

www.safer-networking.org

Patrick Kolla hates spyware. Kolla's Spybot Search & Destroy program is one of the best tools I've found for locating and removing unwanted spyware and adware programs from your computer. This excellent software is continually updated in an effort to keep up with the spyware makers.

Spybot S&D is a free program; Kolla requests a small donation if you use and like the program.

Symantec

www.symantec.com

Unlike many of their competitors, Symantec doesn't offer much in the way of free online testing. But they do offer trial versions of most of their security software products. The trial versions are fully functional but time-limited, so you can only use them for 15 days. If you decide to continue using the software, you can purchase an unlock key online, so you won't have to remove the trial version and install the full version of the software.

General Technology Sites

Check out these sites for useful and interesting tips and info.

ExtremeTech

www.extremetech.com

ExtremeTech is the ultimate destination for hardcore technologists and do-it-yourself system builders. It features intense reviews, complete plans and parts lists for building systems and components, technical resources, and interactive discussions. Focused on work and personal PC technologies, along with a new concentration on building the ultimate home entertainment network, ExtremeTech is led by a team of hardcore, passionate technologists.

ExtremeTech features an active and lively discussion forum where readers can exchange ideas, information, and tips with one another.

PC Magazine

www.pcmag.com

PCMag.com is the premier online destination for technology buyers making brand selections for their company and personal lives. Updated daily, PCMag.com offers all of the editorial content found in *PC Magazine*, plus original content from First Looks and *PC Magazine* columnists. Added features, such as Shop Now, allow visitors to compare prices from leading retailers, after they've made an informed brand decision.

Practically Networked

www.practicallynetworked.com

Practically Networked is a great site that provides advice, reviews, and practical (hence the name) how-to information on home networking.

The review archive contains concise, critical reviews of just about every home network product out there. Each review also contains links to reader comments, so it's easy to see what real users out in the real world think about each product.

Tom's Hardware

www.tomshardware.com

Tom Pabst has never heard the question "So, Tom, tell us what you really think." Dr. Pabst is a medical doctor who decided he prefers poking around inside PCs to poking around inside people. Founded as a hobby in 1996, Dr. Tom's site has amassed a huge following worldwide thanks to the site's cut-to-the-chase, no-holds-barred reviews.

As you might have guessed from the name, the site's primary focus is on performance. You'll find lots of tips and discussions about the hottest new processors, chip sets, and graphics cards. The networking section is heavy on product reviews and how-to articles.

Other Interesting Sites

And finally . . .

The Internet Society

www.isoc.org

If the Internet has a home, this is it. The ISOC is the main clearinghouse for Internet information and education. Subchapters of the ISOC are charged with defining and maintaining Internet standards and protocols.

Nearly every major computer, networking, and software vendor on the planet is involved in the ISOC or one of its auxiliary organizations. If you're looking for information on Internet standards or protocols, this is the place to start.

CIAC Hoaxbusters

hoaxbusters.ciac.org

This is one government-sponsored page that makes me proud to be a taxpayer! The Computer Incident Advisory Capability (CIAC) is a division of the U.S. Department of Energy and is responsible for computer security at DOE. Someone at CIAC had the brilliant idea to create a public Web page to help debunk the torrent of chain letters, e-mail hoaxes, and false virus alerts that have plagued the Internet for years.

This isn't the prettiest site you'll ever visit, but it contains an excellent reference and cross-index of just about every hoax, prank, chain letter, and phony virus alert.

Dynamic DNS Services

www.dyndns.com

DynDNS offers a wide range of dynamic DNS services for home and business users, including a free single-address account. When you create an account, you'll choose a name for your home system, using one of DynDNS's domain names. For example, you might choose the name pcmag.dyndns.org. After you've set up the account, you can connect to your home LAN using the name pcmag.dyndns.org instead of using your router's public IP address (which can change at any time).

To use this service, you'll need a router with a dynamic DNS feature, or you'll need to run a Dynamic DNS updater program on one of the computers on your LAN.

SNOPES

snopes.com

Snopes Webmasters Barbara and David P. Mikkelson are on a mission to save the world from rumors, hoaxes, half-truths, and outright lies. Their site is a virtual encyclopedia of disinformation, and it covers everything from Coca-Cola myths to computer viruses.

Snopes' vast collection of myths, hoaxes, and urban legends is colorfully organized by category, making it easy to zero in on a topic area. They have plenty of simple, non-technical information about computer viruses and e-mail chain letter hoaxes.

Urban Legends

urbanlegends.miningco.com

This site is prettier and more comprehensive than the CIAC site. As the name implies, it contains a database of urban legends, myths, folklore—and Internet hoaxes. This is the first place I go when I smell a hoax, and this site has never let me down.

The only problem with this site is that you can easily spend hours here, lost in a world of weird, wacky, and generally outlandish stuff that some folks actually believe to be true.

Glossary

10/100 Ethernet   Networking equipment that is compatible with both the 10Base-T and 100Base-T specifications. 10/100 Ethernet systems automatically switch speeds to maintain compatibility with both systems, allowing the use of 10 and 100 mbps devices on the same LAN.

100Base-TX   An IEEE specification for running 100 mbps Ethernet signals over unshielded twisted pair cable. 100Base-TX is currently the most widely used local area networking specification. Also known as *Fast Ethernet.*

10Base-2   An IEEE specification for running 10 mbps Ethernet over thin, shielded coaxial cable. Also known as "Cheapernet" because it was much less expensive to install than the original, thick-cable Ethernet. 10Base-2 is now obsolete, having been replaced by 10Base-T and 100Base-T networks.

10Base-T   An IEEE specification for running 10 mbps Ethernet signals over unshielded twisted pair cable.

802.11a   An IEEE specification for transmitting Ethernet signals at speeds up to 54 mbps over a radio signal in the 5 GHz radio band.

802.11a/b/g   A wireless network compatible with all three wireless standards. Also called a *tri-mode* network.

802.11b   An IEEE specification for transmitting Ethernet signals at speeds up to 11 mbps over a radio signal in the 2.4 GHz radio band.

802.11g   An IEEE specification for transmitting Ethernet signals at speeds up to 54 mbps over a radio signal in the 2.4 GHz radio band. 802.11g wireless networks are backward-compatible with 802.11b devices.

802.11g   A proposed IEEE specification for transmitting Ethernet signals at speeds up to 108 mbps using multiple radio signals in the 2.4 GHz radio band. 802.11n wireless networks will be backward-compatible with 802.11b and 802.11g devices.

access point (AP)   A device that acts as a gateway between wired and wireless networks. APs act as a central connecting point for the wireless clients on a LAN.

351

address   A unique numeric or alphanumeric identifier that identifies a specific device or connection on a network. See *IP address.*

Address Resolution Protocol (ARP)   A network protocol that provides for the assignment of IP addresses based on a device's hardware MAC address.

adapter   See *network adapter.*

administrator   The person in charge of a computer, network, or group of computers.

authentication   The process of verifying a user's identity, typically through the use of an account name and password.

bandwidth   A measure of the traffic-carrying capacity of a communications channel, usually expressed in terms of the number of data bits the channel can carry in a second. For example, Fast Ethernet networks have a bandwidth of 100 megabits per second.

broadband   A system that carries digital signals as a secondary service over a network built for a different purpose. For example, cable modems use the existing cable TV network to provide high-speed Internet service, and DSL modems carry data over ordinary voice-grade telephone lines.

browser   Short for *Web browser,* a program used to view pages on a Web server.

cable modem   A device that provides a high-speed, two-way data connection over a cable TV service.

CardBus   An improved, 32-bit version of the original PC Card (also known as PCMCIA) standard for laptop expansion cards. PC Cards will work in a CardBus-compatible device, but CardBus cards will not operate in a PC Card–based computer.

CAT5 and CAT5e   Short for Category 5, a high-grade UTP cable used for Fast Ethernet networks. CAT5e cable can be used with Gigabit Ethernet over short distances.

CAT6   An extremely high-grade UTP cable used for Gigabit Ethernet.

client   A computer (or other device) that makes use of services provided by another device (typically a server) over a network.

client-server network   A networking system where some computers (called servers) provide services that can be used by other (client) computers on the network.

crossover cable   A specially wired patch cable used to connect two computers or two switches together.

default gateway   On an IP network, the IP address of the router or other device that connects the LAN to the Internet.

Digital Subscriber Line (DSL)   A service, available from many local telephone companies, that delivers a high-speed data service using ordinary voice-grade telephone lines.

domain name   A name that identifies an organization and the organization's associated IP addresses. For example, `pcmag.com` identifies the block of IP addresses assigned to PC Magazine. Domain names are used in conjunction with a *host name* to identify individual computers (such as `www.pcmag.com` or `mail.pcmag.com`) on a network.

Domain Name Service (DNS)   An Internet service that translates human-readable names (like `pcmag.com`) into IP addresses.

driver   Software (usually provided with a hardware device) that allows a device to interact with a computer's operating system. Also called a *device driver.*

Dynamic Host Configuration Protocol (DHCP)   A LAN service that automatically provides IP address and routing information to LAN client computers on demand. DHCP servers are typically built into routers, wireless APs, and network servers.

Ethernet   A local area network architecture developed by Digital Equipment Corporation, Intel, and Xerox in the 1970s. The original Ethernet specification operated at 10 mbps; subsequent improvements have increased the speed up to 1000 mbps (1 gigabit).

Ethernet switch   A device that controls the flow of data among devices on an Ethernet LAN. Each device on the LAN connects to a connector (called a *port*) on the switch; the switch monitors incoming traffic on each port and sends the data on to the appropriate destination port. See *switch.*

Fast Ethernet   A high-speed variant of Ethernet that operates at 100 mbps over CAT5 UTP wiring.

file server   A network device that provides file storage space for use by other computers on the network. Windows XP includes a built-in file server feature that allows any Windows XP computer to share files with other computers.

firewall   A device used to prevent unauthorized access to a LAN. A firewall typically connects between a private LAN and the public Internet. A firewall is essentially a special-purpose computer that monitors and regulates all traffic between the LAN and the Internet.

FireWire   A high-speed data connection specification originally developed by Apple Computer and now an IEEE standard called IEEE 1394. FireWire connections operate at 400 and 800 mbps and are most often used to connect high-speed peripheral devices like video cameras and external hard drives.

FTP   An acronym for *file transfer protocol*, an Internet standard for transporting files across the Internet. The term FTP is used to refer both to the protocol itself and the programs that implement the protocol.

gateway   The device on a network that provides connectivity to another network, usually to the Internet.

gateway address   The IP address of the gateway device on a local area network. On home networks, the gateway address is the address of the local router.

Gigabit Ethernet   An IEEE specification for running 1000 mbps Ethernet signals over CAT5e and CAT6 unshielded twisted pair cable.

home gateway   A device that provides a router, firewall, and Ethernet switch (and often a wireless access point as well) in a single, compact box. Home gateways provide a simple, inexpensive way to share an Internet connection among several computers.

Home Phoneline Networking Alliance (HPNA)   An industry trade group that sets technical specifications for transmitting data over home telephone wiring. Also used to describe products compatible with the HPNA specification.

host   A computer that is connected to the Internet. This term is a holdover from the days when most computers connected to the Internet allowed direct remote access to the computer's command-line interface. Today, the term is most often used to refer to Web, mail, and FTP servers.

hub   A device that creates a local area network by combining the signals from several Ethernet devices. Unlike switches, hubs simply repeat the signal from each cable connected to the hub. See *Ethernet switch.*

Internet Corporation for Assigned Names and Numbers (ICANN)   A nonprofit corporation responsible for IP address space allocation, protocol assignment, and domain name system management.

IEEE 1394   See *FireWire.*

Internet Engineering Task Force (IETF)   A large international community of network designers, operators, vendors, and researchers concerned with the evolution of the Internet architecture and the smooth operation of the Internet.

Institute of Electrical and Electronic Engineers (IEEE)   Pronounced "Eye-triple-E," this is a global association of engineers. IEEE members and committees created many of the standards used in data networking today.

Internet Connection Sharing (ICS)   A feature built into Windows Me, Windows 2000, and Windows XP that allows one PC on the network to operate as an Internet gateway for the other computers on the LAN.

Internet Protocol (IP)   A communications protocol that defines rules for the addressing and transmission of data over a network. Each device on an IP network has a unique address, so any two devices on an IP network can communicate directly with one another. IP is the basis of the worldwide Internet.

Internet Service Provider (ISP)   A company that provides access to the Internet, usually over a dial-up, DSL, or cable modem connection. ISPs typically charge a monthly or hourly fee for usage.

intranet   A private wide area network often used by corporations, universities, and other large organizations to link several LANs together into a single, seamless network covering a large geographical area.

IP address   A unique address assigned to each computer and other devices directly connected to the Internet. IP addresses consist of four numbers between 0 and 255, separated by periods, as in 10.1.2.3 or 192.168.0.202.

latency   The amount of time (usually measured in milliseconds, or 1/1000 of a second) that it takes for a data packet to travel from the source (sending) computer to the destination (receiving) computer. Long latency times are certain death for online gaming because they increase the amount of time it takes to respond to an opponent's move. Also called *lag time* and *ping time*.

local area network (LAN)   A network of computers contained in a relatively small area, usually within a building or a cluster of buildings. LANs provide a shared connection that allows for sharing of files, printers, and services (including an Internet connection) among the devices connected to the LAN. See *wide area network (WAN)*.

mapping   A technique used to create an additional, virtual disk drive on one computer that provides a connection to a shared drive or directory on another computer. Also called *drive mapping*.

Media Access Control (MAC) address   A 6-byte address (for example, 00-80-C8-1E-C8-83) that uniquely identifies an Ethernet device. The first 3 bytes of the MAC address identify the manufacturer of the device. The MAC address is not the same as the IP address. See *Address Resolution Protocol*.

Multiple Input Multiple Output (MIMO)   A technique (used in 802.11n wireless networking) for combining the bandwidth of several 802.11g channels into a single, faster channel.

network   A continuous connection between two or more computers that allows the sharing of files, printers, and other resources.

Network Address Translation (NAT)   A technique commonly used in routers and firewalls that allows several computers to share a single public IP address. NAT routers are commonly used to provide Internet sharing and firewall protection for all the computers on a LAN.

network adapter   A device that acts as the interface between a network and a computer. Network adapters come in a variety of form factors, including internal PCI and CardBus expansion cards and external USB devices.

network interface card (NIC)   A network adapter built on a PCI or other removable expansion card.

network media   The cable or wiring used to carry network signals.

patch cable   A short cable used to connect an Ethernet device (such as a computer or printer) to an Ethernet wall plate or switch port.

PC   Short for personal computer, this term was originally used to identify the original IBM Model 5150 Personal Computer. Today, the term is used to identify any desktop computer system, regardless of manufacturer or operating system.

PC Card (also called PCMCIA)   A standard created by the Personal Computer Memory Card International Association that defines the physical and electrical characteristics for small expansion cards commonly used in laptop computers and other portable devices. Although originally designed as a specification for adding memory to portable computers, the PC Card specification has been expanded to include all types of expansion duties, including network adapters, USB, and FireWire interfaces. See *CardBus*.

peer-to-peer network   A network that allows any computer to act as both a client and a server, often at the same time. The built-in file sharing in Windows XP creates a peer network when two or more computers are connected to the network.

Peripheral Components Interconnect (PCI)   A specification that defines the size, shape, and electrical characteristics of internal expansion cards and slots for desktop PCs. Although originally developed by Intel, the PCI specification is not tied to any single computer architecture and is widely used in PC and Macintosh desktop PCs.

ping   A method (and a utility program of the same name) to determine if a specific IP address is active. Most ping programs, including the one included with Windows XP, will also tell you how long it takes to send a data packet from your computer to another IP address and back again. Ping borrows its name from the sonar depth sounding system, which uses an audible "ping" to determine the depth of items below the surface of the water.

plenum cable   Cable certified to be fire-resistant and to produce little or no toxic fumes in the event of a fire. Many local fire codes require the use of plenum cable in office and residential applications.

Plug and Play (PnP)   A technical specification designed to simplify the process of adding expansion devices to a computer system. PC Card, CardBus, USB, and PCI are examples of PnP systems.

Point-to-Point Protocol over Ethernet (PPPoE)   A standard for user authentication over a broadband cable modem or DSL connection. When a broadband device establishes a connection to the Internet, the ISP may request user authentication in the form of a user name and password. Most routers handle the PPPoE authentication automatically.

Point-to-Point Tunneling Protocol (PPTP)   A protocol used in virtual private networks. PPTP uses sophisticated data encryption techniques to securely send data over the public Internet. Although it is possible for someone to intercept the data packets as they travel over the Internet, it is very difficult (but not impossible) to decrypt the data back into readable form. See *virtual private network*.

port   An interface connection (Ethernet, serial, parallel, USB, and so forth) on a computer or other electronic device that provides a connection to another device or network.

print server   A device that connects a printer to a LAN, making the attached printer available to users on the LAN.

protocol   A standardized format that describes the rules and procedures for transmitting data between two devices. There are hundreds of communications protocols in use today, including TCP/IP (Internet Protocol) and Hypertext Transfer Protocol (HTTP, the basis of the World Wide Web). Standardized protocols facilitate the exchange of information between devices made by different manufacturers or between computers running different operating systems.

RJ-45   An eight-pin plastic connector used for telephone and data connections, usually in conjunction with CAT5 cable.

route   The path taken by an IP packet as it travels over a LAN or the Internet.

router   A device that monitors and manages the flow of data between two IP networks. Typically, a router connects between a LAN and a WAN. Most routers sold for the home networking market also include a firewall.

sharing   The process of making a resource on one computer available to other computers on the network, usually on a LAN. Examples include file sharing, printer sharing, and Internet access sharing.

server   A network device that provides services (such as file or printer sharing) that other computers can use.

Stateful Packet Inspection (SPI)   A data filtering technique used in advanced network firewalls. Simple NAT firewalls examine the source and destination address of each data packet to determine the proper routing and disposition of the data. SPI firewalls go a step further by examining the contents of each data packet in order to determine the validity of the packet. See *Network Address Translation.*

switch   In Ethernet networks, a device that examines and forwards data packets between two or more connections. Switches have all but replaced hubs as the central connecting point on Ethernet networks.

Transmission Control Protocol/Internet Protocol (TCP/IP)   A suite of communications protocols originally developed by the U.S. Department of Defense that forms the basis of the worldwide Internet.

Uniform Resource Locator (URL)   A human-readable representation (such as `http://www.pcmag.com`) of an IP address and port number.

Universal Serial Bus (USB)   A high-speed, short-range connection scheme commonly used to connect printers, keyboards, pointing devices, and other peripheral equipment to a personal computer.

unshielded twisted pair (UTP)   A multiconductor cable composed of two or more pairs of wires. Each pair of wires is twisted together to form a single twisted pair. The twist prevents interference from other nearby cables and allows several pairs of wires to share a single outer jacket.

virtual private network (VPN)   A private network of computers connected over the public Internet using a secure "tunneling" protocol. The tunneling protocol uses strong data encryption techniques to provide a secure, private connection among the computers on the VPN.

wide area network (WAN)   A data network that connects computers over a large geographical area. The Internet is the best-known WAN, but many corporations operate their own private WANs using data connections leased from public data carriers.

WiFi Alliance   A nonprofit trade association formed to certify interoperability of wireless local area network products based on the IEEE 802.11 specifications. Formerly known as the Wireless Ethernet Compatibility Association.

WiFi Protected Access (WPA)   An improved security protocol for wireless networks that includes encryption and authentication.

Wired Equivalency Protocol (WEP)   The original wireless security protocol for wireless networks.

wireless access point (WAP)   The central connecting point on a wireless network. WAPs regulate the traffic on a wireless network and also provide a connection between the wireless network and a wired Ethernet LAN.

Index

continued

M

X